# THE SPIRITUALITY OF JOHN CALVIN

Lucien Joseph Richard

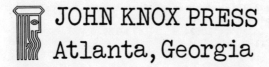 JOHN KNOX PRESS
Atlanta, Georgia

Acknowledgments

This book would not have been written without the financial support and the supportive friendship of my own religious community, the Oblates of Mary Immaculate. I am very thankful to Richard Martin and John Bonowitz for reshaping quite a few of my crooked sentences. I also want to express my appreciation to Carolyn Cross, a dedicated typist who spent many hours typing the manuscript.

*Library of Congress Cataloging in Publication Data*

Richard, Lucien Joseph.
   The spirituality of John Calvin.

   Bibliography: p.
   Includes index.
   1. Spiritual life--History of doctrines. 2. Calvin, Jean, 1509-1564. I. Title.
BV4490.R5    230'.4'20924    73-16920
ISBN 0-8042-0711-9 pbk.

Printed in the United States of America

Dedication

To my father and mother and to Helen
in memory of her son John

TABLE OF CONTENTS

## ABBREVIATIONS

| | |
|---|---|
| AHDLMA | Archives d'histoire doctrinale et littéraire du Moyen Age |
| ARG | Archiv für Reformationgeschichte |
| BHR | Bibliothèque d'humanisme et Renaissance |
| BHPF | Bulletin d'histoire du protestanisme français |
| BSHPF | Bulletin de la Société de l'histoire du protestantisme française |
| DS | Dictionnaire de Spiritualité |
| DTC | Dictionnaire de Théologie Catholique |
| Ev.Th. | Evangelische Theologie |
| JHI | Journal of the History of Ideas |
| JR | Journal of Religion |
| NAKG | Nederlands Archief voor Kerkgeschiedenis |
| NRT | Nouvelle Revue de Théologie |
| PTR | Princeton Theological Review |
| RAM | Revue d'Ascetique et de Mystique |
| RHE | Revue d'Histoire écclésiastique |
| RHEF | Revue de l'histoire de l'Eglise de France |
| ZAM | Zeitschrift für Aszese und Mystik |

# INTRODUCTION

It is only quite recently that the theological tradition in the Catholic Church has admitted the presence of a spirituality in the writings of John Calvin.[1] By spirituality I mean the personal assimilation of the salvific mission of Christ by each Christian and this in the framework of new and ever evolving forms of Christian conduct. Spirituality means the forms that holiness takes in the concrete life of the believer. The concept of spirituality implies that there is the possibility of progress in holiness, that there is a need of working toward perfection, and that there are certain means and ways of attaining such a perfection.

In the course of the Church's history, different patterns of religious conduct, i.e. different spiritualities, have exercised formative influence and have often been charismatic and exemplary realizations of Christian spirituality for a given time and for a given task.

It is my contention that the works of John Calvin circumscribe such a spirituality. And, although the distinctive character of Calvin's spirituality originated in response to the challenge of the sixteenth century, yet this legacy, so unmistakably valid for the world of his time, has a new and unmistakable validity today. As modern emphases deepen Calvin's primordial concepts, they give his vision of the Christian life a new and richer dimension.

Although concrete spiritualities can be grasped less as doctrine than as personal experience, they are not totally resistant to conceptual analysis. Such an analysis is the object of this book. It is my purpose to demonstrate the originality of John Calvin's spirituality as the expression of a new religious epistemology.

## A. The Question of Sources

In establishing the originality of Calvin's spirituality, the question of sources must be dealt with at length. Many currents converged in the religious thought of Calvin. The simplest outline of his work in its historical context lays bare the variety of influences that played upon his thought and personality. The difficulty in discerning the real influences at work on him is illustrated by the opposing and at times

contradictory judgments of scholars.  Innumerable scholars have traced
the intellectual antecedents to almost all of his most characteristic
ideas, finding them in varying degrees in different people and different
movements.[2]

According to A. Ganoczy, the most important movements that influenced
Calvin's thought were nominalism, mysticism, conciliarism, and humanism.[3]
The author underlines the voluntarism of the nominalistic tradition and
its concepts of the omnipotence of God.  In the mystical movement he
underlines the *Devotio Moderna* and its reaction against concern for temporal goods and its insistence on the decadence of scholasticism with
its love of subtle distinctions in theology.  The *Devotio Moderna* preferred a clear and experiential knowledge of God acquired through personal meditation.  And this led to individualism which helped the process of dissolution of the Middle Ages' universalism.[4]

The influence of the *Devotio Moderna* on Calvin has been indicated in
several works.  Karl Reuter has affirmed quite clearly that there is no
essential current of the spirituality of the *De Imitatione Christi* which
Calvin did not digest and incorporate critically in his theology.[5]
Albert Hyma has constantly affirmed the important influence of the
*Devotio Moderna* on Calvin's thought.[6]

According to Warfield, Augustinianism and Bucer are the main sources
of Calvin's theology.

> The system of doctrines taught by Calvin is just the Augustinianism
> common to the whole body of the reformer.  And this Augustinianism
> is taught by him fundamentally as he learned it from Luther, whose
> fertile conceptions he completely assimilated, and most directly
> from Martin Bucer, in whose practical, ethical point of view he
> perfectly entered.  Many of the forms of statement most character-
> istic of Calvin, on such topics as predestination, faith, and
> stages of salvation, the church, the sacraments, only reproduce,
> though of course with that clearness and religious depth peculiar
> to Calvin, precise teachings of Bucer, who was above all others,
> accordingly, Calvin's master in theology.[7]

The extent of Bucer's influence on Calvin is a matter of disagreement
among scholars.[8]  Notwithstanding the disagreement there is some consensus on Bucer's influence in Calvin's doctrine of predestination, sanctification, the manner of approaching the Scriptures, and in a special
manner the doctrine of the Holy Spirit.  Calvin also shows himself to be
acquainted with Anselm, Lombard, and Aquinas, and also quite clearly
read the writings of St. Bernard.

At the same time, by training, Calvin stood squarely in the intellectual tradition of early French Humanism and he derived from that tradition many of his basic perspectives and preoccupations.  Most French
humanists born around 1490 were actually Christian Erasmians, and therefore the question of Erasmus' influence on Calvin must be dealt with.
François Wendel writes:

> Although Erasmus's name nowhere appears in the *Institutes*, it has
> been possible to show that numerous passages on the contempt of the
> world, the longing for death, earthly duties, even upon the notion
> of faith and upon eschatology, present striking analogies with
> parallel texts from the great humanist.[9]

It will therefore be necessary to evaluate in greater detail the
important contribution coming from Erasmus' own piety and spirituality.
Throughout his life he wrote works of piety, from the early *De Contemptu
Mundi* to his extensive tract on preaching, *De Ecclesiastes*.  His *Enchi-
ridion Militis Christiani* endeavors to teach what he considered to be
Christian piety.  This contribution would not have been possible had
Erasmus' spirituality and theology been somewhat superficial as has too
often been said both by older and more recent theologians.

In the field of epistemology the predominant influences seem to have
been nominalism and the Christian humanism of the sixteenth century.
There is controversy concerning the influence of nominalism, particularly that of John Major, on the thought of Calvin.  Karl Reuter has
stressed the influence of John Major and neo-scotistic theology on Calvin's thought.[10]  T. F. Torrance has indicated the same influence in
reference to Calvin's understanding of the knowledge of God.[11]  On the
contrary, A. Ganoczy minimizes the importance of Major's influence on
Calvin's theological thought.  He conceives a possible influence of John
Major after 1540 but not before 1536 and therefore not on the first
writing of the *Institutes*.[12]  For A. Lavalée, Calvin's dependence on
John Major is undocumented and questionable.[13]  The affirmation of John
Major's nominalism and his influence upon Calvin recurs very often in
Kilian McDonnell's book.

> In the pursuit of the knowledge of God, Calvin turns to the knowl-
> edge of himself.  There is in this self-knowledge the remnant of
> that intuitive knowledge found in Duns Scotus and developed by
> Occam, a knowledge which is individual, empirical, and immediate.[14]
>     Calvin was introduced to the personalism of Scotus through John
> Major.[15]

When Calvin came to Paris to pursue his university studies it was the nominalistic theory of knowledge and logic of William of Occam together with the conclusions that the Scotistic scholastics drew from that philosophy which dominated university life.   In 1473 nominalism was under censure and forbidden, but was again allowed in 1481, and after this latter date it reigned supreme at Paris. Calvin had an immediate contact with nominalism through John Major, whose theory of knowledge and logic was simply that of Occam.[16]

Reuter  suggests that the doctrine of the *acceptatio divina*, found in both Occam and Gregory of Rimini, was taken over by Calvin from Gregory through the teaching of John Major.[17]

Certainly the Occamist theory of knowledge helped Calvin build his doctrine of revelation, Calvin filling with scriptural theology the void Occam's distrust of reason had created.[18]

Notwithstanding these affirmations on McDonnell's part, the influence of John Major will have to be more clearly indicated. For instance,  A. Ganoczy has shown in his work on the library of John Calvin's academy that there were no volumes there of any nominalistic origin.  Nothing of Occam, d'Ailly, G. Biel, Gerson.  None of the numerous volumes of John Major published in Paris or Lyon from 1505 to 1530 are in the catalogue.[19]

Although conscious of the numerous possible influences on John Calvin, one must also consider that his mind was far more than a mirror of external events and currents of thought.  It was a profoundly creative mind and when all the influences upon it have been discerned, its character remains authentically his own.  The search for the antecedents to a man's theology often fails to do justice to his originality and individuality.  Other men subjected to the same influence will respond differently, but no man is merely the sum of the influences that affect him.

Although it is necessary to consider and evaluate the different influences at work in Calvin's thought in order to establish his originality, it is also necessary to note the correspondence of certain dominant tendencies in his religious thought to certain basic tendencies in the religious and cultural evolution of the Renaissance period.  It is in noting this that we will approach most closely an understanding of the degree to which Calvin's spirituality was truly original.  It becomes imperative to establish the essential characteristics and problems of the spiritualities of the sixteenth century.

The Renaissance and the incipient Reformation involved a cultural, intellectual and spiritual shift and contained a change in ideas, values and thought.  At the same time in the transition from the medieval period to the Renaissance, elements and problems of the previous period

were inextricably intertwined with new dimensions.   As Mark Curtis
observed,

> though the revisionists who have attempted to make the Renaissance
> a part of the Middle Ages may have failed to prove their case, they
> have demonstrated that some phenomena, once thought uniquely charac-
> teristic of Renaissance culture, were present by more than coinci-
> dence in medieval civilization and second, that important features
> of medieval thought and attitudes persisted as fundamental, consti-
> tuent parts of the Renaissance mind.[20]

B.  *The Influence of the* Devotio Moderna *and the Ecclesiological Dimen-*
    *sion of Spirituality During the Renaissance and on the Eve of the*
    *Reformation*

Renaissance humanism represented a type of reform movement within the
Church.  It issued a call for a purified and more religious Church, and
a less superstitious worship.  Both the driving force and the peculiar
quality of this reform were in large part an inheritance from the combination of lay piety with mysticism and from the zeal for the reform of
the Church which had been endemic in the Northern countries and which
was most fully formulated in the movement known as the *Devotio Moderna*.[21]
The *Devotio Moderna* meant personal reformation through a return to Christian inwardness.  It advocated a certain individualism and favored a
reaction against an overly legalistic piety.

About the year 1515 not only many humanists but also statesmen like
Thomas More and Duke George of Saxony, and bishops such as Warham of
Canterbury, were under the impression that a reform as planned by Erasmus  would renew the Church.  Countless church members were striving for
self-reform.[22]  But none of these efforts were completely successful,
even in such restricted spheres as a religious order or a particular
country, much less in the whole church.  The attempts at reform which
sprouted from the soil of the Church did not come to maturity.  The reasons for this failure must be analyzed, because they point out one of
the most important questions Calvin had to deal with.

According to Gordon Leff, the Church was no worse in the sixteenth
century than she had been in the thirteenth or tenth centuries.[23]  The
old weaknesses were still there, although some of them had become more
acute and there was a growing and intensifying unwillingness to bear
with these weaknesses.  The Church needed housecleaning, but she had

needed that several times before, and it always had been effected without disruption.  If there had been nothing new in the crisis of the sixteenth century, the old methods of reform may have been tried and found
reliable once again.

But there was something new.  There was the appearance of a new style
of piety, that of the *Devotio Moderna*, as mediated by the humanists, and
the Church was too slow to respond to this new style of piety.  In the
sixteenth century the Church was faced with change from a more community-
minded society to a more associational society.  This change involved
the coming of a more individualistic form of life, a form of life that
the Church in its totality failed to share and for a time, actively re-
sisted.  The reason for this resistance seems to lie in the Church's
understanding of the nature of man's relationship to God.  Individualism,
wherein God's relationship to man became exclusively an I-Thou relationship, left the Church out of the picture.  The mediation of the Church
as community becomes unnecessary, at times even a hindrance to a pure
personal relationship to God.  Reacting consciously or unconsciously
against this growing individualism in piety, the Church was defending
her very existence and function.  Furthermore, churchmen reasoned that
an individualistic piety, a *Solus-cum-Solo* piety, arises in and through
a religious tradition.  If this tradition is nonexistent, such an individual's experience will not arise.  Individual piety is not created *ex
nihilo*.  It needs the proper soil to take root and to grow.  This soil
is the Church.  This conviction on the part of the Church explains its
slowness in responding to the new individualistic piety.

Furthermore, the structures of feudal society were underpinned by an
ideology that ran in strict hierarchical patterns.  The hierarchical
order created by God in the Cosmos, for instance, was thought to be
realized and guaranteed on this earth by the basic institutions of em-
pire and Church which were in turn hierarchically structured.  Holiness
consisted in conforming to order and was achieved by obeying the orders
that came from above through which orders God's will was translated for
man in practical terms.  At the heart of medieval ecclesiology was the
conviction that the visible hierarchical institution, in communion with
the vicar of Christ, embodied, in an unqualified way, the reality of the
Church.  This understanding led to an exaggerated view of papal authority, and the mediating role of the Church in the Christian life.  At the

same time, with the distinction introduced by St. Augustine between the
*Ecclesia ab Abel*, which stands for the tradition of truth, and the *Ecclesia ab Cain*, which stands for an equally continuous line of distortion
of the truth, there was an ever-increasing tendency to distinguish between the invisible Church--pure and spotless--and the visible Church
where good and evil co-exist. The link and bond between these two
aspects and dimensions of the Church became problematical. In the context of this distinction, the question of who interprets the scripture
became important. The relation between the authority of the hierarchy
and the doctor of theology in interpreting the scriptures became a divisive question.

The changing outlook and spiritual climate brought about by the *Devotio Moderna* with its tendency toward a more individualistic and inward
religious life was bound to have deep repercussions within the field of
ecclesiology. The ideal, more or less conscious in the minds of the
Renaissance authors, would no longer be a religion of obedience to an
external authority. Religious life had, in some way, to find its ultimate source within man himself. At the time of the Renaissance and on
the eve of the Reformation, the ecclesiological dimensions of the spiritual life clearly came to the fore. The ecclesiological presupposi-
tions of the existing spiritualities were questionable and begging for
new approaches. A great deal of Calvin's efforts were focussed in this
direction.

## C. *Spirituality and Epistemology*

The Renaissance period was not only characterized by a breakdown in
ecclesiological models but also by the birth of new intellectual needs
and of new forms of activities and research. These new needs and problems questioned classical theology in its very structure. They also led
to a new theological approach.[24]

In such a period of transition, theology is very often the very locus
where the cultural and spiritual shifts become reflectively expressed.
According to R. W. Southern,

> the digestion of Aristotle's logic was the greatest intellectual
> task of the period from the end of the tenth to the end of the
> twelfth century. Under its influence, the methods of theological
> discussion and the forms of the presentation of theological specu-
> lation underwent a profound change. It was in theology that the
> change was felt most keenly and fought most fiercely.[25]

Theology is fully and inextricably immersed in the problem of cultural
and spiritual change since its content touches upon everything else that
man knows and does.

From the time of Francesco Petrarch, one can follow the opposition to
the Scholastics, the academic theologians and philosophers of the universities.  What was most criticized was the fact that existing theology
and philosophy nowhere touched man's concrete existence and therefore
provided no inspiration for man's life.  And it no longer corresponded
to the new needs of 16th century man.

As the Middle Ages unfolded, two themes which had been maintained in
tension became separated.  Spirituality ceased to exercise any fundamental role in the understanding of theology.  The change was gradual
and the causes complex, but this unfortunate dichotomy between theology
and spirituality resulted in sterile theology and in a spirituality
nourished for the most part by sentimentality.  Erasmus' life work consisted in a renewal of theology, a renewal based on the desire to unite
piety and theology.[26]  Erasmus could not think of piety as existing in
opposition to theology for theology and piety were both essential and
complementary aspects of a Christian life.

This renewal of theology involved an epistemological shift.  The
epistemological question of the relation of subjective perception to
objective truth and of language to being and the question of the certainty of knowledge had been long-established issues which continually
divided minds.  The Renaissance found, in the confluence of the rediscovery of the importance of eloquence and the dynamism of the biblical
word, new answers to these problems.  At the same time, the importance
given to the power of the Word gave origin to the *theologia rhetorica*,
where the knowledge of God became more of a moral virtue than an intellectual reality, where *sapientia* became intimately related to *pietas*.[27]

Calvin faced squarely the epistemological problems inherent in the
renewal of theology and the implications of this renewal in the realm of
spirituality.  Research in Calvin has never focussed its attention on
the epistemology grounding his spirituality.  In attempting to give proper weight both to the significant continuity of Calvin's spirituality
with preceding and contemporary spiritualities and at the same time to
its remarkable diversity, the focus has to be brought to bear upon Calvin's epistemology.  The originality of Calvin's position is attributable

to his epistemology and to the basic structure of his theory of the
knowledge of God.  The root and reason for the originality and distinc-
tiveness of his spirituality lay within his epistemology.  This epistemology established the proper foundations for the incipient individualistic and personalistic traits of the spirituality of the *Devotio Moderna*.
It also led to a new ecclesiological model and to the resolution of the
question of the mediating role of the Church in the spiritual life of
the believer.

## Notes

1. J. Dedieu, "Calvin et Calvinisme," in *Dictionnaire de Spiritualité*, T. II (Paris, 1953), col. 23-50; L. Bouyer, *La spiritualité orthodoxe et la spiritualité Protestante et Anglicane* (Paris, 1965), pp. 117-131; A. Ganoczy, *Le jeune Calvin: Genèse et évolution de sa vocation réformatrice* (Wiesbaden, 1966), pp. 208-232. In a recent book, G. Harkness, having defined mysticism as communion with God in a personal encounter, denies the presence of this mysticism in Calvin.

> As for Calvin, he seems to have been born to be an interpreter and systematizer of Christian theology, a careful and painstaking expositor of the Scriptures, and a firm disciplinarian in what he believed to be for the glory of God and the right conduct of a Christian community. But if God ever designed him to be a mystic, the plan got mislaid along the way! This is not to say that it would have been impossible, for he was a sincere Christian with a powerful devotion to the God whom he sought to exalt and serve. Augustine, we have seen, was a mystic and at the same time a great theologian and ecclesiastical statesman, but such a combination does not appear very often and it seems to have passed Calvin by.

G. Harkness, *Mysticism: Its Meaning and Message* (Nashville: Abingdon Press, 1973), p. 124.

2. J. Pannier, *Recherches sur la formation intellectuelle de Calvin* (Paris, 1951); P. Imbart de la Tour, *Les origines de la Réforme*, T. IV, *Calvin et l'Institution Chrétienne* (Paris, 1935); W. F. Dankbaar, *Calvijn, zijn Weg en Werk* (Nykerk, 1958); K. Reuter, *Das Grundverständnis der Theologie Calvins* (Neukirchen, 1963); F. Wendel, *Calvin. The Origins and Development of his Religious Thought* (New York, 1963); K. McDonnell, *John Calvin, the Church and the Eucharist* (Princeton, 1967), pp. 3-105; A. Ganoczy, *Le jeune Calvin*, pp. 23-196.

3. A. Ganoczy, *Calvin, théologien de l'Eglise et du ministère* (Paris, 1964), pp. 21-30.

4. *Ibid.*, pp. 57-58.

5. Alongside the development of the *Devotio Moderna* through Jerome to Erasmus, another stream flows from the devout piety of Bernard which comes through Augustinianism (and Augustine himself) and through Luther to Calvin. But Calvin follows the *Devotio Moderna* in the form of Erasmus' conceptual framework and incorporates it critically into his own theology in a fashion proper to a Reformed understanding of Scripture. He presents death and resurrection with Christ, rebirth, conversion to docility-obedience (taken in the Reformation understanding of Scripture), the basic stance to humility, penance, self-denial and submission to God alone and His word consistently with this pattern. He urges the coordination of inner states of mind with external behavior for the sanctification of the Christian. He exhorts to spiritual growth and takes the struggles and sufferings of the Christian as earnestly as he takes the believer's eschatological fulfillment. There is no essential point in the piety of "imitation" that Calvin has not worked over.

K. Reuter, *Das Grundverständnis*, p. 37.

6. "It is now apparent that his remarkable work (Calvin's *Institutes*) is at least in part one of the last fruits of the New Devotion." A. Hyma, *The Christian Renaissance* (Hamden, 1965), p. 284.

7. C. Warfield, *Calvin and Augustine* (Philadelphia, 1956), p. 22.

8. F. Wendel, *Calvin*, pp. 137-144.

9. *Ibid.*, p. 130.

10. K. Reuter, *Das Gründverständnis*, p. 22.

11. T. F. Torrance, "Knowledge of God and Speech about Him according to Calvin," *Revue d'Histoire et de Philosophie Religieuse* 44 (1964) 402-422.

12. A. Ganoczy, *Le jeune Calvin*, pp. 186-192.

13. A. Lavalée, "Calvin's Criticism of Scholastic Theology" (unpublished Ph.D. thesis, Harvard University, 1967), pp. 242-246.

14. K. McDonnell, *John Calvin*, p. 10.

15. *Ibid.*, p. 12.

16. *Ibid.*, pp. 18-19.

17. *Ibid.*, p. 20.

18. *Ibid.*, p. 21.

19. A. Ganoczy, *La Bibliothèque de l'Académie de Calvin* (Geneva, 1969), pp. 106-108.

20. H. M. Curtis, *Oxford and Cambridge in Transition 1558-1642* (Oxford, 1959), pp. 12-13.

21. Although the literature of the *Devotio Moderna* is vast, it has been made quite manageable through R. R. Post's important contribution on the subject. R. R. Post, *The Modern Devotion: Confrontation with Reformation and Humanism* (London, 1968).

22. Cf. J. Cadier, *Luther et les débuts de la Réforme française* (Paris, 1958); L. Febvre, *Au coeur religieux du XVIe siècle* (Paris, 1957); H. Hauser, A. Renaudet, *Les débuts de l'âge moderne: La Renaissance et la Réforme* (Paris, 1938); R. J. Lovy, *Les origines de la Réforme française, Meaux 1518-1546* (Paris, 1959).

23. G. Leff, *Paris and Oxford Universities in the Thirteenth and Fourteenth Centuries* (New York, 1969).

24. Cf. A. Humbert, *Les origines de la théologie moderne. I. La renaissance de l'antiquité chrétienne (1450-1521)* (Paris, 1911); Ch. Goerung, *La théologie d'après Érasmus et Luther* (Paris, 1913); A. Renaudet, *Préréforme et humanisme à Paris pendant les premières guerres d'Italie (1494-1515)* (Paris, 1916); A. Lang, *Die Loci theologici des Melchior Cano und die Methode des dogmatischen Beweises* (Munich, 1925); K. Eschweller, *Die zwei Wege der neueren Theologie. Eine kritische Untersuchung des Problems der theologischen Erkenntnis* (Augsbourg, 1926); P. Polman, *L'élement historique dans la controverse religieuse du XVIe siècle* (Gembloux, 1932).

25. R. W. Southern, *The Making of the M.A.* (London, 1953), p. 189.

26. After his *Epistola de philosophia christiana*, Erasmus published an *Exhortatio ad philosophiae christianae studium* 1519-1520, which in less than twenty years went through 35 editions.

27. Cf. E. Rice, *The Renaissance Idea of Wisdom* (Boston, 1958).

Chapter I

THE *DEVOTIO MODERNA*

A. *General Characteristics*

The *Devotio Moderna*,[1] as a current of spirituality, flourished during
the fifteenth and sixteenth centuries. It influenced such schools of
spirituality as the Erasmian and the Ignatian, and to a certain degree,
contemporary Protestant spirituality as well.[2] According to L. Spitz,
the modern devotionalists influenced nearly every humanist.[3] Until recently the *Devotio Moderna* as a movement was judged too medieval and too
orthodox to have had much influence on the course of reform; but the
work of recent scholars has demonstrated the wider social and intellectual context of the movement.[4]

The movement, known as the "Brothers of the Common Life,"[5] originated
under the impact of Gerhard Groote (1340-1384) of Deventer, who gathered
a following dedicated both to the contemplative and to the active life.
They lived in a community under a regimen like that of monks, calling
for fasts, vigils, readings and prayers, private and communal, inter-
spersed with long periods of silence. The *Devotio Moderna* meant personal reform through a return to Christian inwardness.[6] It was a free
movement, not limited, as were the monastic reforms, to an existing corporation regulated by law, nor burdened by tradition. Hence it was able
to develop in every direction. Like all genuine religious movements it
issued in active work. In fact, Groote himself had been a missionary.
Throughout north and west Germany, the brothers of Deventer and Zwolle
practiced an apostolate of the spoken and printed word through their
schools and writings. There was a pronounced lay dimension to the "devout movement," and by a remarkable coincidence similar lay apostolates
spung up in the southern half of Europe.

All these groups practiced what they called "inner devotion," from
which they derived their name. By this they understood, in general,
deep consciousness of a personal relationship with God and a perpetual
striving to direct all their work, prayer and spiritual exercise to Him.
This presupposed, however, the practice of the virtues of humility,
obedience, purity, mutual love and mortification, out of love of God.
With Thomas à Kempis this devotion was intensified to an exalted

mysticism, a contemplation of God, insofar as it was possible in this
world. Imitating Christ was thought to contribute to progress along
this road; hence constant meditation on Christ's life and passion was
recommended. In the beginning this meditation consisted of a brief reflection, repeated several times during the day before entering into any
activity. Wessel à Gansfort and John Mombaer developed this rumination
into a complex system of meditative exercises designed to focus the mind.
This method resembled meditation in the modern sense. The emphasis upon
inward fervor and conscious inner devotion did not, however, lead the
modern devotionalists to reject such oral prayers as the Hours, the
Rosary, the Psalms and vigils, and they held the holy mass in high
esteem, although they strove, through inward meditation, to prevent both
vocal prayer and liturgy from becoming too formalistic.

## B. Gerhard Groote

Gerhard Groote (1340-1384) is the recognized father of the *Devotio
Moderna*.[7] This is particularly striking in view of the shortness of his
effective apostolate: only ten years, from 1374 to 1384. But they were
years that saw the outbreak of the great schism, the departure of most
of the English masses from the university of Paris and the publication
of Wyclif's *De Eucharistia*. In that decade Groote emerged as the evan-
gelist of the north, and it was during that decade that he resolved--
following a conversion and probably an attendant psychological crisis--
to reject the world while living within it, as a simple penitent.[8] He
included in this conversion all that he desired to abandon or renounce,
now that he wished to direct his life towards the glory of God and His
service. He resolved not to value temporal advantage above salvation of
the soul, that is, never again to desire a benefice, and this liberated
his spirit. Considering freedom the highest good in the spiritual life,[9]
Groote determined to possess only essentials, to be content with what
was in accordance with participation in community life.[10] He did not
wish to enter the gainful service of an ecclesiastical or temporal lord,
and he renounced all profit which he might acquire from learning.[11] In
fact, he originally proposed to abandon all manner of scholarship. Philosophy and theology were not mentioned,[12] but of pagan learning he
would have retained only moral philosophy. And he rejected inquiry
into the secrets of nature in pagan books or even in the Old and New

Testaments. He did not wish to obtain any academic degree in medicine, in either branch of law, or theology.[13] He would not devote himself to any field of study or write any book to enhance his reputation. He wished to avoid public debates, considered those of the university inexpedient, and would not enter into private dispute with anyone. He even refused to continue his studies in Roman law and medicine.[14] What characterized this resolution was its search for spiritual freedom through the deliberate rejection of everything that is not essential. Some of the resolutions stressed the fact that learning itself is not essential.

Groote had a very realistic approach to spiritual life. What was of real importance, in his appraisal, was the conversion of the heart, the virtues, the bearing of difficulties and suffering, the apostolate and, above all, one's own salvation. To attain his eternal goal, man, who is really and truly a sinner, must convert himself. But by himself he can do nothing that is of value. His works are powerless and incapable of personal justification.

> From any complacency in our own selves or in our good works deliver us, Lord; from the thought that we may have done any good by ourselves, deliver us, Lord.[15]

Any thought of self-justification was foreign to Groote, but he did see man as having to choose between two directions. This concept of election was quite important to him.

> It is necessary for any creature to serve God, either a punishing God or a rewarding God; this service may be against its will, and therefore, for eternal punishment, or according to its will, and thus for eternal joy.[16]

For Groote this choice of a way of life was dependent upon man's knowledge of himself and upon his consciousness of the presence of the Spirit in him. Man had to be conscious of the presence of the Spirit,[17] for God really calls us and this call is felt interiorly. For Groote a correlation existed between interiority (the locus where God speaks to man, the life in Christ) and piety (zeal for the glory of God). These different notions made up the concept of devotion, which Groote called *Ynnicheit*. He considered devotion and interiority necessary components of the virtue of religion.

> By the virtue of religion, man is inclined to consecrate himself to the service of God, in order to honor him in an appropriate way.

> The work and interior exercises of religion are an intimate devo-
> tion, interiority and submission to the will of God.  Exterior
> works and exercises consist in adoration and the offering of one-
> self.[18]

Groote thought that this devotion manifested itself in daily life by
prayer, the breviary, examination of conscience and meditation.  It was
manifested in a very special fashion by the imitation of the humanity of
Christ which is the door to any authentic spiritual life.[19]

*Imitatio* does not present itself as the simple reenactment of the
gestures of Christ, although these actions have a role in our lives as
topics of meditation.[20]  Rather, this imitation is more a configuration,
that is, an actualization of the model, the type, that one wants to
become perfected in one's life.[21]  The imitation of Christ demanded by
Groote was really an active way of life, and not merely contemplative.
This active imitation of Christ was to be primarily a humble self-
dispossession.  Groote understood humility not primarily as a moral virtue, but as the very foundation of the spiritual life.  Only humility
can create in the human soul that emptiness that God alone can fill.[22]
If man denies himself, humbles himself, God can empty himself into this
nothingness.

The notion of universal order (*ordo universalis*) was fundamental for
Groote.  It was at the foundation of his understanding of law and morality.  *Ordo*, according to Groote, is a hierarchy of values and goods.  To
this order corresponds the *ordinatio*, which for Groote had two meanings:
From *God's side* this *ordinatio* is the manner in which God disposes everything for man's salvation.  *Ordinatio* is therefore equivalent to God's
will.  Speaking about monastic obedience, for instance, Groote wrote
that God has willed that a monk be saved by obedience to his superior,
and that any resistance to this obedience would be a resistance to God's
*ordinatio*.[23]  From *man's* point of view, *ordinatio* includes all that is
necessary for man to attain the end and purpose of his human life, i.e.
the service and glory of God, the sanctification of the name of God.[24]
*Ordinatio* for man consists in accepting everything God sends and wants
for him.  For Groote this was the only attitude possible for one who
sought peace of mind.

In the conclusion of his book, De Beer[25] characterizes the spirituality of Groote as voluntaristic, practical and not exclusively directed
toward the contemplation of God but toward the love of God and all

things.  Since it had as its main concern the salvation of the soul,
Groote's spirituality acquired an anthropocentric-utilitarian character.
De Beer finds that this was accompanied by a somewhat mercenary spirit
which required a return for effort involved.

Groote had a distaste for all empty formality,[26] although his spiritual life was liturgically oriented.[27]  Conceding that over-emphasis of
externals was always possible, Groote considered that it is not really
the outward state that matters, but the inward state.

Groote's ecclesiology was not without influence on his spirituality
and that of his followers.  Groote exercised an active apostolate during
the outbreak of the great schism.  Although he did not adopt a neutral
attitude towards the two popes but supported Urban VI, Groote did not
think of the schism in legal terms, but viewed it with the eyes of a
believer who saw the one church divided.  He did not regard the split as
a true schism, but as a division resulting from the papal question.  More
important than all this is Groote's view of the unity of the Church.
Groote was aware of the imperfection of the existing Church and consequently consoled himself with the idea of an invisible church of the
Spirit.  He had a tendency to divide the Church in two:  the triumphant,
invisible, spiritual Church, and the visible, institutional and juridical Church.  This distinction was particularly evident in his letter on
the schism.

> The direction of soul purifies the conscience and gives man access
> to the triumphant and celestial church; it unites man to the mysti-
> cal body of Christ; but jurisdiction purifies the militant church,
> composed of good and bad members, it purifies the church in exterior
> matters of some enormous scandals and abuses among its members,
> although the time has not yet come for all the scandals to be sup-
> pressed.[28]

At times Groote seemed to make of the Church militant a simple human
institution.  To emphasize the unity of the Church in a time of schism
Groote insisted on an interior dimension of unity, but at the expense of
external and hierarchical unity.  He reasoned that Christ is truly the
head of the Church and it is from a vivifying and interior order that
unity proceeds.  The pope then can be outside of that Church of Christ;
he may not even be a member of the Church but only the head of that congregation which is called the house of God (caput istius congregationis
vocata domus Domini).  His rule over the Church is purely exterior, and

his power juridical *(secundum iudicialem presidenciam et regnam)*.[29]   In
this same text Groote explained that the faithful are members of the
body of Christ according to their degree of personal holiness.  They are
united to Christ according to their charity *(secundum ligam seraphicam)*
and their faith *(veritatem cherubicam)*.  Groote stressed the bond of love
rather than the ties of authority.  Attachment to the Church is two-fold,
one spiritual, inner, and therefore by nature invisible (that of love
and faith), the other external and necessarily visible (that of authority and direction from a unique head, the pope).  Not having explained
where the pope receives his power, Groote seems to have separated the
spiritual power of Christ over his mystical body from the power of the
pope who became in his view the head only of the juridical institution.
Groote drew a clear distinction between Christ as the head of the Church
and the authority of the pope.  Although he agreed that union with
Christ is always a necessary element to membership in the Church, he
thought it possible that the link with the pope could be totally absent.
The traditional medieval concept of the Church was here put into danger.
Groote clearly accented the primacy of the mystical unity of the Church,
somewhat at the expense of the visible primacy.  Speaking of the Church's
visible unity, Groote stressed that union with the head does not consist
so much in a link with the pope but in unity with the ecclesiastical institution which by nature transcends the very person of the pope.[30]

In the same way that Groote's concept of the Church colored his spirituality and influenced his followers, so did his understanding of the
nature and place of knowledge.  Some of the resolutions occasioned by
his conversion explicitly deal with these notions.  For instance he vir-
tually rejected scholasticism, its study, terrain and methods.  Speaking
of philosophy he wrote:

> Alas, how misguided are the young people today, that they, depend-
> ing only on the personal work of Aristotle, or of another philoso-
> pher whom they esteem very highly, persuade and convince themselves
> of many opinions which they scarcely understand, or indeed even
> before they have penetrated to the heart of them, solely on account
> of the person who expresses them.  But this, which today is only
> one great hindrance to philosophy, arises from the fact that when
> reflecting on the intelligible, people take account of such an
> incidental thing as another's pronouncement on the subject.  There
> is, however, another greater and more widespread hindrance--and
> this lies in philosophy itself--namely, that apart from the first-
> mentioned methods of philosophizing, our students of philosophy,
> when concerning themselves with the essentials of things, their

nature, and their genera and species, do not direct their minds to
reality but for the greater part only to verbal expressions themselves.  I must confess that I have philosophized in this manner
for a very long time.[31]

But his efforts to keep his library well stocked is a sign that he did
not abandon learning altogether nor reject his theological studies completely.  Nonetheless, for Groote, true knowledge was knowledge of the
Gospel.  In one of the resolutions expressed in his *De Sacris Libris
Studendis* Groote affirmed:

I return to learning:  the root of your knowledge and the mirror of
your life is the Gospel of Christ.[32]

He called this knowledge of God a *true philosophy*.

When shall the soul depart from this damp cave and fly up to the
freedom of the celestial, the peace of the devout, the engagement
of the true philosophy which is God?[33]

A great deal of what Groote wrote he inherited from his predecessors.
De Beer gives a list of the books which Groote had copied and which he
liked to possess, and also of the authors to whom Groote constantly referred in setting out his own opinions.  The books that make up the list
comprise nearly the whole of the medieval spiritual literature.[34]

Because of his situation in time, Groote's doctrine was somewhat
ambiguous; it led in different directions.  In fact there are two different and contrary tendencies in Groote's spirituality.  On the one
hand he sought to withdraw from the world, to work in solitude toward
the perfection of his own soul and the continuing self-dispossession demanded by an active imitation of the person of Christ.  Groote was fully
in sympathy with the whole monastic state and extolled it as being the
most perfect way to salvation.[35]  On the other hand Groote also sought
to be an apostle, to reform the Church through his preaching.  He had a
sober sense of reality and his spirituality is intended for a man in
this world.  His spirituality to a large extent can be termed a lay
spirituality.

One or the other of these tendencies will mark the followers of
Groote.  The Brethren of the Common Life will strive to live a religious
life in the world; while the Canons of Windesheimer will further the
monastic tendencies in Groote's spirituality.

## C.  *Groote's Immediate Disciples*

Chief among Groote's followers and helpers was Florens Redewijns
(1350-1400).  He was, with Groote, the co-founder of the Brothers of
the Common Life and was at the head of the devotionalist movement from
Groote's death until his own, that is from 1384 to 1400.[36]  Apart from
a few various *Notabilia Verba*,[37] only two works of his have been preserved:  *Multum valet*[38] and *Omnes inquit artes*.  What characterizes the
spirituality of Florens is its practical aspect.[39]  "There is no true
knowledge unless it is acquired in order to act."[40]  His writings are
didactic and moralizing.  He gave advice on ordering the interior and
exterior aspects of the spiritual life and designated norms for attaining self-knowledge.  He had no concept of the spiritual life as a hierarchical ascension toward union with God; from the different writings
he quoted, he always underlined the purgative and eliminative dimensions
of the spiritual life.  His spiritual doctrine is quite well indicated in
this quotation from his *Notabilia Verba*:  "Whatever man does he must do
it only for the glory of God."[41]  In view of this glory of God Florens
wanted to renew the apostolical life *(vita apostolica)* in and through
the fraternities of the Brothers of the Common Life.

After Groote and Florens, the most important author among the Brothers of the Common Life was Geert Zerbolt van Zutphen (1367-1398) who
wrote two significant treatises:  *De Reformatione Virium Animae* and the
*De Spiritualibus Ascensionibus*.[42]  Both works were widely read and influenced later spiritual writers.

Their contents accord essentially with Florens' two treatises--a description of the practice of virtue and of the way to attain purity of
soul--but these themes are treated in different ways.  In his understanding of the spiritual life, Zerbolt always began with the visible
situation of the sinful man, who must be conscious of his sin and of
the necessity of conversion.  In the very first chapter of his *De Spiritualibus Ascensionibus* Zerbolt emphasized the fact that man is inclined
by nature to turn upwards to God:

> I know, O man, that you are desirous to go upward and that you do
> long earnestly to be lifted up, for you are a creature reasonable
> and noble, endowed with a certain greatness of mind, wherefore you
> do seek lofty heights and ascend thereto by reason of a desire that
> is of your nature.[43]

But the spiritual ascent which realizes itself in different stages has
its starting point in man's own depravity and degeneration, as experienced in original sin, concupiscence, and mortal sin. These are the
direct opposites of original justice.

> From this it comes that now these powers and afflictions are in-
> clined in a direction far removed from that to which God ordained
> them, being prone to evil and going headlong to the desire of that
> which is unlawful. Nay, moreover, reason herself, having become
> blind, wandering and dull, does often take falsehood for truth, and
> enmesh herself in unprofitable curious matters. The will has be-
> come crooked, does often choose the worst part and loves carnal
> things, making light of things spiritual and heavenly.[44]

Zerbolt proceeded from the decline of the soul's powers, which had lost
their energy and direction, to their restoration. In contrast with this
triple deprivation he posited a triple ascension: conversion, ordered
love and sanctification of the faculties. The means to ascend from one
level to the other are, according to Zerbolt, self-knowledge, repentance,
combat of sin, mortification and the practice of humility and obedience
through prayer, spiritual reading and meditation. The highest level to
be attained and last ascent to be made is contemplation. Zerbolt described the way that leads to contemplation, but he did not describe the
state itself.

In this framework of levels and ascents there is a very evident
stress on the concept of order and an existing pattern to which man must
conform.

> Thus it was that God, the first cause of all things, brought into
> actual being those things themselves in fitting fashion and form,
> making nothing save in accordance with the essential and ideal pat-
> tern of all things.[45]

This order is revealed to us in the person of Christ who becomes our
model. The imitation of Christ, the *imitatio Christi*, was central to
Zerbolt's spirituality. Christ is the only model to be followed and
this imitation is realized in three different steps or ascents.[46] The
first imitation is based on an appreciation of Christ's humanity and the
beauty of this humanity. The second imitation is found in the discovery
and appreciation of the divinity in Christ. Since Christ is both God
and man, this imitation demands both great devotion, love and confidence,
and fear and reverence.[47] The third phase of our imitation of Christ is
union with God.

A man does begin to be in a certain manner and spirit with God, to
pass outside himself, to perceive the very truth and to be made
united to God and to cleave to him.[48]

To be able to further one's ascent in the imitation of Christ, besides the exercises of true virtue and true devotion, Zerbolt prescribed
three exercises:  reading, meditation, and prayer.[49]  These three exercises are centered on the very person of Christ.

By meditation is meant the process in which you do diligently turn
over in your heart whatsoever you have read or heard, earnestly
ruminating the same and thereby enkindling your affections in some
particular manner or enlightening your understanding.[50]

A large part of the book, *De Spiritualibus Ascensionibus*, consists of
material for meditation, derived from the last things, death and judgment, and especially the passion of Christ.

D.  *Thomas à Kempis and the* De Imitatione Christi

Thomas à Kempis (1380-1471) is one of the most important representatives of the *Devotio Moderna*, and his treatise, *De Imitatione Christi*,
is one of the great classics of Christian spirituality.[51]  On every page
of the *De Imitatione* one meets thoughts already expressed by Groote,
Florens and Zerbolt.  In fact we have in *De Imitatione Christi* the confluence of most of the important currents and themes of medieval spirituality.  The book served as a channel through which Augustinian, Bernardian and Franciscan spiritualities influenced the sixteenth century
and those which followed.[52]  The very fact that the authorship of the
book has been the object of extensive discussion is a sign of its ecu-
menicity.  The title of the book refers to a very profound and ever-
present theme in the history of Christian spirituality.[53]  Statistical
study of key phrases in the work does not indicate as much the importance of the concept of imitation of Christ, as it underlines the necessity of spiritual combat.[54]

For Thomas à Kempis, the imitation of Christ is the criterion to
measure the vitality of one's spiritual life.

If you desire to be purified from your vices and to progress in the
exercise of virtue, love the life and passion of Christ, whom the
Father sent in the world as an example of all virtues.[55]
The imitation of Christ is the way of the cross, the doctrine of
our salvation, the wisdom of the saints, the will of mankind.[56]

Christ becomes for man primarily a pattern of self-mortification. Self-renunciation and resignation are ranked highly among virtues.[57]  We find in the *De Imitatione Christi* the themes of spiritual nudity, *nuditas*, of self-dispossession, *exspoliari*, and self-detachment, *resignatio*. The one who follows Christ takes pain to bring his entire life into conformity with Christ.  He who strives to imitate Christ will withdraw from love of visible things and transfer his affection to the invisible, for following sensual inclination stains the conscience.[58]  He will find true inward peace by resisting the fleshly passions.[59]  If we were stricter with ourselves and not entangled in outward things, we could taste of divine things.[60]  Suffering and grief are good for us, for they protect us from vainglory and teach us not to hope in earthly things.[61] Self-discipline is called for; one ought to root out one evil habit each year;[62]

> Keep your eye upon yourself in the first place, and especially admonish yourself in preference to admonishing all your friends.[63]

Indeed,

> the more violence you do to yourself, the greater will be your growth in grace.[64]

The imitation of Christ is the way of the cross; in order to go into life everlasting, man must take up the cross and follow Christ.[65]

> There is no other way to life and to true inward peace save the way of the holy cross, and of daily mortification.[66]

The different themes of self-dispossession can be systematically outlined in the following manner:  separation from all created reality effects spiritual poverty.

> Rare indeed is a man so spiritual as to strip himself of all things. And who shall find a man so truly poor in spirit as to be free from every creature?[67]

Self-dispossession causes the purity of heart necessary for the effective contemplation of God.

> Be pure and free within, unentangled with any creature.  You must bring to God a clean and open heart if you wish to taste and to see how sweet the Lord is.[68]

This self-dispossession is primarily achieved through the imitation of Christ:

Strive for this, pray for this, desire this, to be stripped of all selfishness and naked to follow the naked Jesus, to die to self and live forever.[69]

All this self-dispossession finally renews man.

You must put on the new man. You must be changed into another man. You must often do these things you do not wish to do and forego those you do wish.[70]

Underlying this emphasis on self-denial and self-dispossesion is the affirmation that man is in exile, a pilgrim here on earth. Man is a prisoner and his prison is the flesh which continually besets him with obstacles.[71] Not only is he a pilgrim and prisoner on earth, but he is also in a pitiable state. Because of original sin man has lost his beatitude and is constantly attracted to sin *(ad malum semper prona)*.[72] Thomas à Kempis distinctively taught the depravity of human nature.[73] Man has fallen so low that he cannot rise anymore without divine help. But since he was created in God's image, something divine remains in his sinful heart:

For the small part which remains as it were a spark *(scintilla quaedam)*, light hid in the ashes.[74]

This part cannot be animated through man's own activity, however, but only through God's grace. Although the author of the *De Imitatione Christi* insists strongly on man's own activity, as a true mystic he is very much aware of the impossibility of arriving at a vision or intuition of God without God's own intervention. The mystics, more so than others, feel the incapacity of nature to reach God. They are very conscious of man's passivity in relation to God, for without God no holiness is possible.[75] God intervenes in the life of man through his grace. And this grace is continually needed in man's life.[76] With God's grace man is capable of all; without it he can do nothing. This grace given by God is supernatural life, the pledge of everlasting salvation, continually transforming man to a greater resemblance to God.[77]

It is in this framework of grace and its dynamic transforming power that the self-knowledge advocated by the Greek philosophers is understood. This self-knowledge so important to the development of the spiritual life is knowledge of Christ himself, a knowledge that leads to the imitation of Christ.[78] Illuminated by Christ, man realizes the two most important truths about himself: that his own condition is that of

pilgrim and sinner; and that the purpose of his life is to serve God in
humility and obedience in the footsteps of Christ. We have already
spoken of the first truth about man, of his precarious existence and his
need for self-dispossession. Self-knowledge reveals man's fragility,
his tendency to instability and his incapacity to pursue his own true
good.

> How great is the frailty of human nature which is ever prone to
> evil. Today you confess your sins and tomorrow you again commit
> the same sins which you confessed. One moment you resolve to be
> careful and yet after an hour you act as though you had made no
> resolution.[79]
> Man must see himself as he is: nothing, *nihileitas*. Truly to
> know and despise self is the best and most perfect counsel. To
> think of oneself as nothing and always to think well and highly of
> others is the best and most perfect wisdom.[80]

The recurring word is *nihil*: *nihil sum*; *nihil habeo*; *nihil valeo*.[81]
Nothing can be found in man which truly belongs to him. That which constitutes the foundation of his being and his positive value is his dependence upon God. This basic truth about man, his destiny to serve God
and the acknowledgement of his total dependence on God is clearly and
often underlined in the *De Imitatione Christi*.

Man has been called to serve and honor God. "All is vanity therefore
except to love God and serve him alone."[82] The service of God demands
on the part of the servant a fundamental attitude of humility. Humility
seems to rank above all other virtues in the spirituality of the *De Imitatione Christi*.[83] The word humility and its derivatives, humiliate,
humiliation, humble and humbly, function as a key to the understanding
of the spirituality of Thomas à Kempis. Man's intrinsic value is measured in proportion to his humility.[84] Such humility can only be based
upon the acceptance of one's complete dependence upon God. At the same
time it demands a tremendous amount of detachment and mortification. We
have already seen the role of self-denial and self-dispossession in this
spirituality. The stripping of oneself in humility acknowledges the
glory of God. There is no place in man for any self-admiration or appreciation.

> O how humble and lowly should I consider myself. How very little
> should I esteem anything that seems good to me. How profoundly
> should I submit to your unfathomable judgments, Lord, for I find
> myself to be but nothing.[85]
> He who attributes any good to himself hinders God's grace from

coming to his heart, for the grace of the Holy Spirit seeks always the humble heart.[86]

For man's merits are not measured by many visions or consolations or by knowledge of the Scriptures or by his being in a higher position than others, but by the truths of his humility, by his capacity for divine charity, by his constancy in seeking purely and entirely the order of God, by his disregard and positive contempt of self and more, by preferring to be despised and humiliated rather than honored by others.[87]

This radical humility even extends to a willingness to part with divine consolation and to live in tribulation and darkness.

I do not desire consolation that robs me of contrition, nor do I care for contemplation that leads to pride, for not all that is high is holy, nor is all that is sweet good, nor every desire pure, nor all that is clear to us pleasing to God. I accept willingly the grace whereby I become more humble and contrite, more willing to renounce self.[88]

The predominant attitude of the humble man toward all that is not of God is that of indifference. "For nothing among all the wonders of heaven and earth is like to you."[89]

This radical humility is not without its own effects. It is a cause of peace in the humble believer.[90] Humility is the very condition of our understanding of scripture. "If you would profit from it, therefore, read with humility."[91]

This humility which conditions our understanding of scripture leads also to a radical mortification of our desire for vain knowledge which leads man away from God and distracts him from his main purpose in life.

What good does it do to speak learnedly about the Trinity if lacking humility you displease the Trinity. Indeed it is not learning that makes man holy and just, but a virtuous life makes him pleasing to God. I would rather feel contrition than know how to define it. What would it profit us to know the whole Bible by heart and the principles of all the philosophers if we live without grace and the love of God? Vanity of vanities, all is vanity except to have God and serve him alone.[92]

Man makes more progress from forsaking all things than by studying subtleties. Thomas à Kempis seemed to delight in employing the concept of learning in a pejorative context, for example, "Learning without love and grace," "Learning without the fear of God," or "If I should know everything that was in the world."

One striking characteristic of the *De Imitatione Christi* is an almost complete lack of concern with dogma and systematic theology. The author

cautions us of a purely abstract theology, which, in his eyes, is quite
irrelevant to the spiritual life.[93] The author considered scholastic
disputes worthless, empty talk.  This denigration of learning is in the
spirit of Groote's resolution.  This rejection of formal theology and
philosophy as superfluous may be, in part, a reaction against the steril-
ity of fifteenth-century scholasticism.  But it has deeper roots than
that.  It is related to the understanding that everything comes from God
through Christ and this causal relationship of God to man is evident in
a very particular way in relation to the true knowledge which is knowledge of self and of God.  Everything indeed is attributed to God, who
will teach us all things.

> Though you shall have read and learned many things, it will always
> be necessary for you to return to this one principle:  I am he who
> teaches man knowledge, and to the little ones I give a clearer
> understanding than can be thought by man.  I am he who in one moment
> so enlightens the humble mind that it comprehends more of eternal
> truth than could be learned by ten years in the schools.  I teach
> without noise or words or clash of opinions, without ambition for
> honor or confusion of argument.  I within them am the teacher and
> the truth, the understander of thoughts.[94]

Knowledge of God and knowledge of man are understood in revelational
terms as a gift received from the Father.  The attitude of the receiver
is that of pure faith, a submission of reason to faith.

> Submit yourself to God and humble reason to faith.  From the light
> of understanding will be given you so far as it is good and neces-
> sary for you.  Human reason is weak and can be deceived.  True
> faith, however, cannot be deceived.  All reason and natural science
> ought to come after faith, not go before it, nor oppose it.[95]

In the context of this revelational understanding of knowledge and the
concomitant importance of faith, it is easy to understand how important
the Gospel is for Thomas à Kempis.  "Attend to my words which enkindle
the heart and enlighten the mind, which excite contrition and abound in
manifold consolation."[96]  The *Imitation* is remarkable both for the number
of biblical quotations it contains and for the lack of reference to any
other source.  Thomas regarded the reading of Scripture as absolutely
essential.[97]

Divinely given knowledge has different effects upon man.  It can lift
the soul above itself.  It can be characterized by an ecstasy of the
mind *(in excessu mentis stare)*[98] in which sublime truths are understood

without difficulty in light given from above.[99] This knowledge truly
inflames the heart and instills the necessary strength to follow Christ.
For the very source of this knowledge is Christ himself, *magister magis-*
*trorum.*[100]

Returning to the theme of *imitation* the author states that the degree
and level of a man's knowledge depends on the closeness of his conformity to Christ.[101] The theme of conformity, not only of one's life to
that of Christ, but more fundamentally of one's will to that of God, is
predominant in the *De Imitatione.*[102] This conformity of will is the
highest point of humility and a continual source of peace and joy. It
is also the source of unity and source of contemplation.[103] Humility
and mortification, imitation of Christ and conformity of one's will to
the Father's are fully expressed in the concrete love of the believer.
The violence done to oneself, mortification and abnegation, are neither
servitude nor sadism, but a work of love. Love makes the difficult
easy; it feels no burden, it is always ready to do more.[104] Love is the
very essence of spiritual life. Love tends upward to God for it is
basically from God and cannot rest except in God. Love is the dynamism
of all spiritual life.[105] He who has understood the message of Christ
can only pray and hope for one thing: to be dissolved in love, *dilata*
*in amore;* to love God more than oneself and all others in God.[106]

What has been described till now as the essential characteristics of
the spirituality of the *De Imitatione Christi* are indicative of an emphasis on personal piety, on the inner life of the Spirit and direct communion with God.

Except for the fourth chapter, "Concerning the Sacrament," the *De*
*Imitatione Christi* has practically nothing to say about the sacramental
mediation in the spiritual life. And even the sacrament of the Eucharist, the only sacrament considered, seems to be understood more as food
for the Spirit than as a means for salvation. Holy Communion and the
reading of holy scripture are considered the two things necessary to the
faithful soul.

> I feel there are especially necessary for me in this life two
> things without which its miseries would be unbearable. Confined
> here in this prison of the body I confess I need these two, food
> and light. Therefore you have given me in my weakness the sacred
> flesh to refresh my soul and body, and you have set your word as a
> guiding light for my feet. Without them I could not live or write,

for the word of God is the light of my soul, and the sacrament is the bread of life.[107]

The sacrament must be food for inner devotion, and inner devotion must be present at the reception of the sacrament. Thomas respected the status of the priest and recognized in the mass a definite link with Christ's sacrifice on the cross, the commemoration of the mysteries of salvation. Thomas recommended meditation on Christ's life and passion during the mass. This sacramental attitude was accompanied by the insistence that the grace of devotion is obtained through humility and rejection of self. Even in a sacramental context, emphasis was on the inner life of the spirit and a direct communion with God.

A tendency to minimize the importance of the intermediary agencies provided by the Church underlined this emphasis. In his intense preoccupation with the inner life, Thomas à Kempis tends to regard visible symbols and formal acts as mere externals without value unless accompanied by strong internal feeling. There is no questioning of the orthodox beliefs as practices of the Church. But he shows a subtle criticism of the institutionalized religion of the day. There is a fundamental shift in emphasis away from the sacramental and sacerdotal aspects of medieval religion on which the authority of the Church over the lay world was founded.[108] Most indicative of this is the *De Imitatione*'s lack of teaching on the Church. The Church is hardly ever mentioned.[109] We have already indicated to some extent the place of the Church in Groote's theology. Later medieval theology changed from a communal understanding of the Church to a church understood as a means of salvation.[110] In the context of Church understood as communion, the believer's life and union with God is in and through the Church.[111] In the context of Church understood as a channel of salvation, life and union with God can be understood in a more individualistic fashion. The Church is an aid to, not really the locus of, the spiritual life.

The Church is considered as an institution of salvation. This concept is understood clearly when *De Imitatione* describes the function of the priest and the nature of the Eucharist. The priest is a distributor of the Church's treasures.

When the priest celebrates mass, he honors God, helps the living, brings rest to the departed and wins for himself a share of all good therein.[112]

When the effects of the Eucharist are described, the ecclesiological
dimension of the sacraments is not mentioned.  The Eucharist is described as *medicina*[113] and as a *medicamen* and *remedium*[114] as something
for the soul only.[115]  The communicant's main concern is the attainment
of the beatific vision and his own eternal bliss.  Although he may pray
for his neighbor, the devout person should separate himself from others
during mass.

> Let it be granted me to find you alone, O Christ, to open to you my
> whole heart, to enjoy you as my soul  desires, to be disturbed by
> no one, to be moved and troubled by no creature, that you may speak
> to me and I to you alone as a lover speaks to his loved one and as
> a friend converses with friend.  I pray for this, I desire this,
> that I may be completely united to you and may withdraw my heart
> from created things, learning to relish the celestials and eternal
> through holy communion and the frequent celebration of mass.[116]

The Eucharist does not deepen one's incorporation in the Church.  It
does not strengthen bonds established with one's neighbor.  The effects
of the Eucharist are personal.[117]  It has a salvatory and comforting
function, with very little relation to the ecclesial or the cosmic.

     This individualistic approach is also clearly indicated in a treat-
ment of the bridal theme.  In St. Bernard the bride was considered primarily to be the Church and not the particular and individual soul.  If
the soul can consider itself a bride at all it is only within the Church,
which is the true bride.[118]  In the *Imitation*, the whole bridal mystique
lies in the loving encounter of the individual soul with Christ.[119]

     What becomes clear in reading these many texts is a lack of awareness
of the ecclesial reality in the author of the *Imitation*.  Love of neighbor is not clearly seen as related to the love of God.  In fact, love of
neighbor is treated with suspicion.  Participation in the life of others
is rejected in favor of the effort to save one's own soul.  The goal of
one's spiritual life becomes somewhat egocentric.  It is not a joyous
witness to God's love and will for all men, with its outgoing giving,
moral consequences and implication of this.  It is not a striving for an
ideal that is the highest social as well as individual good.  For while
perfection in the *De Imitatione* is a universal kingdom of peace, it is
peace and happiness of the self.

     The main preoccupation of *De Imitatione Christi* is the interior life
of the individual.  There is very little interest in the apostolate of a
service of God and the world.  The spirituality of Thomas à Kempis is

essentially monastic.  It is in essence a personalization of devotion.

E.  *The Later Disciples of Groote and the* De Imitatione Christi

Because of certain external and sociological circumstances affecting
the structures of Christian life, the *Devotio Moderna* moved during the
latter part of the fifteenth century in the direction of a more systematic and methodical approach to the spiritual life.  A series of
authors developed exact exercises to be followed as a sort of spiritual
gymnastic that could assure productive meditation.  The purpose of these
exercises was to help the soul fold back upon itself, defend its own
interiority and develop a personal religious and spiritual life.  One
thing that emerged from all the writings of the *Devotio Moderna* was the
elaboration and gradual popularization of a systematic method of private
meditative prayer which wielded a wide and profound influence.  A "science of meditation" came into being with its own rules and principles,
which, if regularly and systematically observed, was eminently calcu-
lated to strengthen in each individual habits of self-control and perseverance in the struggle for virtue.  Italy, Spain and Germany felt the
impact of this northern spiritual influence which brought order and
staying power, as well as a new devotional warmth *(Innerlichkeit)*, into
spirituality.

Although most of the later authors of the *Devotio Moderna* wrote specifically for monks, the self-control, attention to prayer, perseverance,
virtue and sense of dedication that are necessary in the religious life
apply in some degree to all Christians.  This movement of ordered and
meditative prayer was woven into the traditional doctrine of the three
ways or stages of the spiritual life, the purgative, the illuminative
and the unitive.  And it was eventually the movement's wider task to
reform the laity and clergy alike.

Groote had already recommended meditation upon the life of Jesus in
order to be able to imitate him.  Radewijns had written a small treatise
of spiritual exercises *(Tractatulus de spiritualibus exercitiis)* wherein
he outlined and stressed the importance of the three ways of the spiritual life.  Zerbolt had written his *De Spiritualibus ascensionibus*
which outlined different methods of maintaining one's ascent in the
spiritual life.  John Wessel of Gansfort wrote his *Scala meditatoria*
describing a complete method of prayer, in three stages, subdivided in

different acts:  *consideratio, attentio, explanatio, ruminatio, optio,*
*confessio, gratiarum actio.*

These different methods and exercises were outlined by John Mombaer
(1460-1501) in his book *Rosetum exercitiorum spiritualium et sacrarum*
*meditationum,* an encyclopedia of the spirituality of the *Devotio Mo-*
*derna.*[120]  The aim of the *Rosetum* was to foster the inner life.  Its
purpose was to help in the principal functions of the devotional life--
the praying of the hours, communion and meditation--which could only be
accomplished well by not allowing the mind to wander.  To help avoid
distraction Mombaer elaborated a system called the *chiro psalterium.*  In
praying the psalms one would stroke his thumb along the inside of his
other finger while articulating a prayer or intention.  Each articula-
tion had a different meaning.  On the four fingers of his left hand Mombaer indicated as many as twenty-eight very brief pious reflections or
prayer intentions.  Once someone had learned these by heart and stroked
along each finger in turn, the associated words or texts could arouse
and maintain in him the desired pious thoughts and intentions.  These
were thoughts that very often recur in the psalms:  thoughts on penance,
praise of God, thanksgiving, and so forth.

The popular "ladders," such as the *scala communionis* and the *scala*
*meditationis* were also aids, in their case, in the reception of communion
and in meditation.  The *scala communionis* helped one receive communion
with devotion.  The *scala meditativa* was intended to help focus the mind
on the subject of meditation.  All of these methods were complicated and
artificial and could easily lead to formalism.  There is no doubt that
for Mombaer, meditative inner prayer was of more value than spoken
prayer.  He considered meditation necessary for salvation.  This insistence also colored his understanding of the sacrament of communion, in
which he saw little advantage.  He even considered it detrimental if not
accompanied by inner meditation.  Spiritual communion had all the advantages of sacramental communion, advantages described in very individualistic and non-ecclesial terms.

*F.  Evaluation of the* Devotio Moderna

It may be argued that the *Devotio Moderna* is not discontinuous with
the medieval spirituality.  It seems to be the confluence of some very
important currents of medieval spirituality, acting as a canal through

which Augustinian, Bernardian and Franciscan spiritualities influenced
the sixteenth century and those which followed.  Since, however, its
contemporaries gave it a distinct name, it would seem that they themselves considered it to be distinctive.  In the title *Devotio Moderna*,
there is first of all the word *devotio*, whose meaning characterizes the
nature of this movement.  In the theological language of the fifteenth
century this word essentially meant service of God and had not yet
acquired a pejorative sense.  This *devotio* is said to be modern because
it appeared to be so at the time of its appearance.[121]  The modern devotionalists applied this name, modern,[122] to themselves because they
claimed to possess their own distinctive quality in the domain of piety,
devotion and spirituality.  They did not, however, clearly state in what
this distinctive modern quality consisted, although they constantly discussed their spirituality, their ideals and the application thereof
among themselves.  The originality and modernity of the *Devotio Moderna*
can be overstressed.  But so can the opposite; the *Devotio Moderna* can
be considered as having little that is distinctive or characteristic to
itself.  This, I think, would be a wrong approach.  There is no doubt
that the *Devotio Moderna* is a carrier of important themes of Western
spirituality.  Further, it cannot be treated as a monolithic movement.
We already have mentioned that in the father of the *Devotio Moderna*,
Groote, two contrary tendencies seemed to be present, that of withdrawal
from the world and that of the apostolate.  The spirituality of the *De
Imitatione Christi* is essentially monastic, but missionaries were sent
from Deventer and Windesheim to reform religious communities in Paris
and in other parts of Europe.  In evaluating the *Devotio Moderna* as a
movement one must be conscious of different emphases present in the
movement itself.

In its general thrust the *Devotio Moderna* was a reaction to an ex-
cess of speculation in the spiritual life.  It was a return to the
primacy of love, to a simple conformity with Christ, to the practice of
the virtues of humility and detachment.  The moral and ascetical values
took a primary place as a concrete expression of one's love for God.
There was a spiritual discipline made up of meditation, examination of
conscience, corporal mortification.  Contemplation lost its intellectual aspect and identified itself practically with the perfection of
charity.  The active and contemplative ways are put on the same footing.

The *Devotio* emphasizes asceticism over mysticism, methodological and practical questions over theoretical ones, the extirpation of vice rather than the ascent to ecstasy. Stress was placed upon piety and deportment. Piety was marked by a heartfelt, lyrical devotion to Jesus, an undeviating endeavor to follow in his steps.

One of the most persistent notes in this piety was inwardness. The ideal was the *homo compunctus, internus et devotus*. In its desire for inwardness the *devotio* commanded solitude and silence; in dealings with men it saw only danger and temptation; it claimed that the basis for perfection is self-knowledge. Spiritualistic stress on religious and almost stoical ethical standards led the *Devotio Moderna* to minimize the effectiveness of the sacraments as channels of grace and of the church as the instrument of salvation. Because of its insistence on direct communion and unity of the soul with God, it tended to become individualistic and divorce itself from common liturgical worship and the sacramental life of the Church.

With the fourteenth and fifteenth centuries the Church loses its predominant role in the spirituality and piety. Although many themes remain the same, the spirit is different. The *Devotio Moderna* reflects very clearly this transformation. There is a desire for direct communion and unity of the soul with God. At the same time, there is clearly a democratization of the spiritual life, an anticipation of Erasmus' *Monochatus non est pietas*. There is a growing individualism and at the same time a criticism of the many attempts to press religious life into an organized system of observance for a professional elite. Master Eckhardt spoke of a union of God that was open to all men, and in a special way for those who are free from the structures of organized religious life. With Groote we see the refusal to accept any authorized rule, to bind his followers with any vows. These refusals indicate the desire to discover for oneself a way of life suited to one's own religious experience. In 1490 the rector of the brothers at Hildesheim was asked for his views on the question of legal sanctions against a member who deserted the brothers. He replied in a letter which shows the lasting power of a type of freedom which Groote had secured for his followers.

> We are not members of an order, but religious men trying to live in the world. If we get a papal order compelling those who leave us

> either to return to us or to enter another order, we shall be sell-
> ing our liberty, that liberty which is the singular glory of the
> Christian religion, to buy chains and prison walls, in order to
> fall into line and conform to the religious orders.  We too will
> then be subject to servitude, like slaves who can be corrected only
> by punishment.  I myself indeed once thought we should accept the
> rule and make a profession, but Master Gabriel Biel corrected me
> saying that there were already enough members of religious orders.
> Our way of life springs and has always sprung from an inner kernel
> of devotion.  Let us therefore not bring upon ourselves at once
> destruction of our good name, our peace, our quiet, our concord,
> and our charity.  Our voluntary life as brothers is very different
> from the irrevocable necessity of those who live under the rule and
> statutes of a religious order.  Their monasteries fall into decay
> through the presence of unstable and undisciplined members:  think
> then how much more our life would be destroyed by the enforced
> presence of such people.[123]

These words would not have been intelligible to St. Bernard or St. Bonaventure.  They reflect a new atmosphere and a new search for interior
and exterior religious freedom.

The *Devotio Moderna* represented a deeply Eucharistic piety understood
in individualistic terms, a self-consciousness of man's sinfulness, a
pursuit in more modest forms of religious experience.  Being more personal and subjective, it tended to make people more self-reliant and
independent in an ethical situation.  The individual was also more independent of the clergy in their function as guides and rulers, weakening
in fact the direct influence of the priests.  It tended to restrict the
Church to the community of those whose personal relationship to Christ
found expression in a visible imitation of the life of Christ.[124]

The movement contained elements understood to be dangerous to the
Church, especially as it spread beyond the confines of the cloister and
the houses of the brothers to literate laymen and women who found themselves dissatisfied with the spiritual sustenance offered by the contemporary clergy.  The *Devotio Moderna* represented

> a disquietude at the heart of the Christian conscience in the pres-
> ence of too much ecclesiastical incarnationalism, a doctrine of
> grace which is, perhaps, too efficient and too precise, namely the
> habit of grace seen as a thing, an object, and as an alienable
> claim to glory to the extent that God becomes man's debtor.[125]

It was a movement that seemed to be saying, "Give us less Church and
more Christ."

It is in this alienation from the Church and in its tendency toward
individualism that the *Devotio Moderna* is modern and original.  We saw

in Groote a greater importance given to the invisible Church.  In the
Eucharistic doctrine of the *Imitatione Christi* we see very little ecclesial and cosmic dimension.  This is truly in contrast to earlier ecclesiology and Eucharistic doctrine.  St. Thomas taught that the ultimate
effect, the *res* of the Eucharist, is the unity of the mystical body.[126]
By and through the Eucharist, according to another medieval theologian,
Rupert of Deutz, we are joined to the one body of the Church, "in unum
corpus ecclesiae conjuncti."[127]  The same author spoke about being consecrated in the body of the Church through the Eucharistic communion.[128]
The Eucharistic communion was always understood as being also a communion to and with the Church.  It was always considered in relation to
the communion of saints:  *"Solemnitas eucharistia, ad quam pertinet
sanctorum communio."*[129]  It was considered the mystical principle at the
heart of Christian society which realizes this communion of the saints
in the body of Christ.  The Eucharist was thought truly to effect the
Church.[130]  In the words of Alger of Liege it unites members to one another and constitutes *"universum Christi corpus."*[131]  This understanding
of the Eucharist, as a creative cause of the Church as body of Christ,
presupposed an understanding of the Church as a corporate union of the
whole Christian people into one body, the *unum corpus* of the Pauline
epistles.

The terminology is basically Pauline.  St. Paul had laid particular
stress upon the incorporation of all the faithful into a unity with
Christ, and this idea was considerably developed in the patristic writings, in which the sacraments were frequently held to symbolize the
organic unity between the head of the Church and its members.[132]  Accepted
at first as the Eucharist itself, the term *corpus Christi mysticum* was
not, however, applied directly to the Church before the twelfth century.[133]  By this application it was intended not only to show the uni-
fied nature of the Church, but also its more important non-material
existence, the idea of it as a body with an essence, a personality of
its own.  To describe the society of the mystical body of Christ was
simply an alternative way of saying that it forms a single corporate
entity, one being or person, "universitas est quoddam individuum."[134]
The community of the faithful was thought to form one being in Christ;
the corporate body of Christians to be the earthly counterpart of that
celestial perfection in which Christ and the faithful are united as one.

In essence there was thought to be no real distinction between Christ
and his Church, for the Church forms one body or person, and that person
is Christ. He is, as St. Augustine has said, the *una persona ecclesiae*.
The *ecclesia* is the *unum corpus Christi*. The emphasis here was on the
relationship between the material and the spiritual world. According to
St. Augustine, man as we know him is essentially a corporeal reproduction of himself. He exists in a material body which on earth represents
the soul by which he is animated and given shape. Similarly, according
to a disciple of St. Augustine, the essence of the *ecclesia* is in Christ,
while the earthly *ecclesia*, although clothed in the mundane form of a
body politic, is only an image of the perfectly existing Church triumphant.[135] The *ecclesia* exists on both planes, the material and the
spiritual. "Ecclesia in praesente et ecclesia in futuro est eadem
ecclesia."[136]

For the medieval theologians, monastic and scholastic, the emphasis
upon the corporate union of all Christians stressed the predominance of
the body over the individual. Every individual part had to be totally
subject to the whole into which it was absorbed and which alone really
existed. True happiness lay really in service of the community; the
individual obtained his full stature only through the society to which
he belonged.[137] Man is indeed the image of God, but the *civitas* is a
more perfect image of God than man. In fact, to the Augustinian, the
whole was always prior to the parts, the entire *ecclesia* infinitely more
important than any of its members and existed over and above them. The
individual was significant insofar as he assisted toward the functioning
of the whole.[138]

In the *Devotio Moderna* we have seen an ever-increasing emphasis upon
the individual, the personal, the private. We have seen a piety that
comprises a most intense striving by and for the individual soul.

This individualism was certainly influenced by nominalism. For Ockham the cardinal principle was the belief that everything that exists is
a single thing. The reduction of all existence to individual existence
is the essence of nominalism, and it was this emphasis on the individual
in Ockham's thought which completely reversed the traditional hiero-
cratic view of the relationship existing between the whole and its parts,
between the community and its members. The *ecclesia* was no longer for
Ockham a body whose essence is universal and on a superior plane of

reality; it was basically nothing more than a collection of actually
existing people.[139] The *populus* was only the sum of its individual persons. It was the individual or part which was of primary importance and
upon which the emphasis fell. This highly individualistic doctrine
meant that each person had a value of his own and not merely because he
was part of a whole. He was not simply an instrument of the community,
but an end in himself. It was the individual members who were all-
important. The *ecclesia*, the *congregatio fidelium*, was regarded as a
purely spiritual entity. It was only from the point of view of faith
that all Christians could be regarded as living in one community and in
need of the unity given by one head. The universal Christian society
became no more than a mere unity of faith. In the same way, for Mar-
silius of Padua, the *ecclesia* was a purely spiritual, sacramental community in which believers were connected only by their common faith and
participation in the sacraments.[140] The unity of the *ecclesia* followed
from the oneness of its faith, but this was a mystical, unsubstantial
unity with little material consequence.

In this type of ecclesiology, where the emphasis was on the predominance of individuals, the sacraments came to be considered means of
individual salvation and stimulants of individual devotion. The relation between Church and sacrament was hard to discern. The ultimate
purpose of the sacrament was the spiritual edification of the individual
recipient. But the effective and causal dimension of the sacrament in
relation to the recipient is not emphasized here. What brings about
sanctification is the stimulation of devout feelings in the recipient.
The organic relation in which both the individual and the sacrament
stand to Christ's mystical Body, the Church, is de-emphasized.

The *Devotio Moderna*, as a reaction against the exteriority of religious practices, tended to bring everything to God alone. It was truly
a reassertion of the sovereignty of God. This reassertion was an effort
to disincarnate a Church which had become too comfortable with the world
and to restore its transcendence. A non-sacramental understanding of
the world tells us nothing about God for it is no longer a finite copy
of His infinite essence but only the implementation of His arbitrary
will. Man does not find God in creation, in the visible and the exterior. This attitude is certainly nominalistic in inspiration. Ockham
had maintained that absolutely nothing could be proven about God in the

light of natural reason.  The existence of God is an object of faith,
not of demonstration.  Empirically given things have to be considered in
isolation; one has no right to place them against hypothetically given
things whose existence cannot be verified.  There is no necessary intel-
ligibility in anything and therefore there is no divinely ordained natural order.[141]

In the *Devotio Moderna* the world estranged man from God.  Man escaped
from this estrangement by stressing the invisible, the internal, the inward.  This was a view of deep cleavage between the realm of the spirit
and the realm of the flesh.  The body was truly a prison of the soul, and
the earthly life a transitory stage in the journey toward eternal life.
A doctrine of ceaseless effort and combat against self came to be situated in this context.  One had to do violence to oneself.  The theme
*Miles Christi* and spiritual combat was predominant.  The kingdom of
heaven would be given to the violent.[142]  The doctrine of ceaseless
effort and combat against the self was complemented by the doctrine that
it is really God who does all, beyond the effect of any individual
effort, and that in the ultimate analysis his glory is all that matters,
*Ad majorem Dei gloriam*.  Devotion in the *Devotio Moderna* was that basic
attitude of one who seeks truly the glory of God; true devotion consists
in "offering yourself with all your heart to the divine will, not seeking what is yours either in small matters or great ones, either in temporal or eternal things."[143]

History has shown that the *Devotio Moderna* was a transitional spirituality.  It was absorbed and transformed by other currents.  Its own
ambivalence between the monastic life and the lay vocation was never resolved and led to future difficulties.  At the same time, its lack of
concern for the intellectual life, understood in the context of scholasticism, led to a widening of the existing gap between spirituality and
theology and to future reactions.

Its individualism, which was its most modern characteristic, brought
out sharply the necessity of redefining the individual's relationship to
the Church.  At the same time, the fundamental role attributed to Scripture as an unequalled source of nourishment for the spiritual life
brought into focus the problem of the authority of the Church in the
realm of spiritual life, and the importance of its dogmas in the directing of one's spiritual life.

The predominance given to the interior and inward life and the need of an "experiential" knowledge of God in opposition to the sterile and cold intellectualism of the scholastics demonstrated the need to develop an epistemology directly related to the spiritual life. These are the different issues that the Renaissance in France and elsewhere would face and attempt to resolve.

*Notes*

1.  P. M. E. Dols, *Bibliographie der Moderne Devotie* (Niemegen, 1941);
R. R. Post, *The Modern Devotion. Confrontation with Reformation and
Humanism* (Leiden, 1968).
2.  L. Cognet, *De la Dévotion moderne à la spiritualité française*
(Paris, 1958); A. Hyma, *The Christian Renaissance, A History of the
"Devotio Moderna"* (New York, 1965); W. M. Landeen, "Gabriel Biel and the
Brethren of the Common Life in Germany," *C.H.* 20 (1951) 23-36; P. Mest-
werdt, *Die Anfänge des Erasmus; Humanismus und "Devotio Moderna"* (Leip-
zig, 1917); B. Bravo, "Influgos de la Devotio Moderna sobre Erasmo de
Rotterdam," *Manresa* 32 (1960) 99-112; J. Hashagen, "Die Devotio Moderna
in ihre Einwirkung auf Humanismus, Reformation, Gegenreformation und
spätere Richtungen," *Zeitschrift für Kirchengeschichte* LV (1936 523-531;
L. E. Halkin, *La "devotio moderna" et les origines de la Réforme aux
Pays Bas. Courants religieux et Humanisme à la fin du XV$^e$ siècle et au
début du XVI$^e$ siècle* (Paris, 1959) 35-61; K. Kekow, *Luther und die Devotio Moderna* (Hamburg, 1932); I. Rodriguez-Grabit, "La 'devotio moderna'
en Espagne et l'influence française," *Bibliothèque d'Humanisme et Renaissance* XIX, 489-495.
3.  L. Spitz, *The Religious Renaissance of the German Humanists* (Cambridge, 1963) 7.
4.  R. R. Post, *The Modern Devotion.*
5.  W. Alberts (ed.), *Consuetudines fratrum vitae communis. Fontes
minores medii aevi* VIII (Gröningen, 1959); E. F. Jacob, "The Brethren of
the Common Life," *Bulletin of the John Ryland's Library* XXIV (1940) 37-
58; A. Hyma, *The Brethren of the Common Life* (Grand Rapids, 1950).
6.  E. de Shoepdryver, "La Dévotion Moderne," *Nouvelle Revue de Théologie* 54 (1927) 752-772; J. de Jong, "Karakter en invloed der Moderne
Devotie," *Historisch Tijdschrift* IV (1925) 26-58; G. Villoslada, "Rasgos
caracteristicos de la Devotio Moderna," *Manresa* 28 (1956) 315-350.
7.  K. C. L. M. de Beer, *Studie over de spiritualiteit van Geert
Groote* (Brussels: Nijmegen, 1938) 290-299; Th. van Zijl, *Gerard Groote,
Ascetic and Reformer* (Washington, D.C., 1963); G. Epiney-Burgard, *Gerard
Grote (1340-1384) et les débuts de la Dévotion Moderne* (Wiesbaden, 1970).
8.  Thomas à Kempis, *Opera omnia* VII, ed. Pohl (Freiburg Briesgau,
1922).
9.  Conclusa et proposita, non vota in nomine Domini a magistro
Gerardo edita, in Thomas à Kempis, *Opera omnia* VII, 87-91.
10.  *Ibid.*, 88.
11.  *Ibid.*, 89.
12.  *Ibid.*, 90.
13.  *Ibid.*, 91.
14.  *Ibid.*, 92, 94.
15.  *Gerardi Magni Epistolae*, No. 71, ed. W. Mulder (Antwerp, 1933),
p. 295.
16.  *Ibid.*, Epis. 56, p. 213.
17.  *Ibid.*, Epis. 56, p. 212.
18.  *De Simonia ad beguttas*, ed. W. de Vreese (The Hague, 1950) 25.
19.  "The imitation of the humanity of Christ is the entrance to
eternal pastures," Epis. 9, 31.
20.  "We should contemplate frequently on the passion of our Lord
Jesus Christ," *ibid.*, 238.
21.  Cf. *ibid.*, 232-243.
22.  Het Getijdenboek van Geert Groote narr het Haagse handschrift
133 E 21. ed. N. Van Wijk, Leidse Drukken en Herdrukken, Kleine Reeks 3

(Leyde, 1940) 181–183.

23. *Epistolae* 52.

24. Conclusa et proposita, Thomas à Kempis, *Opera omnia* VII, 88: "I intend to dedicate my life to the glory, the honor and the service of God, and to the salvation of my soul."

25. De Beer, *Studie.*

26. *Ibid.*, 292.

27. *Ibid.*, 298.

28. *De loc. eccl. A.K.J.* VIII, p. 130.

29. *Epistolae* 21, 91.

30. According to Groote, a Christian is not a schismatic until he has severed his relation to the community. *Ibid.* 21, 83.

31. A. Hyma (ed.), *AGAU* XLIX (1942) 24.

32. Pohl, *Opera omnia* VII, 97–102.

33. *Epistolae*

34. De Beer, *Studie*, 249–266; J. Toussaert, *Le sentiment religieux en Flandre à la fin du M.A.* (Paris, 1963); E. Mikkers, "Sint Bernardus en de Moderne Devotie," *Citeaux in de Nederlanden* IV (1953) 149–186; D. De Man, "Heinrich Suso en den moderne Devoten," *NAK* XIX (1926) 277–283; M. Viller, "Le 'Speculum Monachorum' et la 'Devotio Moderna'," *RAM* 3 (1922).

35. "To enter the monastery is to choose the highest state of life and that which pleases God the most," *Epis.* 15, 50.

36. Thomas à Kempis, *Vita domini Florentii, Opera omnia* VII, 116–197; Radewijns Florent, *Florentii parvum et simplex exercitium*, ed. D. J. M. Wüstenhoff, ANK V (1895) 89–105; Tractulus devotus de exstirpatione vitiorum et passionum et acquisitione verarum virtutum et maxime caritatis Dei et proximi et verae unionis cum Deo et proximo, seu Tractulus de spiritualibus exercitiis, ed. H. Nolte (Friebourg-en-Brisgau, 1892); *Het Libellum Multum valet*, ed. J. F. Vregt, Einige ascetische tractaten, *AGAU* X (1882) 383–427; *Het libellus: Omnes inquit, artes, Een rapiarium van Florentius Radewijnns, Inleiding* (I), *Tekst* (II), *Noten en Indices* (III), ed. M. Th. P. van Workum (Louvain, 1950); *Het Tractatulus devotus van Florens Radewijns*, ed. M. Goossens, De meditatie in de eerste tijd van de Moderne Devotie (Haarlem-Anvers, n.d.) 213–254.

37. Ed. M. J. Pohl, VII, 198–210.

38. Ed. J. F. Vregt, *UGAU* X (1882) 383–427.

39. Thomas à Kempis, *Vita domini Florentii, Opera omnia* VII, 116–195.

40. Libellus "omnes inquit artes" I, 20.

41. *Notabilia verba*, ed. J. F. Vregt, *AGAU* X (1882) 422.

42. *Zerbolt De Zutphen Gérard: De reformatione virium animae*, ed. de la Bigne, Bibliotheca veterum Patrum V (Parisiis, 1624); *Middelnedlandse vertalingen van Super modo vivendi* (7de hooldstuk) *De libris teutonicalibus van Gerard Zerbolt van Zutphen*, ed. J. Deschamps, Handelingen (Kon. Zuidnederl. Mattschappiij voor Taal- en Lettern) XIV (1960) 67–108; XV (1961) 176–200; *De Spiritualibus ascensionibus/Van geetelijke opklimmingen*, ed. J. Mahieu (texte latin et traduction) (Bruges, 1941); *Het "Scriptum pro quodam inordinate gradus ecclesiasticos et praedicationis officium affectante,"* ed. A. Hyma, *NAKG* N.S. t. XX (1927) 179–232; *The De libris teutonicalibus by Gerard Zerbolt of Zutphen*, ed. A. Hymna, *NAKG* N.S. XVII (1924) 42–70; *Super modo vivendi devotorum hominum simul commorantium*, ed. A. Hymna, *AGAU* LII (1926) 1–100.

43. Gerard of Zutphen, *The Spiritual Ascent*, trans. A. Landau (1907) 1.

44. *Ibid.*, c.2, 8.

45.  *Ibid.*, c.9, 21.
46.  *Ibid.*, c.27, 55-60.
47.  *Ibid.*, c.27, 59.
48.  *Ibid.*
49.  *Ibid.*, c.43, 193.
50.  *Ibid.*, c.198.
51.  P. E. Puyol, *La doctrine du livre De Imitatione Christi* (Paris, 1898); P. Hagen, *Imitatio, Eine Urschrift des Buches von der Nachfolge Christ* (Lübeck, 1926); Debongnie, "Les themes de l'Imitation," *RHE* 36 (1940) 331ff.; L. Aubry, *Introduction à l'Imitation de Jésus Christ* (Paris, 1950); P. Mesnard, "La conception de l'humilité dans l'Imitation de J.C.," *Mélanges de Lubac* (Paris, 1960) 199-222; F. Vandenbrouche, "Le Christ dans l'Imitation de J.C.," *La Vie Spirituelle* CX (1964) 276-290; R. R. Post, *The Modern Devotion*, 521-551.
52.  F. W. Wentzloff-Eggebert, *Deutsche Mystik zwischen Mittelalter und Neuzeit* (Tübingen, 1947) 139-140.
53.  According to St. Augustine, the spiritual life consists in following and imitating Christ. As God, Christ is the very goal, and as man he is the way. "Deus Christus patria est quo imus, homo Christus via est qua imus." (*Sermo* 123, M.3; PL. 38, 685) All the virtues needed to live are to be found in Christ. Not only is he an example to all virtues but also a source. Christ becomes the very center of our love. (*De Sancta Virginitate*, nos. 55-56)

The theme of imitation and tenderness and compassion for the life and suffering of Christ finds a strong proponent in the person of Anselm. Anselm dwelled with passionate intensity on the details of Christ's sufferings. "Alas that I was not there to see the Lord of angels humbled for the companionship of man, that he might exalt man to the companionship of angels. Why, O my soul, were thou not present to be transfixed with the sword of sharpest grief at the unendurable sight of your Saviour pierced with the lance and the hands and feet of your Maker broken with the nails." (*Oratio* XX; PL. 158, 903)

St. Bernard gave a more robust and lasting expression to the theme of imitation. One's life must be a total and absolute search for the word. It is well expressed in one of Bernard's last writings. (*Incant. Cant. Sermo* 85; PL. 183, 1187) Man's relation to Christ is characterized by Bernard under the expression of the ways of the Lord, *Viae Domini*. (In Psalm. XC, *Serm.* 11; PL. 183, 228) The relationship is both to the humanity and to the divinity of Christ. To arrive at the love of Christ as God, one must begin with the love of Christ as man. Configuration to and imitation of Christ's mysteries are at the very center of Bernard's spirituality. In every one of his elaborations on the love of God, Bernard always establishes as a first thing the meditation of the mysteries of Christ. The spiritual way must be, according to St. Bernard, the way of Christ. (*De Diversis*, *Serm.* 87; PL. 186, 704)

This same doctrine on the humanity of Christ and the necessity to imitate Christ are found also in scholasticism in the person and teaching of St. Bonaventure. The fundamental act of the illuminative way is the imitation of Christ. (*De Triplici Via*, c.3. M.1. T. VIII, p. 12) The incarnate Word is the accomplished model of all perfection "Totius perfectionis splendor, speculum et exemplar." (*A pol. Paup.* c.3, M.8. T. VIII, p. 246) The supreme rule for justice and holiness is the imitation of Christ: "in imitatione actuum Christi qui vitae perfectae informationem respiciunt." (*Ibid.*, p. 243) Above all, Christ must be imitated in his humility, in his love of neighbor, in his adoration of the Father, his abnegation, poverty, patience and obedience. (*Sermo* 21 in *Dom. I Adv.*, and IV p. 42b, 43)

We find the same doctrine at the end of the fourteenth century in a very influential book, the *Vita Christi* of Ludolphus. Perfection of the Christian life consists in the imitation of Christ, and this imitation is expressed in terms of self-denial and the carrying of the cross. Christ's is the way to be followed, a way that leads to obedience and love of neighbor.

54. The following is a result of a word study: Spiritual combat, 419; Humility, 256; Spiritual Consolation, 138; Interior grace, 108; Imitation of Christ, 64; cf. R. Storz, *Concordantia ad Quatuor Libros De Imitatione Christi* (London, 1911).

55. Thomas à Kempis, *Opera omnia* V, p. 3.

56. *Sermones ad novicios, Opera Omnia* VI, 190.

57. *De Imitatione Christi*, c.I, 17; II, 12; III, 32; IV, 8. All translations in English are from *The Imitation of Christ*, trans. A. Croft (Milwaukee, 1940).

58. I, 1.

59. I, 2.

60. I, 11.

61. II, 12.

62. I, 11.

63. I, 21.

64. I, 25.

65. II, 12.

66. II, 12.

67. II, 11.

68. II, 8.

69. III, 37.

70. III, 49.

71. "If you wish to grow in grace, remember always that you are an exile and pilgrim on this earth." I, 17. Cf. also I, 23.

72. I need Your grace in fullest measure, to subdue that nature which always inclines to evil from my youth up. For it fell through Adam the first of men, and was tainted by sin, the penalty of that fault descending upon all mankind. Thus the nature which You created good and upright has now become the very symbol of corruption and weakness, for when left to itself, it leans always towards evil and base things. The little strength that remains is only like a small spark, buried beneath ashes. Yet this same natural reason, though hidden in profound darkness, still retains the power to know good and evil, and to discern truth and falsehood. But it is powerless to do what it knows to be good, neither does it enjoy the full light of truth, nor its former healthy affections.

73. I, 22; I, 13.

74. III, 55.

75. There can be no holiness, Lord, if You withdraw Yourself. No wisdom can avail, if You cease to guide. No courage can uphold, if You cease to defend. No purity is secure, if You are not guard. No watchfulness of our own can save us, unless Your holy care protects us; for if You abandon us, we sink and perish. But if You visit us, we are raised up and live once more. III, 14.

76. Lord, how urgently I need Your grace if I am to undertake, carry out and perfect any good work! Without it, I can achieve nothing; but in You and by the power of Your grace, all things are possible. III, 55.

77.  III, 54.
78.  I, 1.
79.  I, 22.
80.  I, 24.
81.  III, 8.
82.  I, 24.
83.  Basic to the Gospel itself, and at the very core of Augustinian
spirituality, humility became the very foundation of monastic spirituality and the object of a systematic approach.  This following passage in
the rule of Benedict is indicative of the systematic approach to humility:  "Wherefore brethren if we wish to attain the topmost height of
humility and to come quickly to that heavenly excellence which in this
present life we reach by humility, we must raise up, and by our acts we
must ascend, that ladder which appeared to Jacob in his dream whereon he
saw angels ascending and descending.  This ascending and descending
doubtless signify nothing else than an ascent by humility and a descent
by pride.  The ladder itself is our life on earth raised up by God
towards heaven for the humble of heart.  The sides of the ladder we call
our life on earth raised up by God towards heaven for the humble of
heart.  The sides of the ladder we call our body and soul and into these
sides God has inserted steps of humility and discipline for our ascent."
(*Regula S. Benedicti*, Cap. 5)
     With St. Anselm we have again a great importance given to humility.
He recorded entirely the twelve stages described in the rules of St.
Benedict, turned the ladder into a mountain, the twelve rungs into
seven steps, and gave them a more internal character.  (*Similitudines*,
Cap. c-cix; PL. 182, 941)  One of St. Bernard's first literary works was
a treatise on St. Bernard's twelve steps of humility.  (*De Gradibus
Humilitatis*; PL. 182, 941-972)  Here Bernard traces an ascent from self-
knowledge and self-control through neighborly compassion to perfect contemplation of the truth.  According to St. Bernard, the man who desires
to approach God must first of all practice the virtue of humility.  And
what is humility, if not the sincere knowledge of oneself, of one's own
misery and at the same time also of one's noble calling and vocation?
This self-knowledge which leads to humility and is at the very foundation of one's own serious spiritual life, constitutes also for St.
Bernard the very first moment of the knowledge of God.  Humility here
again is for St. Bernard the only real way.  "Haec est via et non est
alia praeter ipsam."  (In *Ascensione Domini, Sermo* 2, M.6; PL. 183, 304)
With St. Francis of Assisi, humility accompanied by poverty becomes the
characteristic virtue of the Franciscans.
     With St. Thomas Aquinas we find a new approach to theology of humil-
ity, an approach influenced by the rediscovery of Aristotelian philosophy.  Humility becomes moderation and submission to God.  (*S.T.* IIa
IIae, Q. 161, a.2, a.3)  St. Bonaventure reacted violently to any Aristotelian approach to Christian humility.  The unique foundation of
Christian humility is our belief in Christ.  Man being doubly nothing,
both in the order of nature and in the order of grace, there is a dual
humility, humility of knowledge *(humilitas veritatis)* which takes its
origin through its knowledge of one's nothingness as a created being,
and a humility of austerity *(humilitas severitatis)* which is the result
of consciousness of sin.  (*De Perfectione Evangelica. Quaestio de
Humilitate*. Ad. 1, Opera. t.5., Quaracchi [1891] 123)
84.  III, 7.
85.  III, 14.

86. III, 42.
87. III, 7.
88. II, 10.
89. III, 21.
90. III, 3,3.
91. I, 5.
92. I, 1; I, 2,1.
93. I, 3; III, 7.
94. III, 43.
95. IV, 18.
96. III, 43.
97. The first thing that strikes us in reading the works of the medieval monks is their familiarity with the Bible. St. Bernard, William of St. Thierry, Richard of St. Victor and others lived in a scriptural atmosphere; their thinking was molded by Scripture. Cf. J. Leclercq, *The Love of Learning and the Desire for God*, pp. 87-109.
98. III, 31.
99. The more closely a man is united to You in pure simplicity the more varied and profound the matters which he understands without effort, for he receives light and understanding from heaven. I, 3.
100. III, 43.
101. But many people, although they often hear the Gospel, feel little desire to follow it, because they lack the spirit of Christ. Whoever desires to understand and take delight in the words of Christ must strive to conform his whole life to Him. I, 1.
102. Give what You will, as much as You will, and when You will. Do with me as You think good, as pleases You best, and is most to Your glory. I am in Your hand; Guide me according to Your will. I am indeed Your servant, and am ready for anything. I wish to live, not for myself but for You alone; how I wish I could serve You perfectly and worthily. III, 15.
103. II, 2; III, 56; II, 10.
104. III, 5.
105. III, 5.
106. III, 5.
107. IV, 11.
108. P. Dabin, *Le Sacerdoce Royal des Fidèles* (Paris, 1900).
109. The word *ecclesia* is found four times in the *De Imitatione*.
110. M. Wilks, *The Problem of Sovereignty in the Later Middle Ages* (Cambridge, 1963).
111. In earlier monastic spirituality, the Church as a community of salvation is the model and setting of the monastic community. Cf. J. Chatillon, "Une écclesiologie médiévale: l'idée de l'Eglise dans la théologie de Saint Victor au XII^e siècle," *Irenikon* 22 (1949) 115-138, 395-411. All individuals, monks or lay, must achieve this destiny within the Church.
112. IV, 5.
113. IV, 3; IV, 4.
114. IV, 11.
115. IV, 3.
116. IV, 13.
117. In contrast to this: cf. Eucharistic doctrine of Thomas Aquinas: in 4 Sent. d. 12, 13; S.T. IIIa qu. 73, a.1,a.3; q. 83, a.4, ad 4 um.
118. Y. Congar, "Die Ekklesiologie des hl. Bernhard" in *Bernhard von Clairvaux Mönch und Mystiker*, ed. J. Lortz (Wiesbaden, 1955) 76-119.

The whole Bridal theme as developed by St. Bernard is basically about the relationship that exists between the Church and Christ before it exists between the soul and its spouse. Bernard's faith in the mysteries of Christ is a faith based on the presentation of these mysteries by the Church in her liturgy. Christ communicates himself to man only through men. "These are Peter and Paul, two great luminaries, which God constituted in himself and in the body of the Church. These are transmitted to us in masters and in mediators, and through these it becomes possible for me to ascend to the Mediator." (In *Fest. SS. Pet. et Paul*; PL 183, 405) His fidelity to the fathers of the Church seems to be inspired by the same conviction. (*De Baptismo, Praefat. et Cap*. 2. M.8) Because of this faith in the visible mediation of Christ, Bernard always insists in founding his piety and doctrine on the teaching of the visible Church (*East*. 174, M.2), and in particular on the Church of Rome. The ecclesial dimension of Bernard's spirituality comes to the fore when he describes the relationship of the soul to Christ. There is no question here of direct relationship or any kind of individualism. The unity between the Spouse and the Bride is accomplished within the corporate group. The ecclesial dimension of our union with Christ is expressed in his sermons on the *Canticle of Canticles* 77, 78, 79. The Church is predestined by the Father to answer his need of communicating himself; it is created and constituted by the Son and animated and inspired by the Holy Spirit. (*Incant. Cant., Serm*. 85, M.13) In everything which he does on the supernatural level, the Christian acts as a member of the Church. Christ loves us individually but not separately: he loves us in his Church. Our personal destiny can work itself out only in the common salvation of the Church. It is in His Church that God looks upon us and loves us, in her that He desires us and we encounter Him and in her that we cleave to Him and are made blessed.

The role of the Church is the background, the very fabric of thought and feeling of every spiritual theme elaborated by St. Bernard and his immediate followers. Personal experience and direct relation between the human soul and Christ are sought within the framework of the Church, and in and through the sacramental life.

119. III, 1; III, 21.

120. H. Watrigant, "La méditation méthodique et Jean Mauburnus," *RAM* 4 (1932); P. Debongnie, *Jean Mombaer de Bruxelles abbé de Livry, ses écrits et ses réformes* (Louvina, 1927); *idem*, "Exercices Spirituels," *Dict. De. Spiritualité* IV, pt. 2 (1902-1933).

121. Contrary to certain authors, the *Devotio Moderna* does not owe its name to the *via moderna* of the Nominalists. This does not mean that it was in no way influenced by the *via moderna*.

122. M. Ditsche, "Zur Herkunft und Bedeutung des Befriffes Devotio Moderna," *Historisches Jahrbuch* LXXIX (1960) 134-145.

123. *Annalen u. Akten der Brüder des Gemeinsamen Lebens im Lüchtenhofe zu Hildesheim*, ed. Doebner (Quellen u Darstellungen zur Gesch, Neidersachsens 1903, ix) 113. Quoted by R. W. Southern, *Western Society and the Church in the Middle Ages* (London, 1970) 345.

124. W. Spoelhof, "Concepts of Religious Non-conformity and Religious Toleration as Developed by the Brethren of the Common Life in the Netherlands, 1374-1489" (unpublished Ph.D. thesis, University of Michigan, 1946).

125. K. McDonnell, *John Calvin*, 37.

126. Thomas Aquinas, *Summa Theologica*, IIIa qu. 79, "The Eucharist was not instituted to satisfy for our sins, but to nourish us spiritually

by uniting us to Christ and to his members."

127. Rupert of Deutz, P.L. 170, 381.

128. Rupert of Deutz, P.L. 169, 483 A.

129. Luc de Tuy, *Adversus Albigenses*, I, 2.

130. H. De Lubac, *Corpus Mysticum* (Paris, 1944).

131. Alger of Liege, P.L. 180, 847A-B: "Cum enim altaris sacrificum, signando ipsius Ecclesiae et Christi unitatem, universi corporis Christi sit sacramentum, non conficitur ibi Christus, ubi non conficitur universus. Et ideo non fit ibi Eucharistia, ubi unitatis totius dominci corporis non administratur gratia."

132. Saint Augustine, in *Joannis evangelium tractatus* xxvi, 15, P L. 35,1614: "Hunc itaque cibum et potum societatem (Christus) vult intelligi corporis et membrorum suorum quod est sancta Ecclesia."

133. E. Mersch, *Le corps mystique du Christ* (Paris, 1936); M. Roberti, "Il corpus mysticum di S. Paola nella storia della persona giuridica," *Studi in onore di Enrico Besta* IV (Milan, 1939) 37-82.

134. Thomas Aquinas, *Summa Theologica* Ia IIae, q. 81, a.1: "Omnes homines qui sunt unius communitatis reputantur quasi unum corpus, et tota communitas unus homo." Cf. I. T. Eschmann, "Bonum commune melior est quam bonum unius," *Mediaeval Studies* VI (1944) 62-120; P. Gillet, *La personalité juridique en droit ecclésiastique* (Malines, 1927).

135. Aegidius Spiritalis, *Libellus contra infideles*, 112-113: "The militant church is constituted to the image of the celestial church."

136. Thomas Aquinas, *Comm in Ep. ad Coloss.* I, lect.5.

137. G. de Lagarde, "Individualisme et corporatisme au moyen age," *Recueil de travaux d'histoire et de philologie*, 2e serie, xliv (1937) KTB 478-480.

138. Augustinus Triumphus, *Summa XLIV*. 3, p. 242.

139. For the idea of the "Ecclesia" as a corporation in Ockham, cf. B. Tierney, "Ockham, the Conciliar Theory and the Canonists," *Journal of the History of Ideas* XV (1954) 40-70.

140. A. Gewirth, "John of Landeed and the Defensor Pacis," *Speculum* XXII (1948) 267-272.

141. This is in opposition to the belief that there is a divine order in the world and that the world itself is a reflection of this divine order. Divine order becomes simply an object of faith. According to Thomas Aquinas, God has placed a twofold order in creatures: that of things to one another and that of the whole universe to himself. The order of the universe to God explains all that is to be found within the universe. In this order of the universe God manifests his perfection, he is the principal cause of the order of the universe and created agents are the instrumental cause. Cf. J. H. Wright, *The Order of the Universe in the Theology of Saint Thomas Aquinas* (Rome, 1957).

142. Blessed is the man who for Your sake, Lord, bids farewell to every creature, and, forcibly overcoming his natural inclinations, crucifies the desires of the flesh by the very fervour of his spirit, in order that he may offer You pure prayer with a quiet conscience. Having excluded all worldly things from his heart and life, he will be worthy to take his place in the choir of angels. *De Imitatione Christi*, I, 3.

143. *Ibid.*, III, 25.

Chapter II

THE *DEVOTIO MODERNA* AND THE SPIRITUALITIES OF THE 16TH CENTURY:

THE CONTEXT OF JOHN CALVIN'S SPIRITUALITY

A. *Introduction*

My interest in this chapter will be to describe the spirituality of
the 16th century French humanism in order to establish the immediate
context of John Calvin's thought.

France, in the short space of one century, experienced all the forms
of humanism which in Italy had evolved over a period of three centuries.[1]
French humanism represented a fusion of classical humanism with evangelical piety.  Out of this combination evolved a positive program for religious reform and for the reorientation of theological study.  Christian humanism was in large part an inheritance from the mystical lay
piety and zeal for reform of the Church which had been endemic in the
northern countries for two centuries.[2]  French humanism was a movement
which possessed, aside from the uneasy coexistence within it of medieval
and modern characteristics, certain distinctive traits and a high degree
of cultural vitality.[3]  The more we learn about the sixteenth century in
France, the more clearly we see how complex and variegated a time it
was.  Generalizations about this period are nearly impossible.  The
humanists in France, as in Germany and England, were subject to many
currents of thought coming from all directions, both in time and place.
Sensitivity to the major influences is an absolute prerequisite in establishing the characteristics of the spirituality of sixteenth century
France.

It is quite clear that from the first the *Devotio Moderna* imparted to
French humanism a distinctive character which clearly differentiated it
from Italian humanism.

In France the most popular of the spiritual writings of the *Devotio
Moderna* was the *De Imitatione Christi*.  The first printed French copies
appeared at Toulouse in 1488.[4]  Other writings of the *Devotio Moderna*
were also read in France.  Zerbolt's *De Spiritualibus Ascensionibus* was
widely read.[5]  Mombaer's *Rosetum Exercitiorum* was printed twice, in 1493
and again in 1510.[6]

Books were not the *Devotio Moderna*'s only outlet in France.  Among

the advocates of this spirituality some actually lived in Paris in the
early sixteenth century.  John Standonck, for example, was instrumental
in promoting a program of ecclesiastical reform in Paris, based on the
principles of the *Devotio Moderna*.  In 1483 he became the principal of
the Collège de Montaigu and through him the principles and literature of
the *Devotio Moderna* were made available to a large number of students.
The library in the dormitory founded by Standonck at Montaigu contained
chiefly the mystical productions of the *Devotio Moderna*.

> La bibliothèque mystique formée par Standonck en 1499 contenait
> sans contredit les oeuvres de l'école de Windesheim.[7]

Marcel Godet describes the Collège de Montaigu as little more than a
reproduction of a house of the Brothers of the Common Life, a "succur-
sale."[8]

To speak of a decisive influence of the *Devotio Moderna* upon the
French humanism of the sixteenth century is somewhat difficult.  Many
different ideas converged to shape French humanism.  The *Devotio Moderna*
has been described as a transitional spirituality.  To a large extent
it was absorbed by other currents and movements.  Contributing in varying degrees to the spirituality of the French humanism were the spiritual thought of Gerson, Petrarch and Erasmus.  Erasmus exercised an
important influence on the early French humanists.

B.  *The Spirituality of Jean Gerson (1363-1429)*

Gerson was truly a middleman, a channel for the different currents of
French sixteenth century thought.[9]  He functioned not only as a point of
departure but also as a point of arrival.[10]  He influenced the whole history of the following century.  He was a major figure standing in the
crossfire of a very difficult period in the Church.  His writings were
used by Luther and Melanchthon and he was mentioned ten times in the
Lutheran confessions.  And Gerson was one of the main sources of French
humanism as well.[11]

What seems to have been the motif of Gerson's career and life was his
understanding of the need for reform, and this quest made up the essential part of his life.[12]  This reform, according to Gerson, had to be in
the real of the spiritual life.  He consistently sought to return the
clergy to holiness and to reconcile theology and piety, which were as

intimately linked for Gerson as they were for the humanists.[13] He saw
spirituality and contemplation of God as the very first condition for
any reform. The means for spiritual advancement were prayer, self-study
and humility.

Distrust of pride and the importance of humility were at the very
root of Gerson's insistence on the possibility of contemplation and mystical experience for all men. He did not consider mystical theology the
special field of a few learned men; rather, he thought that it was
acquired through intensive exercise of moral virtues which prepare the
soul for purification, illumination and perfection.[14] In order to present the layman with a simple means of attaining a closer union with
God, Gerson wrote *The Mountain of Contemplation*. He began by affirming
that simple people could, if they had faith, rise to union with God. In
this book Gerson distinguished two tendencies in the mystical life, the
speculative and affective. He pointed out that, although knowledge is
necessary to the ascent, humility above all must be the basis of any
contemplation. Contemplation is the outreach of the soul to a union
with God through the desire of love, which resides not in the intellectual but in the affective power of the soul; its object is not the *verum*
but the *bonum*.[15]

> If you wish to know the secret of love, from the theology of the
> intellect to the theology of the affective power, from knowledge to
> wisdom, from cognition to devotion.[16]

Gerson considered the ultimate in religious experience something
which takes place in the emotions rather than in the intellect. This
experience is not contingent upon intellectual attainment; consequently
it is equally available to all. The highest religious experience attain-
able by man occurs when the highest thought of the cognitive power of
man passes into the affective domain, at which point the extent of theological knowledge is irrelevant to man's religious experience. The
resultant act of love is called the *supermentalis excessus*. In terms of
human psychology it is possible for the affective power to move beyond
the cognitive to a higher experience of God.[17] Centered in the affective powers, Gerson's mystical theology was as available to unlettered
folk as to trained theologians.

For Gerson, contemplation was not a necessary and integral part of
everyone's religious experience, even though everyone was encouraged to

seek it. The *via propria* of faith, hope and love remained the necessary
religion, beyond which one could strive to go. Mystical experience was
still a special gift of the Holy Spirit. But Gerson did not limit this
gift to people in certain vocations.

Gerson considered the Holy Spirit the source of spiritual experience
on any level. Contemplation for example must be approached through repentance, but this is also instilled by the Holy Spirit.

> While the Holy Spirit fills man, the resident of the world, he
> raises him up, not of necessity as has been said, but by his spon-
> taneous will, so that he rises to the pinnacle of contemplative
> perfection.
> And so not in this but in the aforesaid ways a certain transforma-
> tion occurs in the soul through the Holy Spirit: from the glory of
> faith into the glory of knowledge; from the glory of reason to the
> glory of understanding; from the glory of the intellect to the
> glory of the experiential awareness and the affective power. There-
> upon follows swooning or falling or ecstasy.[18]

The fabric of Gerson's spirituality--and also an element of his re-
form--consisted in his continual endeavor to bridge the gap between theology and piety. In many of his writings he advocated a radical change
in theological direction. The concluding statements of his lecture *Contra Curiositatem Studentium*, which deals with the abuses and vanities of
speculative theology, indicate the type of atmosphere in which theology
should be studied.

> The clear and savory understanding of those things which are be-
> lieved in the gospel is called mystical theology, and it is to be
> acquired more through penitence than through human investigation
> alone. In this regard the question will be treated whether it is
> through penitential affection more than through intellectual in-
> vestigation that God is known in this life.[19]

The kind of theology advocated by Gerson can be characterized as a
theology of love active in works. Mystical theology has consistent
allegiance to the Aristotelian principle that only by working well does
one become good[20]--and the basis of this theology is again humility. The
prime requisite of all learning is the virtue of humility. It is pride
in fact that produced the lamentable state in which theology found itself. For the theologian one thing is necessary: a humble recognition
of the inscrutability of the divine. By himself man cannot attain to a
knowledge of God. It is necessary that God reveal himself, and he does
so in a variety of ways.

And because the divine precepts, insofar as they relate to God as
he is blessed, cannot be known to the rational creature by the
natural light alone, revelation will need to be added in whatever
way it may occur, whether through angel or man or by inner illumination, as the Apostle says regarding philosophers to whom he says
that the hidden things of God have been revealed.  Thus the theologians think that God is not absent from anyone, wherever he may
be, who does the best he can, namely by using well the gifts he now
has, and that God in fact divinely illuminates him regarding the
truths necessary for salvation, as Peter says in Acts.[21]

This is why for Gerson the scriptures were the very foundations of theology.  He himself exemplified this.  *Poenitemini et credite evangelia*
(Mark 1:15) proclaimed Gerson in his attempt to introduce the gospel and
piety in the faculty of theology in Paris, in place of *curiositas* and
useless discussion.

Steve Ozment summarized in Gerson's own words his understanding of
*Theologia Mystica*:

> ...mystical theology is (1) an extension of the soul *(extensio animi)*
> to God through the desire of love *(per amores desiderium)*, or (2) a
> transcendental movement *(motio anagogica)* to God through fervent
> and pure love *(per amorem fervidum et purum)*, or it can be described
> as (3) experiential knowledge of God *(cognitio experimentalis habita
> de Deo)* acquired through the embrace of unitive love *(per amoris
> unitivi complexum)*, and finally it is characterized as (4) wisdom,
> a savory knowledge *(sapida notitia)* of God achieved when the high-
> est affective power, the synderesis, is joined and united to him
> through love *(per amorem coniungitur et unitur)*.[22]

Gerson's *mystica theologia* was in effect an effort to avoid the ex-
tremes of intellection or affection.  The *theologia mystica* was an integration of *devotio* and *scientia*.  (Gerson was convinced that the only
*devotio* worthy of the Christian was that which was *secundum scientiam*
and the only *scientia* worthy of the Christian was that which was *secundum devotionem*.)[23]  His criticism of scholasticism was not a criticism
of the intellective powers per se but of attempts to obtain knowledge of
God without the affective powers.  His whole treatment of this issue was
cast within the structures of the question:  whether the knowledge of
God can be better acquired through penitent affective power than through
the intellect.  Gerson answered the question in favor of the penitent
affect.  For Gerson the most common error of scholastic theology was
that it theologized with the mouth and not with the heart.[24]  He held
that theology could not be abused when it was truly a theology of the
heart.[25]

The mystical knowledge of God is not only equal to the speculative knowledge, but superior to it. As love excels knowledge, will the intellect, and the virtue of love the virtue of faith, so the knowledge of God attained in mystical theology through penitential affection is more desirable and perfect than the knowledge which is attained through intellectual investigation and the contemplation of symbolic and speculative theology. In his mystical theology Gerson attempted to relate to God in a subjective and personalistic fashion, through an affective relationship. In this relationship, Gerson in no way wanted to break loose from the moorings of scriptural revelation or of churchly tradition. He did not admit that the mystic was freed from his obligation to ecclesiastical and divine law. A creature, however high a level of perfection he attains, remains unable to escape the subtle limits of the established order. His understanding of God can never break through the boundaries of revelation. The Christian is always intellectually and ethically dependent upon the teachings of the Church.[26] The affections of the heart have to be regulated by the law of Christ and this law is sufficiently revealed in the Decalogue and authoritatively unfolded by the apostles and Holy Doctors.[27] In Gerson there was no opposition between spirit and law. The doctrine of the Church was a final standard; this doctrine had priority not only over individual doctrine, but also over holy scripture, since it was the Church that separated the canonical from the non-canonical books.[28] It is important to note that the priority of the Church over holy scripture was not only the practical priority of Augustine's *commovere* but also a theoretical priority of *approbare*, and it is the Holy Spirit who provided the Church with the proper interpretation of holy scripture.

Gerson accepted with favor most of the tenets of the *Devotio Moderna*.[29] He had the same appreciation for a more interior spiritual life; he had the same distrust of a too speculative and arid theology. But at the same time this distrust of existing theology did not lead him to a sterile contempt for the intellectual life; his whole spirituality attempted to bridge the gap between theology and spirituality. His efforts did not go unnoticed by the French Humanists.

C. *The Spirituality of Francesco Petrarch (1304-1374) and its Influence*
   *in France*

In Italy, at an earlier date, an important contribution toward a more
interior and personal spirituality had been made by Francesco Petrarch.[30]
This spirituality penetrated into France through Guillaume Fichet (1433-
1480) and his disciples. Petrarch's spirituality expressed itself in
terms of *pietas*; his humanism was synonymous to *docta pietas*. It was
first of all the protestation of a Christian believer against the per-
version of Christ's message by the pagan philosophy of Aristotle.[31]   A
kind of Socratic movement, Petrarch's humanism represented a return to a
morality in psychology, a return from the objective to the subjective.[32]

In conformity with the fundamental Augustinian methods, Petrarch
issued a call for introspection.  He considered the knowledge man has of
himself and his destiny the only really valuable knowledge.[33]   This self-
knowledge leads to questions about God and his search for God as in St.
Augustine.[34]  Piety is therefore a predominant virtue.  Petrarch's ideal
was *docta pietas*, a knowledge that respects the mystery in itself.  This
is why Petrarch could affirm again with St. Augustine that *pietas est*
*sapientia*.[35]  He was convinced of the superiority of love over knowledge
and will over intellect.

For Petrarch the epistemological problem concerning the knowledge of
God was resolved in the act of faith, in the infinity of divine benevo-
lence.  If one believed that one had been saved or could be saved
through divine mercy and power then the epistemological problem became
insignificant.  For Petrarch faith in the truth of divine revelation
followed from faith in divine mercy.

> God is omnipotent and all-benevolent, nothing can be imagined so
> magnificent that he cannot do it, so beneficent that he does not
> wish it.  Whatever faith constructs on this foundation will stand
> solid and unshaken by all the undermining and battering rams of the
> enemy, and whatever he has brought up, its impetus and force will
> be blunted by ready and easy obstacles.  Once these things are re-
> ceived in faith everything is plain...[36]

Man's knowledge necessarily came from faith given to him by grace.

> Who will explain, I do not say by human words, but who will con-
> ceive in the human mind either the magnitude of his grace or the
> height of his wisdom towards the sons of man?  Certainly divine aid
> is needed for measuring the divine gift, and to know the grace of
> God is by the grace of God.[37]

Man's natural knowledge of himself led only to a knowledge of his misery, and without faith, to despair. Knowledge of self without knowledge of faith or God could only lead to despair.

According to Petrarch, man's self-knowledge and faith was made possible by the Incarnation. Here the gap between man and faith was bridged. Through the Incarnation man was lifted above his condition of misery.

> ...by an unchanging law of divine wisdom from eternity humanity was to be raised up, divinity bent down. And both equally having happened, there occurred a solitary and celebrated union without which humanity would have lain sick and torpid forever. Neither one could be done without the other; or rather it could be done through none other than through him, who bowed down his heavens and descended, who looked upon earth and made it tremble. And so through him it was done and not through another. Oh, indescribable sacrament! Where could humanity be lifted higher than that man consisting in irrational soul and human flesh, mortal man subject to accidents, dangers, our necessities, and, as I briefly shall say it, true and perfect man, man ineffably adopted by the Word, the Son of God, consubstantial with the Father and co-eternal to God and to the unity of person, should join together two natures in himself by a marvelous aggregation of wholly unequal things? Where I ask can man ascend higher than that man should be God?[38]

This affirmation of the Incarnation was directly related to Petrarch's concern with the verification of faith and knowledge in faith. Faith demanded the acceptance of the authority of the written word and the testimony of history without subjecting either to logical or rational criticism.

> For if we only believe what we see, then each one will see neither immortal God, invisible, nor anything spiritual, nor his own soul, and finally nothing eternal at all, since, as it is written, "the things which are not seen are eternal" for if anyone in order that he might believe should ask that miracles that have once happened be done again, he would again with like temerity that the entire events of the Gospel be repeated. Thus it would suffice nothing that Christ one time acted for our salvation, nor twice even, or four times, since also what we would have seen, by hereditary right of madness, posterity would seek again in different ages, than which nothing more insolent or unfaithful can be imagined; certainly there ought to be some difference between knowledge and faith; certainly, moreover, while faith comes from listening, through a lust of this kind is reduced to sight and touch so that it cannot any longer be called faith, but experience. Brothers, to demand or even to think this does not befit a faithful and devout soul. Suffice it to us to have seen what we believe through the eyes of the saints and apostles; we believe, they know.[39]

Petrarch pinpointed the necessity for a trust in the authenticity of
the whole historical experience of Christians.

> Sufficient to us should also be the wounds of the martyrs and the
> holy blood flowing from them whence our faith has been inscribed in
> pious minds, and unless they have accepted its adequate promise
> never should they hasten more boldly and more gaily to punishment
> and perdition. From all this, brothers, the pious ought to be con-
> vinced that these are windy and frivolous disputations by which,
> not the truth of Christ, but the favor of the crowd is sought, and
> all either vain investigations of things beyond the possibility of
> examination, or lust, especially for miracles, is the sign of ob-
> stinacy and curiosity, not of faith.[40]

Faith and belief are inesparable from Christian action.  And for Petrarch
this faith, made up of psychological reassurance and trust in the historical record, constituted the nature of wisdom itself.

Wisdom understood in this manner can be identified with *pietas*.  The
way to share this God-given wisdom is not through dialectics but rhetoric; the understanding of it leads not to a *theologia dialectica* but to
a *theologia rhetorica* or *poetica*.

Petrarch asserted the claim of the great Roman authors Cicero, Seneca
and Horace:

> They stamp and drive deep into the heart the sharpest and most
> ardent stings of speech, by which the lazy are startled, the ailing
> are kindled, and the sleepy aroused, the sick healed and the pros-
> trate raised, and those who stick to the ground lifted up to the
> highest thoughts and to honest desire.  Then earthly things become
> vile; the aspect of vice stirs up an enormous hatred of vicious
> life; virtue in the shape, and as it were, the face of honesty, are
> beheld by the inmost eye "and inspired miraculous love" of wisdom
> and of themselves, as Plato says.[41]

Wisdom and eloquence are necessarily related.

Petrarch and Gerson were to some extent concerned with the same problem:  to bridge the gap between the spiritual and the intellectual life.
They chose different paths:  Gerson write about the *theologia mystica*,
about an experimental knowledge of God; Petrarch developed the concept
of *docta pietas*, a wisdom that bridged both the spiritual and the intellectual needs of man.  Both men influenced the French Renaissance.  From
Gerson the French Humanists inherited a greater preoccupation with and
concern for the more contemplative aspect of the spiritual life.  Petrarch
bequeathed some important epistemological elements concerning the theological process and the knowledge of God.  His *docta pietas* expressed,

to a great degree, the spirituality of French Humanism.

## D.  Erasmus and the Spirituality of the French Renaissance

Erasmus had the most important influence on the spirituality of the French Renaissance.[42]  A majority of the French Humanists born around 1490 were Erasmians, men like Lefèvre d'Etaples, Guillaume Budé and others.  Erasmus found France congenial to his temperament and interests, and his *Enchiridion Militis Christiani* (1503) was conceived on French soil and enjoyed great popularity in Paris.

In the *Enchiridion*[43] Erasmus offered a comprehensive guide to Christian piety *(ars pietatis)* which at the same time was intended to be a new method in theology.  The *Enchiridion* advocated in a short and precise form a "method of living which might help you achieve a character acceptable to Christ."[44]

Erasmus' program, as elaborated in the *Enchiridion*, was a new form of Christian theology which emphasized education rather than dogma.  To the theology of the medieval *Summae* and *Sententiae*, he opposed the simple evangelical doctrine of Christ accessible to everyone and not only to abstract minds trained in the methods of scholastic logic.  In 1518, in a new edition of his *Enchiridion*, Erasmus wrote by way of preface a letter to his friend Paul Voz, where again he expressed his main concern: to produce a simple Christian way of life.

> It would in my opinion be very practical to choose and bring together some learned and devout men for the following task:  to extract from the most pure sources of the Gospels, the apostolic writings and their best commentators a kind of résumé of the whole "philosophy of Christ," a résumé in which simplicity would not detract from erudition, nor brevity from precision.  All that is of faith should be condensed in very few articles, and the same should be done for all that concerns the Christian way of life.  Those who would receive such instruction would then understand that the yoke of Christ is not heavy, but sweet and acceptable; they would understand that they had found fathers, not tyrants; shepherds, not robbers; that they were called unto salvation, not dragged into slavery.[45]

The *Enchiridion* was written for laymen and expressed in many different ways a lay spirituality.  What characterized the spirituality of this guide was a persistent emphasis on the inner life of the spirit in contrast to all external observances and ceremonies.  This doctrine was based on a very elevated doctrine of reason and soul.  For Erasmus reason and spirit were the same. "What the philosophers call reason, Paul sometimes refers to as spirit, sometimes as the inner man, sometimes as the law of the mind."[46] The spirit is of divine origin and "makes us Godlike; the flesh brutish."[47] The soul or reason has the "capacity for the divine which enables us to surpass even the nature of the angels and be made one with God. If you had not been given a body, you would be part of the Godhead."[48]

This doctrine of the soul, at the very core of Erasmus' spirituality, was expressed in terms of a *docta pietas*. Erasmus found the essence of Christian religion in the attitude of the individual toward his Creator: the concept of *pietas*. Expressions like *consulere pietate* appear with such frequency in the writings of Erasmus that the central influence of *pietas* must be emphasized. Piety meant reverence, devotion, commitment. Genuine piety could not remain an attitude of mind alone, but had to reveal itself in works of charity. This *pietas* was opposed to *devotio* understood in a pejorative sense as external practice and found its perfection in the interior, the invisible.

> Consider perfect piety to be constituted in this one thing only, that thou attemptest always to progress from things visible which are for the most part imperfect or indifferent toward things invisible according to the vision of man already discussed. This precept, indeed, pertains to the matter, since through a neglect or ignorance of it, most Christians are superstitious rather than pious and, except for the name of Christian, are not far removed from the superstitions of the gentile.[49]

Not that Erasmus condemned all formal observances, but he thought that they were secondary and could easily degenerate into superstition.

> These things are not to be omitted, but other things it is necessary to do. Corporeal works are not to be condemned, but God is not pleased save by invisible piety. God is a spirit and is moved by spiritual sacrifices.[50]

The very core of Erasmus' thought was the belief that piety is a matter of the spirit.

It was this primacy of interior religion that inspired Erasmus with distrust for external works and devotional practices. Considering the views of his time, Erasmus was justified in this reaction. He was totally against superstition, formalism and legalism. He did not attack the ceremonies as such but the exaggerated importance and credit given them. Therefore, for Erasmus, "in affectibus est Christi perfectio non in vitae genere." But Erasmus is not preaching a religion of pure spirit. For him as for the whole tradition of the *Devotio Moderna*, the primacy of interiority did not at all mean that intention suffices. It was still the execution which authenticated this disposition of the heart.[51] Nevertheless, the validity of the act came from the intention. Therefore, interiority *(animus, cor, spiritus, mens, intentio, affectus, pectus)* qualified all acts.[52] The *ex opere operato* needed the *ex opere operantis*.

Erasmus also stressed the personal dimension of the Christian life: belief involves the gift of oneself to Christ. His whole theology was marked by an enthusiastic personalism. He was sensitive to religious realities only insofar as they directly concerned the individual. For him the goal of theology was not a matter of speculation, but in the words of the *Ratio Verae Theologiae* "to teach Christ in a pure fashion." Thus in the *De Libero Arbitrio* Erasmus was at his best when describing the experience of freedom, the spiritual attitude by which the sinner confesses his responsibility and attributes to God all that is good in him. Erasmus underlined that in the scriptures everything concerns us, everything is for our instruction and for our education. The meaning of this personalism was expressed by Erasmus in terms of interiority. To find Christ one must seek him in one's own interior self. "Christ is not in corporeal realities."[53] There is a constant appeal in Erasmus to the individual conscience. One of the major themes of the *Enchiridion* is "know thyself." To know oneself became a very basic principle of the spiritual life, and one needed to constantly examine his motives. For Erasmus the Christian's combat was an inward and personal one, a matter primarily concerning the individual man. Knowledge of God came through knowledge of self.

A quest for the immediacy of the divine, independent of the sacramental system, was reflected in the deep current of what Imbart de La-Tour terms "évangélisme"[54] with its heavy Pauline overtones. The fact that St. Paul was converted on his journey to Damascus without the mediation of word and sacrament pointed to a more immediate relationship with God than the established order of sacramental grace. The spirituality of Erasmus was deeply rooted in this element of Pauline theology, but the immediacy of the divine did not do away with the mediation of the person of Christ. Erasmus' piety was essentially Christocentric.

"Look only to Christ as the unique and absolute good, love nothing else."[55] To be "transformed in Christ," this is the ideal of the baptized, in such a way that Christ becomes the unique goal of all of our actions.[56] Christ is truly for us the *caput, centrum, harmonia, petra, ignis, unicus auctor.* He is also our model, our example, the very archetype of piety, *archetypus pietatis.*[57]

In Erasmian Christian life, spirituality consisted in the imitation of Christ, but not essentially in imitation of the Christ of history. The Christ in Spirit, the mystery which vivifies, was the subject of imitation. It is according to the Spirit that Christ is born in us, *nascitur in nobis,* in that we must imitate him in crucifying in us the man according to the flesh.[58] Erasmus in no way slights the historicity of Christ. He upheld the realism of the incarnation against anyone who would alter it in any fashion.[59] In fact for Erasmus the mystery of God was Christ in his salvific action, in the *kenosis.* In the very humanity of Christ, God adapted his language so we could understand him. "Since Christ is the absolute simplicity and truth, there can be no dissimilitude between the archetype and the world."[60] This accommodation *(accommodatio)* was the manner in which God gave himself to man. Outside of Christ there was no other way to know God. In the very same fashion there was no other way to be saved. In this Christocentric perspective, revelation and salvation coincided. God revealed his mysteries in a salvific gesture which was the very person of Christ. This revelation concerned the whole man. In the tradition of Origen, Tauler and Gerson, Erasmus distinguished in man three levels of being: *caro, anima,* and *spiritus.*[61] Christ was the mystery of God; he addressed himself to the total man but in a very special way to the *spiritus.*

This revealed mystery was a gift, a grace, and a historical and transhistorical reality. It was also a call and an invitation to participate substantially in an incorporation in Christ, in order to live according to the spirit of Christ. This spirit of Christ was opposed to the flesh and changed all reality.[62] Only faith made this transformation possible and the very power of the spirit fostered a continual and necessary growth. On earth this growth was never finished and sanctification was always in process.[63]

In this whole synthesis of the spiritual life, what was the place of the Church? Erasmus' Christocentrism guided his whole ecclesiology. The

Church was defined as the Body of Christ.[64] His supernatural and mystical reality made of the Church a community of love where the reality of the body of Christ was lived in love.[65] All authority in the Church had to be based on love.

> The people are not there for the benefit of the bishops, but the institution of bishop has been established for the benefit of the people. Let the bishop therefore rule over the people, but then as a father rules over his children, as a man rules over his beloved bride.[66]

The threat envisioned by Erasmus in all his theological work was that of the invisible Church being absorbed into the visible. His conviction on this point flowed from his spirituality. There can be no doubt that Erasmus tended to neglect the notion of the Church as an external institution. He found that the superstructure of the Church hindered his attempt to make religion a more dynamic part of everyday life.

Notwithstanding his distrust of the visible Church, Erasmus accepted fully the authority of the Church. He pinned his faith on tradition and the authority of the Church. In 1527 he wrote:

> How much the authority of the church means to others I do not know: to me it means so much that I could have the same opinion as the Arians and Pelagians if the church had accepted what they thought. The words of Christ are enough for me, but people should not be surprised if I follow the church as their interpreter; convinced of its authority, I believe the canonical scriptures. Perhaps others are wiser or stronger; I for one find tranquillity in nothing safer than settled decisions of the church. There is no end to reasoning and argumentation.[67]

For Erasmus Church authority and tradition were explicitly recognized; they had to function as regulative principles. Together with scripture Erasmus accepted them as *fundamenta ecclesiae*.

While there is in Erasmus revealed here the same persistent emphasis on the inner life of the spirit as in the *Devotio Moderna*, his *ars pietatis* was at the same time an attempt to renew theology and to reunite it to spirituality.

Erasmus was critical above all else of the fact that theology had become so polluted and overgrown with philosophical dialectic that it was no longer possible to discover Christ beneath this accumulation. Writing to the Archbishop of Canterbury in 1506, he lamented the depraved notion of the divine resulting from the nonsense of the sophists.[68] Theology as it was taught by the over-speculative, hair-splitting

scholastics was entirely too complicated to be of any possible use in
living a pious life.  Who could possibly find his way through the laby-
rinth of the disputations they multiplied?  Who could find the gospel
behind the wall of quiddities and haecceities that the scholastics had
constructed?  It was necessary for a Christian philosophy to be presented in a way that everyone could understand and benefit from.  His
words grew bitter when he pointed out that for most theologians Aristotle meant more than Christ.  The theologians of his time with their
complicated sophisms, their rationalistic formulae and their ever-
increasing dogmatism had made any real penetration of the faith of the
gospel impossible.  Therefore, the aim of Erasmus' theology was an interiorization, a spiritualization of religious practice, a more personal relationship between the individual and God.  On one of the very
first pages of the *Ratio theologiae* the author stated that the unique
purpose of studying theology was:  "To be inwardly changed and transformed into that which you learn from scripture."[69]  It is primarily in
this sense that Erasmus' theology was therefore biblical.[70]  In his
*Paraclesis*, Erasmus affirmed:

> Why do we not concern ourselves explicitly with Holy Scripture?
> Why is it that such an important part of our lives be consecrated
> to Averroes and not to the scriptures?  Why should most of our
> lives be lived in the company of commentaries and their contradic-
> tory opinions?  Scripture itself will be without doubt the school
> of the future great theologians.[71]

Particularly fundamental in Erasmus' interpretation of the nature of
theology was his emphasis that the scriptures share to some extent in
the divine mystery.  For Erasmus the very mystery of God was also the
mystery of scripture.[72]  It was then impossible to separate the knowledge of divine things and the knowledge of the scriptures.  Exegesis
belonged to theology; it could not be reduced to a purely scientific
knowledge of scripture; for it was a prophetic knowledge.  By his docil-
ity to the spirit the theologian was made capable of explaining the very
mystery of scripture.[73]  The mystery of scripture was hidden in the very
letter itself.[74]  From this letter it was extracted, opened.  Theological research could not penetrate the divine mystery both concealed and
revealed in the Bible.  The purpose of biblical interpretation was to
draw a man into a continuing interaction with the divine revelation contained in the scriptures, so that God's own speech and God's own spirit

could make an impact upon him.

To understand this aspect of Erasmus' theological method, one must appreciate his perception of language and *eloquentia*. Erasmus understands language as a vital force in constituting *humanitas*. Language carries more than symbolic power:  it is truly sacramental. Language can affect the hearer; it can convey the wisdom of the speaker. For Erasmus the highest form of *eloquentia* and *sapientia* is the Divine Word first expressed in the Person of Christ and in his Scriptures. The Word of Christ is the most powerful of teachers; it is a living and active reality. Because of the Word's dynamic nature, the hearer of the Word can encounter God in a personal way.

In 1519 Erasmus inserted into the second edition of the New Testament a long essay on "The Method of Attaining to True Theology." In it he challenged the validity of the theological studies of the past 400 years and proposed a radically different curriculum in their place. At the base of his disagreement with the traditional theologians lay a fundamentally different conception of what was "true theology." Dialectics he rejected as the principle tool of learning and substituted philology and history; all medieval glosses and commentaries he passed over, insisting that the student confront study of the scriptural texts as they were originally written. The first requirement for the training of theologians, he argued, should be a thorough knowledge of the three ancient languages; the second, a general training in the humane disciplines, especially history, grammar and rhetoric. As for the dialectic and the learned system, of St. Thomas, Scotus, and Lyra, they might better be ignored. They merely tended to obscure the meaning of the sacred scriptures. For the most part, Erasmus felt that scholastic theology was irrelevant and had little to say to mankind concerning Christ.

> I see the simple multitude longing after food for their souls, desiring to learn how they can return to their homes better people, and then the lecturer *(theologaster)* ventilates some frigid and perplexing question from Scotus or Occam.[75]

In the *Enchiridion* he wrote that

> Scotus seems to have given these men such great confidence that, without ever having read the sacred writings, they still think themselves to be unlimited theologians.[76]

Erasmus saw at the very root of any renewal of theology the need of a philology.

> I see it as madness to touch with the littlest finger that princi-
> ple part of theology, which treats of divine mysteries, without
> first being instructed in Greek, when those who have translated the
> sacred books have in their scrupulous interpretation so rendered
> the Greek phrases that even the primary meaning which our theolo-
> gians call literal cannot be understood by those who do not know
> Greek.[77]

The basic element of Erasmian theology was a philological, critical
approach to scriptures.  Through philological research the theologian
performed best his task as servant, since with this knowledge he could
overcome the temptation to set his opinions in the place of divine revelation.  Severely critical biblical research would produce a theology
which was obedient to revelation and remained its servant.

Any theology that did not submit itself to the primacy of divine initiative was led astray.  Theology could never be man's words about God,
but man listening to God's word addressed to him and leading him to love
and service.  We can understand now why Erasmus considers as his major
theological work his New Testament exegesis and paraphrase.[78]  This exegesis is a complete act; it comprehends dogmatic theology, moral theology, spirituality and pastoral preoccupations.

To be able to grasp more fully what Erasmus understood about theology,
a few words must be said about his hermeneutics.  The starting point for
Erasmus' hermeneutics seems to have been the neo-Platonic conception of
the contrast between flesh and spirit, a contrast which is grounded in
the nature of the world and of man.  Canon V of the *Enchiridion* states
the central principle of Erasmus' piety and theology:

> One maintains perfect piety if one seeks always to proceed from the
> visible things which are either imperfect or neutral to the invis-
> ible according to the higher aspect of man.[79]

In this connection Erasmus linked his doctrine of scripture with his
doctrine of the Incarnation.  In Christ, humanity hides divinity just as
in scripture the letter hides the spiritual meaning.

> Whoever wonders why the divine spirit wishes to hide his riches in
> these wrappings will wonder also why the eternal wisdom assumed the
> person of a poor, humble, spurned and condemned man.[80]

The hermeneutical distinction between flesh and spirit directed Erasmus'
exegesis and thus influenced all his thought.  The passage from the
flesh (the appearance, the figure) to the spirit (the substance, the

truth, reality) the passage from the world and man to God characterizes
Christianity.  In the *Enchiridion*, the theme appears as the ascent from
the visible to the invisible; in the *Ratio* it is described as the pro-
gression from the exterior to the interior.

The scriptures, according to Erasmus, make us know the *mysterium* by
and through a process of interiorization, a process which leads from
literal exegesis to spiritual exegesis.  The hermeneutical "circle," as
Erasmus put it, is "a circle of human progress."[81]  Scripture was first
given its meaning by the Spirit:  the hermeneutical process--that is,
passage from literal exegesis to spiritual exegesis--is accomplished by
the Spirit in the heart of the believer.

The attitude of the exegete is fundamental in discerning the spiritual or allegorical.  He who would understand these meanings of Scripture must approach the Bible not only with the tools of literary and
historical criticism, but also with purged emotions,[82] a clean heart,[83]
and supreme purity of mind.[84]  For it is necessary to be spiritual to
judge rightly spiritual scripture.[85]  From the *Enchiridion* to the *Ecclesiastes*, Erasmus held to the necessity of a mystical and ethical as well
as a philological understanding of scripture.  His own emphasis was
rather more upon the moral than on the mystical side.

Erasmus held that the correct interpretation of scripture required
more than a literal understanding.  It required a spiritual understanding with both subjective and objective aspects.  Objectively it had to
do with a recognition of the spiritual content, that is, the allegory or
tropology which was hidden in the letter.  Subjectively, it had to do
both with the spiritual and moral perception which made possible the
recognition of a spiritual content and with the realization of this content in one's own life.

Erasmus proposed a form of theology which could unite intelligence
and spiritual affectivity.  The right way to understand scripture, he
wrote, was through meditation and prayer, the methods indicated and contained in scripture itself.  They are more fruitful methods of understanding scripture than the *questio* and the *disputatio*.  For theological
learning is better approached with prayer than with argumentation; it is
life rather than disputation, regeneration rather than reasoning.

The following quotation sums up Erasmus' approach both to theology
and Christian piety:

> This kind of philosophy, that is, the philosophy of Christ, which
> lies in the state of mind more truly than in syllogism, is a way of
> life rather than a disputation, inspiration rather than erudition,
> transformation more than reason. To be learned falls to the lot of
> but few, but there is no one who cannot be pious; I may add this
> boldly, no one who cannot be a theologian.[86]

Theology then pretends less to attain the mystery than to dispose the
believer to open himself and receive this mystery with joy, to meditate
upon it and to contemplate it, to be nourished by it, to be inspired and
transformed; to live the mystery.

Theology for Erasmus is therefore doctrinal and mystical and at the
same time practical and pastoral, since its purpose is to conform the
Christian to the mystery which he had meditated on and contemplated.
His  theology was the conjunction of *pietas* and *eruditio*, resulting in a
*pia doctrina*. Erasmus re-established the synthesis between theology and
spirituality in what he called his *philosophia Christi*. The two aspects
of this synthesis were the *pia doctrina* and the *docta pietas*. His theology was spiritual and his spirituality theological. Erasmus discussed
clearly the theologians' perspectives: they all took their origin in
the *mysterium fidei*. While his theology was neither speculative nor
dialectical, it did not lack a systematical dimension. It involved the
entire person of the believer *(in affectibus verius quam in syllogismis)*
and invited the believer to develop in his life *(vita magis quam disputatio)* under the motion of the Spirit, the virtualities of his faith in
baptism *(orans magis quam argumentans et transformari studens magis quam
armari)*.[87] Contemplation as proposed by Erasmus was essentially defined
by its theological content. It did not involve any theory about the
mystical or psychological states.

Erasmus' entire work was religious in its motivation and purpose,
*eruditio* and *pietas*, the two goals of the Christian humanists, Erasmus
drew into a synthesis, and at the same time subordinated the former to
the latter. All studies, he insisted, must converge in the *philosophia
Christi* of which the mystery of Christ was the energy, the content and
the object; its two aspects, the *pia doctrina* and the *docta pietas*, were
distinct but not separated. The *eruditio* was the discipline. If Erasmus recommended the study of profane disciplines which were not Christian in themselves since, in his own words, "they do not treat of Christ
nor do they originate from Christ,"[88] it was on the condition that these

disciplines be referred to Christ, *omnia ad Christum referentur.*[89]

Theology was not a *scientia*, but a *sapientia*, not a systematically ordered body of true and certain knowledge derived from principles of revelation, but a *doctrina sacra* derived from the scripture, a holy rhetoric in the service of the text, unprofaned by Aristotelian philosophy and syllogism. The goal of this theology was not to know God in his fullness, but to love God.

It is in this new vision of theology that Erasmus' original contribution was made. It is here also that he differed most from the *Devotio Moderna*. Instead of abandoning theology as being a distraction to the spiritual life, Erasmus integrated theology into it.

To a larger extent than the *Devotio Moderna* but with the same intent Erasmus endeavored to democratize spirituality. True piety consisted in applying the very spirit of Christ to the daily life of Christians. This obligation was laid upon all men, not only upon professional religious: *monochatus non est pietas.*

> It is a hard thing indeed and known to a very few men, even of monks, to die to sin, to die to carnal desires, to die to this world. And yet this is the common profession of all Christians. Either we must perish or we must without exception take this road to salvation whether we be kings or poor ploughmen. For as it falls not to every man's lot to achieve perfect imitation of Christ, yet all must toil hand and foot to ascend thither. He has a good part of Christian piety who with a sure mind desires to be a Christian.[90]

Here Erasmus attacked the double standard of Christian living which grew out of an over-emphasis on the institutional church in which it was assumed that salvation was more within the range of the monk than the layman. For Erasmus there was but one salvation within Christ and therefore but one way to approach it.

God was not seen in himself, as a metaphysical entity, an object of abstract speculation foreign to man and his destiny. But he was seen in his movement toward man, the revealing God known in the mystery of his salvific action. For Erasmus, every word about God was a word about man. If God turned towards man, man became radically for God. Erasmus reasoned that God in himself is incomprehensible, but he also maintained that man in himself does not exist and man for himself is absurd. In his relation to man God is independent and always holds a free initiative. The movement of God to man is a free gift; man's relation to God

is considerate of his nature and of his salvation.  This type of theological perspective was not exclusively anthropocentric but essentially
soteriological.  It constantly considered man and God, the two poles of
the dialogue.

In this framework the concept of contempt of the world, *comtemptus
mundi*, and the very theme of humility as a basic virtue of man was given
a new direction.  In one current of medieval spirituality (one which had
its influence on the *Devotio Moderna*), the notion prevailed that perfect
sanctity could be found only in monastic-ascetic detachment from the
world.  There appeared in the ascetical literature a *nihil sum* attitude
of disparagement, an attitude which regarded the world and man with contempt and opposed to it the truth of human dignity.  Owing to the promi-
nence of such negative attitudes, the existence and validity of other
spiritual principles were almost overlooked.  In this spirituality there
was no more effective way of preparing for the coming of the kingdom of
God than through contempt and renunciation of the world.  The monastic
way of life, with its strict discipline, became for many the model to be
followed.  The Third Orders originally were intended as a substitute for
the real monastic life, designed for all those who had to remain in the
world.  This was an attempt to pattern life in the world after life in
the cloister.

Yves Congar summarizes very well this current of spirituality:

> Medieval Christianity was the result of two factors:  namely an
> innate logic which forced it to direct all worldly activities to-
> ward the goal of eternal salvation, and the historical circumstances
> of its development under the influence of austere monasticism.  It
> inspired a spirituality which was monastic through and through....
> It imitated the characteristics which were peculiar to a monastic
> life, such as the orientation of life toward eternity and an ab-
> sence of any evaluation of earthly realities and achivements for
> their own sake and in themselves.[91]

Erasmus distinguishes himself from the *Devotio Moderna*.  In contrast to
Thomas à Kempis, Erasmus did not take an either-or attitude toward the
created world:  he endeavored rather to see in created things a world
which man was called to direct toward Christ.  The Christocentrism of
the *Devotio Moderna* typified in the *Imitatio Christi* was too exclusive.
For Erasmus, everything was from Christ and must serve to project Christ
into the world.  The monkish ideal with its flight from the world might
have been an answer for an earlier period.  But Christianity had to be

adapted to the changing times. The new world of the merchant, banker
and financier made the casuistry of the cenobite obsolete. The theme
that Innocent III had imposed on his world, that man was formed out of
dust and was born to labor, sorrow and fear, was losing its hold on the
sixteenth century mind. Individualism was fragmenting medieval universalism. The fifteenth-century problem of the proper relationship between the individual and society was one of which Gerson and, in a special fashion, Erasmus were extremely aware. The *vita contemplativa* and
the *vita activa* could no longer be defined in the old religious terms.
The kind of *contemptus mundi* advocated by Erasmus was related to an interior world. Separation from the world was separation from one's interior world. The world to be avoided and despised was not an exterior
reality. The cloister in no way separated us from this world.[92] If
monasticism was an authentic contempt for the world, then every Christian had to be a monk. A monk is nothing but a pure and simple Christian.[93] Erasmus arrived thus at the concept of "the monk in the world."
"What else is a city but a large monastery."[94]

It was Erasmus' *docta pietas* and *monochatus non est pietas* that had
the most influence on the French Humanists. At the same time Erasmus
carried the spirituality of the *Devotio Moderna* to them.

## E. *The Spirituality of Jacques Lefèvre d'Etaples*

The wide variety of influences contributing to the formation of Christian humanism in France is particularly evident in the career of Jacques
Lefèvre d'Etaples (1450-1536).[95] For three decades after his return
from his first visit to Italy in 1491-1492, he was the acknowledged
leader of the reforming humanists at the University of Paris. Indeed,
except for him and Erasmus, French humanism would have been but an eru-
dition and a literature. Through him and Erasmus it became an awakening
of spirituality and a reorientation of theology itself.

Lefèvre's interest centered on the spiritual life. He was a humanist
who firmly believed in the necessity of restoring solid learning as a
basis for true piety, and who regarded the decadent scholasticism of the
Parisian terminists responsible in a very real sense for the decline of
religion. He was deeply influenced by the *Devotio Moderna* as well, as
is conclusively demonstrated by L. Salley.[96]

While the influence of the *Devotio Moderna* upon Lefèvre must be

affirmed, his main preoccupation was to breach the separation between
theology and spirituality. Here Erasmus' influence was certainly at
work. This unity was achieved by stressing the unique role of scripture.
In the preface of his *Commentatorii initiatorii in quatuor evangelis*
(1522) Lefèvre affirmed the Gospel as the unique source of piety, of the
interior life and of all truth.

Lefèvre expressed his spirituality in his concept of *theologia vivificans*. This vivifying theology was a theological exegesis uniting
spirituality and theology. It was based on an intuition of the primacy
and sufficiency of the world. *"Verbum Dei sufficit."*[97] The word of God
alone is sufficient means to attain one's end for it can guide one's
life. The study of the Gospel is a spiritual life, an *itinerarium mentis ad Deum*, and the propaedeutics are less a knowledge of dialectics
than moral and religious qualities. This understanding of the scriptures presupposes a spiritual life which it nourishes in turn. In 1498
Lefèvre wrote in the preface of his *Theologia Vivificans*:

> The life is much more dazzling when one is nearer the sun. The
> Holy Scripture ought therefore to obtain the greatest respect and
> the greatest authority. In order to apply oneself to sacred stud-
> ies, attention, devotion, piety, religious feeling, respect, humil-
> ity are needed. Those who do not possess these feelings become
> worse by the study of the holy scriptures.[98]

Lefèvre bifurcated the mind's knowledge. On the one hand was knowledge
from above: divine, spiritual humbling to man and always joined with
the love of God. On the other hand was knowledge which was not from
above: human, carnal, self-inflating, and unrelated to the love of God.

For Lefèvre the doctrine of Christ took precedence over all learned
discourse. The intellectual process, the theological exegesis, was primarily an asceticism and a science, a contemplation in which study became a spiritual life. He saw in the three levels of the spiritual
life---purification, illumination and perfection--a description of the
levels of exegesis. Lefèvre placed his commentaries, such as those on
the Psalter and St. Paul, on the first level, that of purification, and
prayed God to give others the gift of writing commentaries on the other
two levels. At these different levels, only the spiritual sense was
true and fruitful, and only the eyes of faith illuminated by the Holy
Spirit were capable of discovering this spiritual meaning. This spiritual knowledge was a gift of the Holy Spirit infused in those who were

humble and conscious of the incapacity of human reasoning.

Lefèvre's argument was as follows:  the spiritual meaning of the scriptures illuminated by the Holy Spirit is the mystery of Christ himself.  Since the spiritual meaning of the scriptures is Christological, the spiritual life should then consist in becoming Christ-like.  And the Holy Spirit is the true interpreter of the scriptures.[99]

It is through the Holy Spirit that the Christological sense is revealed to us.  He is the doctor *par excellence* who illuminates the faithful.  He communicates a "sense of faith" which is above that of "reason and intelligence."[100]  Since the Spirit is at the source of the scriptures, it is through the Spirit that we ourselves must listen.

The centrality of Christ in the spiritual life Lefèvre interpreted as an indication of the democratic nature of the spiritual life.  Since there is but one spiritual life, one foundation and goal, all who serve Christ and are incorporated in Christ should be called "religious of Christ."[101]  The spiritual life, the vocation to intimate relation with God, is not only for a privileged class but for everyone.  But the preeminence he assigned to scripture as a unique source of truth and the importance he attributed to a direct and personal relationship between God and man overshadowed somewhat his concerns with the ecclesial and communal dimension of salvation.[102]  Nevertheless Lefèvre in no way denied the dogmas of the Church on the sacraments.  Although he had little to say about the sacraments, he did not repudiate them, nor did he reject papal authority.  In fact, he clearly asserted the obligation to obey the pope.[103]  He upheld the holiness of the church.  In the thought of Lefèvre the Church was blameless and without error.  "Let us avoid making the Church a teacher of error, for the holy and apostolic Church in which we believe does not commit error."[104]

Lefèvre d'Etaple's was the most representative of the French spiritualities current in the early part of the 16th century.  In its basic tenets it was a great deal more ambiguous than that of Erasmus, owing perhaps to the strong influence the *Devotio Moderna* had upon him.  But at the same time it had at least four characteristics in common with the spirituality of Erasmus.  It assigned a preeminent role to scripture and to the exegesis of scripture; it unifies, through the exegesis of scripture, theology and spirituality; it stressed the role of the Holy Spirit as an interior teacher; and lastly it had the same difficulty in attributing an important role to the Church in the spiritual life.

F. *Conclusion*

It was in the elaboration of the *Theologia vivificans* of the *philoso-phia Christi* that the spirituality of early French humanism expressed itself. This spirituality was an attempt to bridge the gap between the spiritual life and the intellectual life, through the elaboration of a theology that was at the same time a *sapientia* and a *pietas*. Behind this preoccupation lay an emphasis on the Pauline dualism of a spiritual soul and a sinful flesh. A very high doctrine of the soul and reason prevailed. Spirituality became a form of education with its main pur-pose the enlightenment of reason through self-knowledge and the knowl-edge of God.

Fundamental to this orientation was a common aspiration to interiority and inwardness. There was a strong need for a simplified religion, un-cluttered by a multitude of devotions and practices. This ideal could hardly find satisfaction within the framework of late medieval Christian-ity, and therefore led to tension.

Much of the inwardness which we find in this period was colored by a strong subjectivism, marked by a primacy of the personal and moralistic. This piety was comprised of intense striving for salvation by an indi-vidual soul. In fact this endeavor of the soul was central to it. Even in the context of a true sacramental life and a prevalent understanding of the subjective holiness of the Church, the piety of this period to some extent was that of an individual set apart from the objectivity of the liturgical and sacramental life of the Church. What exact measure of influence the emerging spirit of individualism had upon the humanism of this period is difficult to ascertain. Nevertheless it does seem that there was a growing awareness of personality and a keener sense of individual autonomy than had been possible in the political and social conditions of the Middle Ages. But this individualism contributed to, and at the same time was a sign of, a lay piety that stressed the indi-vidual man's direct communion with God.

This lay piety tended to shift the emphasis from the Church and sacra-ments as means of salvation to the individual's direct relationship to God. At the same time the claim that the Holy Spirit guides us and teaches us in the daily reading of the scriptures gave rise to an idea of Christian freedom as absolute dependence upon God and as freedom from the institutional, hierarchical and sacramental Church.

The humanists of the sixteenth century, exemplified by Erasmus, could not accept monasticism as being the unique way to salvation. Every Christian must separate himself from the world, but this world is inside man; it is not the outside world. Separation from the world is not guaranteed by physical presence in a monastery. Neither the habit nor the structure is important, but only the personal choice: *monochatus non est pietas*. Piety is not contempt for created reality but the understanding that what is important is man's own inner life and the acceptance of his dependence on God. Created reality has a value, but it is a relative value; it has autonomy, but a relative autonomy.

Many and varied influences shaped the spirituality of the early 16th century in France. From the *Devotio Moderna* it inherited its lay and democratic characteristics: its desire for a simple Christian way of life, its Christocentric thrust, its persistent emphasis on the inner life and its opposition to external practices; its preoccupation with a constant ascent from the visible to the invisible; its fundamental concern with self-knowledge; its neglect of the mediative role of the Church in the spiritual life accompanied by an explicit acceptance of the authority of the Church; its individualism and constant quest for immediacy with God through the work of the Holy Spirit.

But although in continuity with the *Devotio Moderna* in many of its tenets, the spirituality of the French humanists differed from the *Devotio Moderna* in its most original contribution: its integration of the intellectual and spiritual life. This integration of theology and spirituality began under the influence of Erasmus and resulted in the elaboration of a *docta pietas*. Theology through the conjunction of *pietas* and *eruditio* became a *pia doctrina*.

This *pia doctrina* established, at the outset of the Reformation, a deep yearning among serious people for a religion of inward experience. As an attempted conjunction of theology and spirituality, the *pia doctrina* led to new epistemological problems. It also led in the direction of a greater intellectual and spiritual freedom.

*Notes*

1.  A. Tilley, *The Dawn of the French Renaissance* (Cambridge, 1918).
2.  L. W. Spitz, *The Religious Renaissance of the German Humanists* (Cambridge, 1963).
3.  G. Toffanini, *La religione degli Umanisti* (Bologna, 1950); F. Hermans, *Histoire doctrinale de l'humanisme chrétien* (Paris, 1948); L. Bouyer, *Autour d'Erasme. Etude sur le christianisme des humanistes catholiques* (Paris, 1955); J. C. Olin, *Christian Humanism and the Reformation* (New York, 1956); P. M. Cordier, *Jean Pic de la Mirandole, ou la plus pure figure de l'humanisme chrétien* (Paris, 1957).
4.  P. Fitzgerald, *The World's Own Book or the Treasury of à Kempis; An Account of the Chief Editions of "The Imitation of Christ"* (London, 1895) 5.
5.  J. van Rooij, *Gerard Zerbolt van Zutphen* (Nijmegen, 1936) 362-372.
6.  P. Debongnie, *Jean Mombaer*, 331.
7.  M. Godet, *La congrégation de Montaigu (1490-1580)* (Paris, 1912) 98.
8.  *Ibid.*, 43.
9.  "Par Gerson, cette influence de Saint Bonaventure s'étend au domaine de la spiritualité moderne, elle enrichira désormais et occupera pendant des siècles la conscience chrétienne" (E. Gilson, *La philosophie de Saint Bonaventure* [Paris, 1953] 393). "Au milieu du XV^e siècle, Gerson qui résume de façon personnelle tous ces courants, l'emporte sur tous les autres." (P. Debongnie, "*Devotio moderna*," *Dictionnaire de Spiritualité* IV [Paris, 1958] 743)
10. "Placé aux confins du moyen age et des temps modernes, ce grand théologien qui fut un spirituel admirable, résume en lui la scolastique la plus haute en même temps qu'il annonce l'evangélisme d'Erasme." (A. Combes, "Gerson et la naissance de l'humanisme," in *Revue du Moyen Age latin* I [1945] 259)
11. *Ibid.*, 281-283.
12. E. Delaruelle, *L'Eglise au temps du Grand Schisme et la crise conciliaire* I (Paris, 1962) 322-323.
13. "Jean Gerson. Encore un nom célèbre, qui pose de nouvelles questions, mal étudiées: rapports du moninalisme et de la mystique...; relations surtout entre la 'théologie scolastique,' oeuvre dialectique, matière de l'enseignement universitaire, et la 'théologie mystique,' qui se réfère à une cognitio experimentalis et que l'on pourrait croire réservée aux cloîtres. Aux difficultés spéculatives se trouvent liés dans ces esprits les problèmes pratiques de réforme religieuse." (P. Vignaux, *La pensée au Moyen Age* [Paris, 1958] 182-183)
14. *Opera omnia*, ed. Ellies du Pin III (Antwerp, 1706) 406.
15. *De mystica theologia specu*, Cons. 28E, *Opera omnia* III, 384 B.
16. *Oeuvres complètes*, ed. P. Glorieux, III (Paris, 1962) 127.
17. *Opera omnia* III, 1241 A.
18. *Ibid.* III, 1242 B-C.
19. *Contra curiositatem*, *Oeuvres complètes*, III, 249.
20. *Ibid.*
21. *Ibid.* III, 131.
22. S. Ozment, *Homo spiritualis. A Comparative Study of the Anthropology of Joannes Tauler, Jean Gerson and Martin Luther (1509-1516) in the Context of their Theological Thought* (New York, 1969) 78-79.
23. *Ibid.*
24. *De myst. theol. spec.*, cons, 44, 120, 8ff.

25. *Cons*. 32 I; *Opera* III, 387 D f.

26. *Cons*. 8 P; *Opera omnia* III, 369 A.

27. *Opera omnia* II, 661 C.

28. "...nulla auctoritas cuiuscumque scripturae aut doctoris habet efficaciam ad aliquid probandam...nisi inquantum doctrinae ecclesiasticae congrueret; aut ab ecclesia approbaretur....Non solum doctrinae doctoris sed etiam ipsi canonice praefert (Augustinus) ecclesiam." (*Opera omnia* I, 463)

29. Many editions of the *De Imitatione Christi* appeared from 1498 to 1500 under the name of Gerson. Cf. A. Renaudet, *Préréforme et Humanisme à Paris (1494-1517)* (Paris, 1916) 370.

30. P. Gerosa, *La cultura patristica del Petrarcha* (Turin, 1929); *idem*, *L'Umanesimo agostiano del Petrarcha* (Turin, 1927); A. Tripet, *Pétrarque ou la connaissance de soi* (Geneva, 1967).

31. Petrarca, *De sui ipsius et multorum ignorantia*, tr. H. Nachnod, in *The Renaissance of Man*, ed. E. Cassirer (Chicago, 1948) 59-60.

32. Y. Congar, *Vraie et fausse Réforme dans l'Eglise* (Paris, 1950) 32, 64-65.

33. Petrarca, *De sui ipsius*, 62-63.

34. *Ibid.*, 104-105.

35. Petrarca, *De Remediis Utriusque Fortunae. Opera omnia*, ed. S. Herold (Basel, 1554) 45.

36. Petrarca, *De Officiis*, ed. G. Rotondi, Studi e Testi 195 (Vatican, 1958) 26. Trans. C. Trinkaus, *In our Image and Likeness* (London, 1970) 32.

37. *Ibid.*, 36.

38. *Ibid.*, 37.

39. *Ibid.*, 38-39.

40. *Ibid.*, 39.

41. Petrarca, *De sui ipsius*, 104.

42. Cf. M. Bataillon, *Erasme et l'Espagne. Recherches sur l'histoire spirituelle du XVIe siècle* (Paris, 1937); J. Ehenne, *Spiritualisme Erasmien et théologiens Louvainistes: Un changement de problématique au début du XVIe siècle* (Louvain, 1956); E. W. Kohls, *Die Theologie des Erasmus* (Basel, 1966); C. Bene, *Erasme et Saint Augustin: ou influence de Saint Augustin sur l'humanisme d'Erasme* (Geneva, 1969).

43. Cf. J. B. Pineau, *Erasme, sa pensée religieuse* (Paris, 1924) 101-132; R. B. Drummond, *His Life and Character as Shown in His Correspondence and Works* I (London, 1873) 114-115; Spitz, *Religious Renaissance*, 197-236.

44. Erasmus, *Enchiridion Militis*, trans. R. Himelick, *The Enchiridion of Erasmus* (Bloomington, 1963) 37.

45. Letter 858, 14 August 1518; *Opus epistolarum* III, ed. P. S. Allen (Oxford, 1906) 365.

46. *Enchiridion Militis*, 72.

47. *Ibid.*, 80.

48. *Ibid.*, 63.

49. *Ibid.*, 101.

50. *Ibid.*, 126.

51. Erasmus, *Opera omnia*, ed. J. LeClercq (Leiden, 1703) V, 34 (hereafter LB).

52. LB V, 36a.

53. LB VI, 125 D.

54. F. Imbart de la Tour, *Les Origines de la Réforme* III (Paris, 1948) 398.

55. *Enchiridion*, 94.

56. "But in order that you may press forward to felicity by a more trustworthy course, take this as your fourth rule: that you set Christ before you as the only goal of your whole life and direct all your efforts, all your activities, all your leisure, all your business in His direction." (*Ibid.*, 94)

57. LB V, II, 39, 40, 45, 88, 89, 92.

58. LB V, 31f-32a.

59. LB V, 92e-94b.

60. LB V, 32a.

61. LB V, 19.

62. LB V, 43a.

63. LB II, 771d-772d.

64. LB V, 45-46.

65. On Erasmus' concept of the Church, see the following: J. Leclerc, *Histoire de la tolérance au siècle de la Réforme* I (Paris, 1955) 133-149; Kohls, *Theologie* I, 159-171.

66. LB IX, 1197-1214.

67. Allen, 7 (1893) 62-70.

68. *Ibid.*, 1, 419.

69. LB V, 77 B.

70. Cf. E. W. Kohls, *Theologie*, says that Erasmus consistently represents a living scriptural theology. He claims that Erasmus developed a purely biblical theology already before his debate with Luther.

71. *Paraclesis*, ed. Holborn 148, 5-2.

72. LB IX, 90 A.

73. *Ibid.*

74. LB IX, 85 E, 87 F.

75. Holborn, 3, 301.

76. *Ibid.*, 34, 1.

77. Allen, 149, 21.

78. Cf. Kohls, *Theologie*, 216.

79. LB V, 271.

80. Preface to the 1516 edition of the New Testament, Allen, II, 373.

81. LB V, 180 D.

82. Holborn 3, 179.

83. *Ecclesiastes* (1535); LB V, 774 D.

84. LB V, 88 C.

85. "Ut enim de artificio nemo judicat nisi artifex, ita de spirituali Scriptura nemo vere pronunciat nisi spiritualis." (LB V, 825 E)

86. Holborn I, 144.

87. LB VI, 4.

88. LB X, 1728e.

89. LB V, 8a.

90. *Enchiridion*, 59.

91. Y. Congar, *Lay People in the Church* (London, 1962) 384.

92. LB V, 65c.

93. "Nec aliud tum erat monachus quam pure christianus." (LB V, 1261e-1262c)

94. "Quid aliud est civitas quam magnum monasterium?" (Allen, e, 276) Cf. also G. di Napoli, "*Contemptus mundi* e *Dignitas Hominis* nel Rinascimento," *Rivista di filosofia neoscolastica* XLVIII (1956) 9-41.

95. J. Dagens, *Humanisme et évangélisme chez Lefèvre d'Etaples* (Paris, 1959).

96. C. L. Salley, "The Ideas of the *Devotio Moderna* as Reflected in the Life and the Writings of J. L. D'Etaples" (Dissert. Abstracts XIII [1953] Micro F; Andover-Harvard Theological Library).

97. *Commentarii initiatorii in quatuor evangelia*, ed. Andreae Cratanchi (Basel, 1523) fo. a2, v°.

98. *Theologia Vivificans* (Paris, 1498) a III, V° IIII R°.

99. "What are transmitted in types and figures are allegorical; what are not transmitted in types and figures are not; nor do these realities require any other sense than that which is expressed and which the author intends, who in this case happens to be the Holy Spirit. This sense is also called the literal sense, because it is without type or figure. But this sense is also spiritual. How could it not be a spiritual sense since it has the Holy Spirit as author?" (*Sancti Pauli Epistolae XIV, Commentarius* [Paris, 1515] *In Gal.* IV, fol. 159r)

100. *Commentarii in Epistolas catholicas* (Basel, 1527) *Comm. in I Petr.* III, 26, 30r.

101. "...religiosos Christi se nominare debent." (*Comm. Ep. Pauli,* fo. 106, r° and v°.

102. Cf. E. Hamann, "Lefevre d'Etaples," *D.T.C.* (Paris, 1926) 144.

103. "Omnes...ecclesiasticae dignitates et ordines debent sacro monarchae parere in sanctis institutionibus ut summus pontifex est; non autem ut peculiaris est alicuius loci pontifex." (*Comm. Ep. Pauli,* 98 f. in Ro. 13.

104. *De una ex tribus Maria* (Paris, 1518) fol. 38, v.-fol. 39r.

Chapter III

*DEVOTIO* AND *PIETAS*: A LINGUISTIC APPROACH TO JOHN CALVIN'S SPIRITUALITY

In a way words are merely devices of sound which have come to signify one idea rather than another. But words are also invested with overtones which are very real, though not easily defined. In fact what differentiates man from animal is not primarily his capacity for verbal expression but the inarticulable properties of thought and experience upon which verbal language depends. Man's personal participation in speech is such that his unspoken knowledge and thought are of decisive importance to its understanding. This is particularly true of words which express spiritual man's values. What has been said by H. Delehaye of the word "saint" is applicable to innumerable other words:

> If we ask, finally, what is the real meaning of the word "saint," at the end of a long evolution we can say that it is vaguely charged with all the nuances through which it passed through the different ages in the profane domain as well as in the religious domain.[1]

*Devotio* and *pietas*, words well worn by popular use, are vaguely charged in the general consciousness with all the nuances through which they have passed in the course of the ages. For no other word-concepts penetrate to more intimate psychological depths than those which symbolize the relationship of the spirit to God. The history of words and the history of ideas are two different fields, but fields that are inseparable.

The goal of this short language study is to elucidate an area in the history of spirituality which is at one time a system of ideas and a phenomenon of culture.

A. *Devotio*

*Devotio*[2] signifies total dedication. Chronologically, the word in Latin first meant the action of devoting or consecrating (for good or evil) by vow; it later came to signify the condition of being devoted, devotedness, loyalty, allegiance. It also meant the condition of one set apart for a unique purpose. And it conveyed a sense of the inner, intimate side of worship.[3]

From the very beginning, Christian writers found in the word *devotio* an ideal expression of man's proper disposition toward God. Different Christian authors of the early church, remembering the primitive meaning of *devotio*, used the term to designate certain ritual acts prescribed in Scripture. Although the word *devotio* as found in the Vulgate usually designates an external practice or act, this external *devotio* includes an internal act. And while the internal dimension of this *devotio* was not specifically considered in the earliest Christian literature, yet the Vulgate clearly does contain that meaning which later Christian writers developed so explicitly. According to the Vulgate, external devotion can be the act by which one gives interiorly to God what he wills to offer in fact.[4]

*Devotio* in liturgical texts[5] was used to designate the cycle of feasts, and, more particularly, the paschal cycle.[6] But *devotio* was not limited to an external meaning; it could also signify an internal disposition of faith, or the fervor that one must have during cultic acts.[7]

Among the early Christian writers, *devotio* retained the basic meaning of consecration and service which had characterized it in its classical usage. But for the Christian writer it became consecration to the service of God. Understood as service of God, *devotio* became a highly complex reality. We see, for example, that for Ambrose *devotio* as the service of God was the very first of all the virtues and the foundation of all the others.[8] Although St. Augustine rarely used the term (he preferred *pietas* and contributed largely to the development of the word in Christian Latin), when he employed it, he gave it the same meaning of "service of God."[9] As service of God, *devotio* was a fundamental attitude of the creature before his Creator.

As we move from the age of the Fathers to the medieval period, we find in the writings of St. Bernard the greatest single influence on the development of the word *devotio*, and of spirituality itself. It was through St. Bernard that the rising stream of Christocentric devotion issuing from a predominantly Benedictine (and therefore practical, biblical and liturgical) spirituality was channeled. In this task St. Bernard was not alone; his way was prepared by the work of his predecessor, St. Anselm.

Anselm, like Bernard, was a Benedictine and an initiator: he is usually described as being at once speculative and affective. One may read

many pages of his work without finding the colorful and moving language
of St. Bernard, but at those times when Anselm did consider the humanity
of Christ, the scenes of the Gospel and the glories of Mary, or when he
composed his prayers, he frequently surpassed Bernard in the use of
affective language.[10]   Certain passages of Anselm's *Meditations on the
Christ Theme* are strikingly similar to St. Bernard's even in vocabulary.
For both, Christ is regarded as the source of our devotion and our spiritual consolation.   Their new use of *devotio* accounts for the apparently
sudden efflorescence of the word in the twelfth century.   It still possessed its earliest Christian connotations:  devotedness towards a person, loyalty, the ardent desire to follow and imitate.   But in the writings of Anselm and Bernard, *devotio* came to be the consideration of God
in the person of Christ, a consideration accomplished in sentiments of
love and gratitude.   Such an approach to Christ had not been emphasized
in earlier times, but under the influence of St. Bernard, it became
overwhelmingly dominant in the Middle Ages.[11]

Thus the humanity of Christ emerged as the central object of devotion.
St. Bernard confessed, although with regret, that he found the humanity
of Christ more attractive than his divinity.[12]   St. Thomas agreed with
this view.[13]   During the Middle Ages, the term *devotio* reached its
height of semantic development as importance was increasingly attached
to the concept of devotedness to the human person of Christ.   St. Bernard wrote:  "The human heart through bodily love is touched by the consideration of Christ as man."[14]

Meditating on the humanity of Christ moved many to devotion.   Such
meditation constituted the main element of "affective spirituality."
Words such as *afficio, affectus,*[15] occurred frequently in conjunction
with *devotio* and sometimes replaced it.[16]   In many texts *devotio* is sur-
rounded by notions of humility, compunction, and reliance upon grace
followed by joy and consolation.[17]   *Devotio* became the spiritual joy
attendant upon purification, confession of sins and conversion.   This
conjunction of devotion and compunction was pointed out by Hugh of St.
Victor:  "Man experiences compunction when his heart is touched by the
inner pain which the memory of his past sins causes.   *Devotio* is the
pious and humble affection for God which originates from compunction."[18]
*Devotio* was even at times employed as a synonym for compunction.

The question of "sensible devotion" enters here.   In the spirituality of many Christians devotion was limited to the level of the senses. For the mystic and the mystical theologian this "sensible devotion" occupied a contingent and non-essential place, occurring only when events in the superior part of the soul broke into the inferior part and then into the senses. Others preferred the *affectus devotionis* to *cogitatio* as the means of contemplation. Here humble devotion and illuminated love can comprehend God where language and reason fail. Faith supersedes reason, but faith nourishes love and adapts it to this vision; while devotion leads to pure faith.

The adjectives "fervent" and "ardent" were often applied to *devotio* to emphasize its meaning; "fervor" and "ardor" sometimes served as synonyms for *devotio*.[19] The intimate relation between *devotio* and *contemplatio* led to a particular type of theology: the monastic theology. Thus *devotio* became an intimate part of *theologia*. In the monastic theology immediately preceding scholasticism and existing concurrently with early scholastic thinking, we find a unity of spirituality and theology; at the same time there is a certain distrust of the intrustion of reason in the theological process.[20] The purpose of monastic theology was not speculative knowledge but a certain love of truth and of God. This theology demanded a certain gift from God to teacher and student. God is truly the teacher. In this perspective there was no theology without prayer, without a real spiritual life. What counted here was not the *quaestio* but the *desiderium*, not *quaeritur* but *desideratur*, not *sciendum* but *experiendum*.

St. Bernard affirmed, "One seeks in a more dignified way and finds in an easier fashion, praying than disputing *(orando quam disputando)*."[21] Reverence for God's mystery which characterized the monk's theology came from what St. Bernard called the reverence of prayer. If you are a theologian you will pray in truth and if you pray in truth you are a theologian. Experience of the realities of faith was at one time the condition for and the result of monastic theology. Monastic theology was the outgrowth of the practice of monastic life. "On the whole," writes Dom Jean Leclercq, "the monastic approach to theology, the kind of religious understanding the monks are trying to attain, might be better described by reviving the word *gnosis*, on condition naturally that no paradox, nuance, be given it. The Christian *gnosis*, the true *gnosis*, in its original, fundamental, orthodox meaning, is that kind of higher knowledge

which is the consummation, the fruition of faith, and which reaches com-
pletion in prayer and contemplation."[22]  Here learning and spiritual
life are intimately combined.

The Christian authors from the very beginning found in the word *devotio* an ideal expression for the singular relation existing between man
and God.  *Devotio* was understood as a total subjection of man to God.
St. Thomas Aquinas understood *devotio* as an act of the virtue of religion, a virtue which subordinates man to God and at the same time urges
him to serve God as he should be served.  Man serves God through his
intellect, his will and all of his body, and to these three faculties
correspond three acts:  prayer, devotion and adoration.  St. Thomas then
defines *devotio* as the promptitude and readiness of the will to serve
God:  *devotio* becomes a function of the will.[23]  *Devotio* was considered
the most important act of the virtue of religion, because it is through
the will that man can truly be united to God as a person.  Union through
the intellect is only intentional in nature.  This is why *devotio* played
a role in every other act of religion:  prayer, adoration, sacrifice,
religious vows.  By definition, then, every act of religion must flow
from devotion.  In this sense, prayer, sacrifice, adoration and all the
rest must be devout to be truly acts of religion.

According to Thomas, feeling and emotion were not to be mistaken for
devotion since devotion is an act of the will, while feelings and emotions are activities of the senses.  Because man is substantially one,
however, when the act of devotion is intense, feelings of love, desire,
and pleasure may accompany *devotio*, but the reality and truth of *devotio*
cannot be measured by these feelings.

With Saint Thomas, the concept of *devotio* gained a greater specific-
ity.  But this concept did not assume for him an important role in the
*theological* process.  *Devotio* had an integral place in monastic theology,
but the *fides quaerens intellectum* was not immediately recast in intellectual terms.  Any ascent to God had to be made in terms of love.  The
words of Saint John cannot be forgotten:  "He who does not love does not
know God, for God is love."  The *fides quaerens intellectum* interpreted
by some of the scholastics in very intellectual terms was expressed by
St. Bernard as the *anima quaerens Verbum*.[24]  This is a variation of the
*fides quaerens intellectum*, but it is very indicative of the nature of
monastic theology.  For the more abstract terms, faith and understanding,

Bernard substituted the more concrete terms of "soul" and "word," the soul in search of the word.

The *fides quaerens intellectum* as understood by scholasticism was strongly optimistic of rational knowledge. Faith and evidence seemed to coincide and to be proportionate to one another. The scholastic method of the Middle Ages was an intellectual attempt to discover and articulate the whole range of truth from reason and revelation. In the process of setting up this all-embracing system, the intellect became the predominant faculty. One word which came to be used with increasing frequency from the early twelfth century on to express this ideal ordering of knowledge was the word *summa*.[25]

Scholasticism launched a theology of its own, preoccupied with scientific techniques. And beginning with St. Thomas Aquinas a clear distinction was made between theology and philosophy, both becoming autonomous to some extent. But, for Thomas Aquinas,[26] theology had to integrate the valid conclusions of philosophy. He considered theology a construct of reason founded on faith, and yet, notwithstanding this intimate link with faith, for him theology remained an activity of reason. He considered theology an intellectual wisdom acquired through intelligent effort. Its primary concerns were with knowledge and understanding, both as the tools of theology and as its goal. St. Thomas' appreciation of reason and his integration of reason and faith had the inherent danger of leading to rationalism. Through his methodology, he risked the possibility of losing his sense of the unity and the uniqueness of the Christian realities.

Although primarily speculative in nature[27] and therefore in some opposition to the monastic concept of theology, Thomas Aquinas' understanding of theology also had an important practical dimension. Indeed, the very goal of theology required that it be a living dialogue between the theologian and God and not merely an abstract discipline. Practical and speculative theology alike demanded that the theologian's work be wedded to his spiritual life. The grace of God, piety and personal holiness were required to deepen his understanding of his beliefs.[28] An exercise of *fides quaerens intellectum* had to contribute both to the theologian's external effectiveness and to his own contemplation, for man's cognitive powers are affected by his moral status.[29] But unlike the monastic discipline, love and *devotio* were not integral to Aquinas' theology.

The medieval period may be regarded as a period dominated by two opposing tendencies manifested in the schools of St. Bernard and of Thomas Aquinas. Their opposition lay in the dominantly affective character and spiritual teachings of the one versus the dominantly speculative character and dogmatic teaching of the other. Thomas spoke of *devotio* as an act of the virtue of religion. Bernard and his followers spoke of *devotio* as an affective state.

The later medieval period as a field of linguistic study in the area of *devotio* is far from sterile. Language kept pace semantically with the conflicting and rapidly moving trends of this time. Some of the new modes of expression were rich in import for later developments. For example, in the writings of Jean Gerson, *devotio* was considered in the context of affective spirituality, linked on the one hand to *compunctio* and on the other hand to *oratio*.[30] He thought *devotio*, being midway between the carnal and the spiritual, and associated with reason, meditation and will, prepared the soul for *contemplatio*. Although Gerson used the word *devotio*, his spirituality expressed itself basically through the notion of *pietas*.

The *Devotio Moderna* which also emerged in this period was a spirituality which did express itself in terms of *devotio*. What is important here in our own study is to understand how this current of thought related to other currents. The word *moderna* is variously explained. According to A. M. Lücker, *moderna* comes from the same source as *via moderna*, which according to the author means the turning to experience.[31] According to Hashagen, the adjective *moderna* expressed consciousness of a greater simplification and interiorization in the spirituality itself.[32] Thomas à Kempis in his *Dialogus Novitiorum* used the word *moderna* somewhat in the sense of "contemporary," "today's devotion." Speaking to novices, he wanted to show them "who were those primitive fathers through whose influence the modern devotion bloomed again."[33] In fact the novices themselves asked to be told about the contemporary saints. The use of the word *devotio* with the designation *moderna* implied a sense of continuity as well as a thrust in a new direction.

Among the adherents of the *Devotio Moderna* the word *devotio* seemed to have kept its generic meaning of service to God. But this service was understood in a very special way as conformity of one's will to that of God, and this in the imitation of Christ. As service, affection and

charity, it also implied the ancient meaning of consecration or spiritual unction. Zerbolt of Zutphen (1367-1398) stressed the affective
aspect of *devotio*. But he also warned his readers not to overemphasize
this characteristic since he saw a danger of giving too much importance
to the experiential dimension of the spiritual life. *Devotio* was spoken
of in the context of interiority. Zerbolt wrote of Mary and Martha that
they were "being occupied only with that inward devotion from which
Martha was unwillingly thrown away."[34] *Devotio* was understood also as a
quality of meditation. "And this you do when you meditate upon the passion with circumspection, with gravity and with devotion."[35] "For by
this means you do look upon Christ with more devotion and with greater
reverence."[36]

Devotion was something that could be increased through reading. "But
do choose a book which as a whole may suit your purpose, inform your
manner and increase your devotion."[37] "If at times you do read holy
scriptures, let the passages be chiefly such as deal with some matter of
devotion."[38] The way of devotion lay in religious exercises.

> In the third place, you ought to exercise yourself so as to attain
> effectual devotion, which seems to consist in two things, namely,
> that you should have fear and reverence for the reception of this
> sacrament, and, further, that you may be moved by effectual love
> and longing for union with Christ.[39]

According to Thomas à Kempis, *devotio*[40] was essentially an affection
which was to be transferred into *exultatio* and *jubilatio*. He considered
devotion an interior disposition of the spiritual man. "Cum his obser-
vationibus fit homo compunctus, internus, devotus." *Devotio* was a grace
of fervor and consolation to be asked for in all humility and which
might or might not be given.[41] Devotion was expressed as affection,
fervor and desire for God.[42] Interiority, inwardness, consecration and
dedication to the service and glory of God became characteristic of the
*Devotio Moderna*'s spirituality. The adjective *moderna* was attached to
the word in order to distinguish it from an unacceptable meaning of *devotio*. For there was a pronounced increase in the late medieval period
of a tendency to concretize both religion and devotion. This tendency
was expressed in the usage of the word *devotio* in its plural form. In
this form it designated all of one's prayers and acts of religion, often
with special reference to the mass and communion. Places of pilgrimage
were described as devout. Even the images of saints came to be called

devotions. *Devotio* shifted from subject to object, from active to passive. The transition from *devotio* in the singular, with its dimensions
of interiority and its demand for a total involvement of the whole person, to *devotio* in the plural, with its stress on the external, objective and bodily dimension, involved a risk: the weakening and degrada-
tion of the spiritual life. While devotions were, when rightly employed,
helpful instruments and tools, they could easily tend to become ends in
themselves. As external manifestations and expressions they have meaning and value only as long as they are joined to the interior dimension.
This link is tenuous and can be easily broken. Whenever this happened,
the word *devotio* took a pejorative sense and was gradually replaced by
the Renaissance authors with the word *pietas*.

This breakdown in the usage of the word *devotio* was accompanied by a
disintegration of the unity of theology and spirituality.[43] The *Devotio
Moderna* was not only a reaction against the externalization of *devotio*
but also against the arid intellectualism of contemporary theology. A
great deal of the theology of the time proliferated in pure problems of
logic. The only reaction against this divisive tendency came from Jean
Gerson, whose new approach had a great deal in common with monastic theology.[44] His *Theologia Mystica Speculativa* was written as an attempt to
reform an overly intellectual theology.[45] Gerson saw himself as a theologian obliged to deal with things which edify. The unity of theology
and the spiritual life, of reason and faith, was expressed in Gerson's
concept of *theologia mystica*. For Gerson this type of theology resulted
in what he called a *cognitio Dei experimentalis* in which both the intellectual and affective powers operated.

## B. Pietas

In its classical meaning, piety implies habitual reverence and obedience to the gods; it signifies godliness, devoutness, religiousness. It
also means faithfulness to the duties naturally owed to parents and
superiors. The broad range of its connotations - compassion on the part
of God, charity toward the neighbor, piety towards God - was represented
from the beginning of Christianity, as these examples demonstrate. Fraternal charity: "Pietate autem amorem fraternitatis, in amore autem
fraternitatis charitatem." (2 Pet. 1:7) Piety towards God: "Si quis
aliter docet et non acquiescit sanis sermonibus Domini nostri Jesu

Christi, et ei, quae secundum pietatem est, doctrinae." (1 Tim. 6:3).
The second passage is of utmost importance as it so explicitly identi-
fies *pietas, amor* and *charitas*, at least in the sense implied. Another
point of contact in these three words is that each may be understood as
directed from God to man, from man to God, or from man to his fellows.
But the use of *pietas* in the sense of piety (man towards God) declined
after the first centuries of the Church, although it did not entirely
disappear. One of the principal reasons for this was the semantic
growth of *devotio*.

The word *pietas* did not experience the same evolution and use as the
word *devotio*. In the Middle Ages *pius* and *pietas* were far more prevalent than in earlier usage, but almost entirely as applied to God and to
the Blessed Virgin in considerations of their mercy: "piisime spiritus,"
"pie Jesu," "materne pietas." *Pietas* was also associated with sentiments of tenderness and gratitude which in succeeding generations, from
St. Bernard to Gerson, would be resolved into "pity" and then "piety."
This was stimulated by considerations of the humanity of Christ, especially in his infancy and Passion.

In his article *De Pietate*,[46] Thomas Aquinas presented a lucid survey
of the reciprocal relationships to be found from antiquity in the area
of *pietas*. Thomas began by citing St. Augustine, who strongly influenced the semantic course of *pietas* in Christianity: "*Pietas* denotes,
properly speaking, the worship of God which the Greek designate by the
word Eusebia."[47] According to St. Thomas, God is considered primarily
as father and is, therefore, both pious and deserving of filial piety on
the part of men. St. Thomas continued in the body of the article,

> The cultus due to our parents includes the cultus given to all our
> kindred, since our kinfolk are those who descend from the same
> parents. The *cultus* given to our country includes homage to our
> fellow citizens and to all friends of our country. The greater in-
> cludes the lesser: wherefore the worship *(cultus)* due to God in-
> cludes the *cultus* due to our parents in particular. Hence it is
> written (Malachi 1:6) if I be a father where is my honor? Conse-
> quently, the term *pietas* extends also to the divine worship.[48]

*(Nomen pietatis ad divinum cultum refertur.)* Clearly the point of
reference for all this reasoning was the relationship to a father. St.
Thomas completed the circle with a final quotation from St. Augustine
which directly illustrates fourth century usage.

> As Augustine says (*De Civitate Dei*, Bk. 10, c.1), the term *pietas*
> is often used in connection with works of mercy, in the language of
> the common people; the reason for which I consider to be the fact
> that these works are more pleasing to him than sacrifices. This
> custom has led to the application of the word pious to God him-
> self.[49]

At this period of its semantic evolution, one of the differences between *pietas* and *devotio* was that *pietas* remained a background word.
It was understood as a basic affection, apt to be more essentially
stable than *devotio*. Those transient states of the sense and the will
leading to external expression were usually signified by *devotio*.

In the same way that the idea of compunction frequently accompanied
*devotio*, the notion of humility was often coupled with *pietas*. Humility
was the foundation of true *pietas*. As we approach the latter part of
the Middle Ages, we see two different tendencies. In Petrarch the word
*devotio* is rarely employed; he expressed himself in terms of *pietas*.
Like Augustine, Petrarch equated *pietas* with *sapientia*. St. Augustine
had written *sapientia est pietas*. "Man's wisdom is piety."[50] And further, "God is the highest possible wisdom and the worship of God is
man's wisdom."[51] For Petrarch this *pietas/sapientia* was acquired in
humility. *(Nihil altius ascendat quam humilitas operosa.)* Through an
identification of *sapientia* and *pietas* he saw the fear of God as the
beginning of wisdom, and defined piety as the knowledge and worship of
God. This knowledge-wisdom was transformed from an intellectual to a
moral virtue.

In Gerson we have a man who sought one word to carry the burden of
his constant occupation with an interior spiritual life. He looked for
a concept which could be opposed to the vain and excessive speculation
of the scholars of his day. He found his word and concept in *pietas*,
which he seems to acknowledge explicitly as deriving from Augustine and
Bonaventure, and in some opposition to Thomas.[52] Gerson spoke of *doctrina et vita pietatis*. It was, in fact, the *doctrina secundum pietatem*
which caught the interest of Gerson's age. Against a welter of vain doctrines, he proposed a doctrine of piety, affective, interiorizing and
spiritual. This *doctrina secundum pietatem* was an echo of Augustine and
of Petrarch's *pietas est sapientia*.

But Gerson's effort to restore *devotio* to *pietas* seems to have been
practically isolated. The *De Imitatione Christi* contained no mention of

*pietas*. In explanation it must be said that Gerson was an intellectual, while the Brothers of the Common Life, and especially the author of *De Imitatione Christi*, rejected any intellectual approach to spirituality. Gerson contested only the abuses of scholasticism. He made a conscious attempt to introduce the concept of *pietas* because of a deterioration in the use of the word *devotio*. He hoped that *pietas* would bolster an interior and affective spirituality in contrast to the sterile discourses of a decadent scholasticism.

The history of the words *devotio* and *pietas* up to this point indicates that the problem of semantic change is largely one of ascent and decline in a scale of spiritual values. With the coming of the Renaissance and the Reformation we reach another phase in the development of these words. To some extent it parallels the development which we noted in Petrarch and Gerson. In various authors *devotio* was replaced by *pietas*. *Devotio* acquired a clear pejorative sense; it became identified with a spiritual life based on external practices, in antithesis to interior life.

In the *Enchiridion Militis Christiani* of Erasmus *pietas* and its derivatives occur quite frequently. It is used in contrast to *devotio*, which is considered pejoratively as an external practice. *Pietas* finds its perfection in interiority, in the invisible. "You may evaluate perfect piety by this one principle: you should always try to advance from things visible to things invisible."[53]

For Erasmus piety meant reverence, devotion, commitment; it enriched the concept of humanity by the addition of gentler Christian qualities such as compassion, patience, longsuffering, forgiveness, humility, and self-effacement. *Pietas* for Erasmus was a cordial and affective knowledge of God. Like Augustine's *pietas est sapientia*, Petrarch's *docta pietas* and Gerson's *doctrina secundum pietatem*, Erasmus' understanding of *pietas* was directly related to knowledge and was well expressed in his *Philosophia Christi*. *Pietas* was wisdom defined in the *Enchiridion* as *precatio et scientia*, knowledge of God activated by prayer. This *sapientia-pietas* was a knowledge of *salutares opiniones*, of things which would assure man of salvation. As the preface to the fifteenth and eighteenth editions of the *Enchiridion* states, the *salutares opiniones* are nothing but the words and deeds of a good, pure and simple life. Christ Erasmus depicts as *sapientiae auctor*, or, better still, wisdom

itself.  What one must know of him is his law which supplements the
Mosaic law.  This law is crystallized in the action of the human Christ.
Beginning as a knowledge of Christ, wisdom becomes an active imitation
of Christ, whose life on earth was that of a conscious exemplar and
moral pattern.[54]   *Pietas* is truly a *sancta eruditio*.

Erasmus continually stressed that his Christian view of life was more
a concern of the heart than of understanding, more life itself than
learning.  In the same spirit, he placed his theology in the framework
of religious behavior.  For him the only effective theology was accompanied by piety, since theology and piety are intrinsically bound up
with one another.  His preference for the theological writers of antiquity was based to a certain extent upon the fact that he considered them
pious men; they reflected *pia doctrina* and *docta pietas*.  According to
Erasmus a true theologian lives the things he reads and preaches.  It is
not enough to comprehend the scriptures with the understanding; he must
penetrate his own heart as well, for a theologian who does not understand himself cannot understand truth outside himself.  To discover a
simpler and more pious theology the Christian (theologian) had to return
to the sources:  the scriptures and the writings of the Fathers.

The substitution of the word *pietas* for *devotio* in the early part of
the Renaissance was not limited to northern Europe.  It was already a
fact for some of the Italian humanists.  We find it also in Spain, especially in the writings of Juan de Valdes.[55]   In his *Dialogo de Doctrina
Christiana*, de Valdes, speaking through the person of the Archbishop
Pedro de Alba, deplored contradictions between vain devotions and true
Christianity and lamented the false pharisaism of the time which prided
itself on external works while diminishing the interior disposition.[56]
In Juan's *Commentaries* the words *pio, impio, piedad* and *impiedad* were
frequently employed.[57]  Piety could be used as a synonym for justification.  Piety, justice and faith were inseparable.[58]   In his ninth Consideration Juan outlined in detail his understanding of piety and some
of its implications:

> All the good works to which we are excited in this life can be
> attributed either to our human nature or to our piety.  The fact
> that we are men leads us to sympathize with and help each other;
> that is to say, in all things that belong to the comfort of life.
> Piety leads us to confide in God, to love him, to depend upon him:
> leads us to confide in Christ, to love him and to preach him:
> leads us to modify our fleshly affections and lusts:  and leads us

to condemn all that the world prizes such as honor, status and
wealth.  On the other hand the person who is decidedly pious, exer-
cising himself in the practice of duty and incidentally to humanity, practices himself in piety, because his principal design is
the glory of God which is the characteristic of piety.[59]

Piety was in the very first place the knowledge of God.  "Pious is
the man who knows God."  This knowledge could not be attained by reasoning or science but "by experience and revelation."  Valdes made numerous
connections between piety and religious knowledge, between piety and
sound and true doctrine.  (1 Tim 6:3; Tit 1:1)  Piety identified itself
with religion.  It manifested itself principally in the realm of conduct, foreign to all types of vain speculation.  For de Valdes the mystery of piety is Christ himself.  (1 Tim 3:6)

## C.  *Wisdom and Piety*

A careful study of the texts, in particular of the writings of Erasmus, reveals that during the Renaissance most writers concurrently held
two fundamentally different ideas of wisdom:  one, an infused grace of
God; the other, an acquired virtue.  The writers of the Renaissance,
Erasmus included, accepted the idea of a divine wisdom whose modes and
objects of knowledge differed from those of acquired and natural wisdom.

*Sapientia* remained for many Renaissance writers a revealed knowledge
of divine things, understood in an explicitly Christian sense.  Wisdom
came from God.  According to Erasmus, *sapientia* is a knowledge of God
whose very nature is virtue and who is the source of all virtues.

> Wisdom thus flows from God whose central attribute is virtue, from
> a scriptural revelation described as a code of conduct, and from a
> Christ whose function was to illustrate that code by his life.[60]

For John Colet, Erasmus' friend, Christ is the wisdom of God:  "Sapientia tandem quasi humanata in persona humana."[61]  According to Colet wisdom comes from God alone.  It is caused by divine illumination and can
only be grasped by divine illumination.

> This faith is a kind of light infused into the soul of man from the
> divine sun, by which the heavenly virtues are known to be revealed
> without uncertainty or doubt; and it far excels the light of reason
> as certainty does uncertainty.  The wisdom of the intellect is
> faith...the illumination and infused light, by which the soul may
> see perfect truths, is faith.[62]

The tentative secularism of some of the humanists concerning the

source and origin of wisdom was paralleled by the profoundly religious
attitude towards wisdom which emerged in this period. Wisdom itself,
both on the infused and natural levels, was transformed; what was formerly considered an intellectual virtue became an ethical reality. Indeed, *sapientia*, both infused and natural, became identified with
ethics; the pursuit of the truth was the pursuit of the "good." This
pursuit of the good demanded obedience to the fundamental command of
self-knowledge. Colucio Salutati († 1404) defined wisdom as the *eruditio
moralis*. Beginning as an intellectual *eruditio*, the concept of *sapientia* developed into a moral virtue; once regarded as theoretical knowledge, now it was understood as probity in action.

The Petrarchan concept of *sapientia* contained an incipient moralism
which became increasingly important in the sixteenth century. Wisdom,
deserving of its name, could not be separated from virtue. For Erasmus,
wisdom united the ethical insights of learning with the practice of virtue. In his *Commentary on Corinthians*, Colet underlined the fact that
*sapientia* was achieved not by an intellectual analysis of ideas, but by
the passive reception of understanding given by God to those who are
morally good. Let man seek moral virtue and God would give him truth.[63]

The ethical dimension of *sapientia*, with its affirmation of the primacy of the will and love, led to a greater emphasis on the experiential
dimensions of the knowledge of God and also to the development of rhetoric. Wisdom had the responsibility, not merely of demonstrating the
truth of given realities, but of directing people to a better life.
Hence a rhetorical dimension was added to wisdom. A persuasive wisdom
was required, one which would bring men to guide their lives according to
its teachings.

This short history of two important words in the vocabulary of Christian spirituality has clarified both the continuity and discontinuity
between the *Devotio Moderna* and the spiritualities of the early Renaissance. This discontinuity is exemplified by the substitution of the
word *pietas* for *devotio*. What is really indicative of the originality
of the Renaissance spirituality beyond that of the *Devotio Moderna* is
its identification of *pietas* with wisdom, that is, the knowledge of God.
Although the Renaissance authors shared the objections of the *Devotio
Moderna* against the *eruditio* of the scholastics, they in no way opposed
learning. True piety was a *sancta eruditio*. For them a false knowledge

of God was the greatest danger to a spiritual life since it made man's obligation of worship impossible to fulfill. Petrarch's concept of *docta pietas* and Gerson's *doctrina secundum pietatem*, Lefèvre's *theologia vivificans* and Erasmus' *philosophia Christi* all were expressions of the same concern. They attempted a synthesis of piety with true knowledge of God, a knowledge which in no way left aside acquired knowledge. Without knowledge, both acquired and received, the true worship of God and the spiritual life could not be attained. Calvin would use *pietas* as the word to express his own spirituality. In so doing, he placed himself to some extent in the tradition of the Renaissance.

The integral relation existing between *pietas* and the knowledge of God posed more sharply the question of the epistemological structure of spirituality. It is here that Calvin offered some valuable solutions.

*Notes*

1. H. Delehaye, *Sanctus, Essai sur le culte des saints* (Brussels, 1927),58.
2. J. Chatillon, "Devotion," *Dict. Spir.* 3 (Paris, 1957) 702-716.
3. Cf. *Thesaurus linguae latinae*, t.5 (1910) devotio, devotus and devovere. Devotatio, imprecatio. Devotio, 1) execratio, dedicatio, deditio, incantatio; 2) obedientia, fides, pietas (erga homines, deum, leges); 3) tributum; 4) votum. Devotare, 1) maledicere; 2) vovere. Devovere, 1) consecrare (dei, personae); 2) (latiore sensu) offerre, proicere, destinare. Devotus, 1) execrabilis; 2) deditus (homini, deo, rei). Devote, fideliter, submisse, pie.
4. Cf. Numbers 6,21: "Juxta quod mente devoverat, ita faciet ad perfectionem sanctificationis suae."
5. A. Daniels, "Devotio" in *Jahrbuch für Liturgiewissenschaft* 1 (1961) 40-60.
6. Tertullian used the word *devotio* to designate the cycle of liturgical feasts. Cf. De jejuniis 14; PL 2, 973.
7. This is the meaning that *devotio* has each time it is used in such expressions as *solida devotio; devotio quieta; pia devotio; gratia devotionis; affectus devotionis*. Cf. Daniels, *Jahrbuch* 57-60.
8. *In Ps.* 118, v. 25; PL. 15, 1259d.
9. *Contra Donatistos* II, 8, 17; PL. 43, 61.
10. "Martha ministered, Lazarus sat and Mary anointed. Mary's gesture should be hours: break the alabaster of your heart, and whatever you have of devotion, of love, of desire, of affection, pour all on the head of your spouse...." *Meditatio* XV; PL. 158, 788.
11. J. Vernet, *La spiritualité médiévale* (Paris, 1928) 73.
12. *Ibid.*, 118-120.
13. *Ibid.*, 119. "St. Thomas dit que la divinité en droit, est ce qui excite le plus à l'amour et, par conséquent, à la dévotion, mais que, en fait, l'humanité du Christ touche d'avantage notre nature sensible, que l'humanité est la voie qui mène à la divinité. D'où la troisième partie de la Somme théologique: 'Du Christ qui, en tant qu'homme, est la voie vers Dieu.'"
14. *In Cant.* XX, 6; PL. 184, 105.
15. Cf. H. Flasche, "Pascal y Bernardo de Clairvaux," *Phil.* VIII (Num. 14, 1951) 31-50.
16. Cf. *Dom. inf. oct. Assumpt.*, 1-2.
17. This is true of St. Bernard and his disciples.
18. S. V. Hugh, *De modo orandi*; Wilm., p. 182
19. St. Bern., *Serm.* 250-251.
20. J. Leclercq, *L'amour des lettres et le désir de Dieu* (Paris, 1957) 179-251.
21. *De consid.* V, 32; PL. 182, 808.
22. J. Leclercq, *L'Amour des lettres*, 215.
23. "Devotion is a special act of the will...and therefore since devotion is a special act of the will, the act of a man offering himself to God in order to serve Him..." *S.T.* IIa IIae, qu. 81, a.1, ad 1um.
   Cf. also W. Curran, "Thomistic Concept of Devotion," *Thomist* 2 (1940) 410-443, 546-580.
24. *Serm. In Cant.* 85-86; PL. 183, 187.
25. M. D. Chenu, *Introduction à l'étude de Saint Thomas d'Aquin* (Paris, 1954) 256-258.
26. *S.T.* Ia, q. 1.

27. In *Boeth. de trin.*, q. 2, a.1; in I Sent., *prologus*, q 1a.3, col. 1.

28. *S.T.* IIa, IIae, q. 2, a.10.

29. *S.T.* IIa, IIae, q. 15, a.3.

30. *De Mystica theologia speculativa*, cons. 21; *Op. Omnia* 3, col. 378.

31. A. M. Lücker, *Meister Eckhart und die Devotio moderna* (Leiden, 1950).

32. J. Hashagen, "Die Devotio Moderna in ihre Einwirkung auf Humanismus, Reformation, Gegenreformation und spätere Richtungen," *Z. f. Kirkeng* 55 (1936) 523-531.

33. Ed. J. Pohl, VII, 30.

34. *De spiritualibus ascensionibus*, c. 68, trans. A. Landau (London, 1907) 153.

35. *Ibid.*, c. 32, 73.

36. *Ibid.*, c. 32, 73.

37. *Ibid.*, c. 44, 97.

38. *Ibid.*, c. 45, 101.

39. *Ibid.*, c. 31, 68.

40. In the *De Imitatione Christi* the words *devotio* and *devotus* are used 88 times.

41. You must seek the grace of devotion with earnestness, ask for it with real desire, wait for it with patience and trust, receive it with thankfulness, keep it with humility, use it with diligence, and commit to God the time and manner of His heavenly gift. Above all, humble yourself when you feel little or no inner devotion, and do not be too depressed or discouraged, for God often grants in one short moment what He has withheld for a long while. And sometimes He grants in due time what He delayed to grant at your first request. *De Imitatione Christi*, Bk. 4, c. 15, trans. Leo Sherley-Price (Baltimore: Penguin Classics, 1968) 211-212.

42. "Devotion is nothing other but the soul's desire for God." (T. de Kempis, *Opera*, VII, 209) "Devotion is the pious and humble affection for God." (Mombaer, *Rosetum* tit.V, alph.16, par.4)

43. This tendency is quite clearly indicated by the fact that beginning with the 15th century in the *Tabulae Fontium Traditionis christianae* (J. Creusen and E. Van Eyen) a separate section for works in mystical theology is inserted: *Theologia ascetica et mystica*.

44. H. de Lubac, *Exégèse médiévale* I (Paris, 1959) 94-110.

45. Cf. Gerson, *Contra vanam curiositatem in negotio fidei*, *Opera*, ed. Dupin, t. L, col. 86-106; *De reformatione theologiae*, col. 120-124; P. Glorieux, "Le chancelier Gerson et la réforme de l'enseignement," *Mélanges Etienne Gilson* (Paris, 1959) 285-298.

46. *S.T.*, IIa IIae, q. 101.

47. *Ibid.*, ad 1.

48. *Ibid.*

49. *Ibid.*, ad 2.

50. "Hominis autem sapientia pietas est. Habes hoc in libro sancti Job: nam ibi legitur quod ipsa Sapientia dixerit eo loco pietatem, distinctius in graeco reperies theoseibeian qui est Dei cultur." *Enchiridion* II; PL. 40, 231.

51. *De Trinitate*, XIV, 1; PL. 42, 1037.

52. *Tractatus in Cantico.*, ed. Du Pin, IV, col. 53.

53. *Enchiridion militis*, *Opera Omnia* V (Louvain, 1704), trans. R. Himmelick (Bloomington, Ind., 1963) 101.

54. "The exemplar of all piety is sought most fittingly in Christ Himself." *Enchiridion*, 111.

55. The importance of John de Valdes for the history of spirituality has been conclusively shown by J. Nieto, *Juan de Valdes and the Origins of the Spanish and Italian Reformation* (Geneva, 1970).

56. "Verdaderamente no se como no tienen empacho unos hombres, que sin mostrar en toda su vida señal deste amor, por no sé qué ceremonias y *devociones* que ellos se inventan, se tienen por más que christianos; y lo que más es de notar, y aun de llorar, en los tales, es que al que veen que no toma y adora sus frias y vanas *devociones*, aunque este tal claramente biva coniorme a la le de dios, no le tienen por christiano. Esta es sin dubda ninguna la justicia pharisaica, que ensalca sus obras exteriores y disminuye y tiene en poco las interiores de los otros." *Dialogo de Doctrina Christiana*, ed. M. Bataillon (Coimbra, 1925) fol. 8v.

57. M. Morreale, "Devocion o piedad. Apunctiones sobre el lexico de Alfonso y Juan Valdes," *Revista Portuguese de Filogia* 7 (Coimbra, 1956) 379.

58. *Ibid.*

59. *Spiritual and Anabaptist Writers, Evangelical Catholicism as Represented by Juan de Valdes*, ed. A. Megal (Philadelphia, 1957) 347-349.

60. Quoted by E. Rice, *The Renaissance Idea of Wisdom* (Cambridge, 1958) 161.

61. John Colet, *An Exposition of St. Paul's Epistle to the Romans. Delivered as Lectures in the University of Oxford, 1497*, trans. J. Lupton (London, 1873) 44.

62. John Colet, *An Exposition of St. Paul's Epistle to the Corinthians*, trans. J. Lupton (London, 1874) 12.

63. For any one to see the truth "Then he must wholly strip and lay bare himself, laying aside all the thoughts of his mind...by which he deemed that he had learnt something." Just as primal matter, in order to be formed is naked, that there may be nothing in it to counteract the formation, so it is needful that a man should strip off his powers...if he would be enlightened by inspiration to understand things divine...For those things of the intelligible world, unalloyed reasons, divine and spiritual...none are qualified but those of the very highest power, those who are wholly concentrated on the One, and who despising the body and the world stand unshaken in the loftiest mental pinnacle: on the one indivisible center. Colet, *St. Paul's Epistle to the Romans*, 45.

CHAPTER IV

*THE SPIRITUALITY OF JOHN CALVIN: ITS GENESIS, DYNAMICS AND CONTENT*

A. *Spirituality in Calvin's Early Writings*

It is the purpose of this chapter to present Calvin's spirituality within the context of his cultural and historical background and to investigate the major influences on the formation of his religious thought. I will begin by outlining the main characteristics of Calvin's initial spirituality, expressed in his earliest writings: the *Institutes* of 1536, the *Institutes* of 1539, and the *Reply to Sadoleto* of 1539.[1] This will be followed by a systematic development of the major themes of John Calvin's spirituality, drawing on the principal sources, especially the *Commentaries*.

The fundamental aspects of John Calvin's spirituality are already present in the first edition of the *Institutes* (1536) which Calvin prefaced with a confessional address to King Francis I of France. The *Institutes* of 1536 was a small booklet, a *libellus*. The 1536 title page bore the inscription "Christianae Religionis Institutio." A remarkable continuation of the title, which admittedly could have been added by the publisher rather than by Calvin himself, is very indicative of the content:

> Containing almost the whole sum of piety and everything it is necessary to know in the doctrine of salvation, a work very well worth reading by all those who love piety and very recently published.[2]

The word "Institutio," which in its Latin sense signifies "instruction," can also be translated "manual" or, more exactly, "summary," according to the publisher's use: *totam fere pietatis Summam*. In other words, here was a book that professed to teach the elements of Christian religion. The important words in this introduction were *Summam pietatis*. They expressed the purpose of the *Institutes*, reaffirmed in the first words of Calvin's letter to King Francis I:

> My intention is only to offer some basic rudiments *(rudimenta)* through which those who feel some interest in religion *(studio religionis)* might be trained to true piety *(ad veram pietatem)*.[3]

The first words of an important document such as a letter to Francis I,

a letter which defined the purpose of the *Institutes*, were carefully
chosen and count as indicative of what was most important to John Calvin.
In his preface of the *Commentary on the Psalms*, moreover, Calvin, speaking about his conversion, again affirmed the source and purpose of this
theological writing:

> Having therefore received some taste and knowledge of true piety I
> was suddenly fired with such a great desire to advance that even
> though I did not forsake the other studies entirely I nonetheless
> worked at them more slackly.[4]

The spirituality of John Calvin from the very beginning was expressed in
terms of *pietas* and *eruditio*.

The *Institutes* of 1536 was made up of six chapters.  Of the six chapters, four were devoted respectively to the Law, the Creed, the Lord's
Prayer, and the Sacraments of Baptism and the Lord's Supper.  This conformed to the classical pattern of the then existing catechism.  The
last two chapters were polemical in nature and dealt respectively with
false sacraments and Christian liberty.

The first chapter of the 1536 *Institutes* opened with this sentence:

> One might say that the whole of sacred doctrine *(summa fere sacrae
> doctrinae)* consists of these two parts:  knowledge of God and of
> ourselves *(cognitione Dei ac nostri)*.[5]

We have knowledge of God when we recognize Him as the source of all wisdom, and believe that "all things in heaven and on earth have been made
for His glory."[6]  These two affirmations imply a response from us of
obedience and service.[7]

Knowledge of ourselves implies recognition of our humble state, of
our primitive state of righteousness, and of the result of the fall in
which "this image, this godlikeness was cancelled, effaced."[8]  The result of this cancellation is that there is nothing left of man save
"ignorance, iniquity, impotence, death and judgment, stripped and de-
prived (as he is) of all wisdom and righteousness."[9]  And yet even in
this sad state we have to honor God.

> Yet the very thing we cannot supply, we do not cease to owe.  As
> God's creatures, we should serve His honor and His glory, obey His
> commandments.[10]

The only way to fulfill our obligations in our present state is through
Christ.

> In Christ our Lord, God gives us all these benefits: free forgive-
> ness of sins, peace and reconciliation to God, gifts and graces of
> the Holy Spirit...Apart from him we are nothing...in him we become
> God's children.[11]

The result of true knowledge of God and of ourselves is humble dependence upon God, expressed in the form of true worship, which is the
authentic *pietas*. "From it we learn to humble ourselves, cast ourselves
before God, seek his mercy."[12]

The summary of the *Institutes* of 1536 reviews the major themes of
Calvin's spirituality. Knowledge of God and of man; the necessity of
honoring the glory of God, demanding, on the part of man, faith, service
and obedience; total dependence upon God's word incarnated in Christ,
and the practical attitude of man expressed in piety and worship.

The theme of the knowledge of God and self, while treated only briefly
in the two opening paragraphs of the edition of 1536, was basic in the
mind of John Calvin and assumed a central importance in later editions
of the *Institutes*. This knowledge is revelational in nature, the fruit
of the word of God incarnate, a word full of power. "God's word which
promises us these things is power and truth."[13] The word of God is the
foundation of the Christian life, sufficient in itself as the source of
all life. It is the word spoken by and in Christ, the *verbum Christi*.[14]
This word becomes the norm and criterion of all truth and justice.[15]
Nothing can be added or taken away from this word.[16] It is evident that
Calvin's first synthesis gives an important place to the person of
Christ. He is truly our wisdom, the source of our justice and the
ground of our hope.[17] At various times Calvin described Christ as the
wisdom of God and man. This seems to have been a recurrent theme.[18]
Real knowledge of God and therefore of ourselves is possible only in the
Son.[19] Christ is truly the *solus mediator*, the "only way which leads to
the Father."[20] This doctrine of *solus Christus*, Christ as sole mediator
and unique way, led Calvin to emphasize the need for an imitation of
Christ. But to imitate him was not simply to copy his actions; it was
to be inserted into the mysteries of Christ's life, death and resurrection.

> Another benefit of baptism is that it shows us our mortification in
> Christ and new life in him. 'Know you not,' says the apostle,
> 'that as many of us as were baptised into Jesus Christ, were bap-
> tised into his death? Therefore we are buried with him by baptism

into death,' that we 'should walk in newness of life' (Rom. vi.3,
4). By these words, he not only exhorts us to imitation of Christ,
as if he had said, that we are admonished by baptism, in like manner as Christ died, to die to our lusts, and as he rose, to rise to
righteousness; but he traces the matter much higher, that Christ by
baptism has made us partakers of his death, engrafting us into it.
And as the twig derives substance and nourishment from the root to
which it is attached, so those who receive baptism with true faith
truly feel the efficacy of Christ's death in the mortification of
their flesh, and the efficacy of his resurrection in the quickening
of the Spirit. On this he founds his exhortation, that if we are
Christians we should be dead unto sin, and alive unto righteousness.[21]

The importance given to the mediation of Christ underlines the primacy of the Father in Calvin's thought. He expressed this primacy in
terms of the glory of God and of our need to worship and obey the father.
In all of the *Institutes*, the concept of the glory of God is present.[22]
The first sentence directly affirms that God alone is God, that everything that is not God exists to serve the glory of God.[23] And His glory
should be constantly before our eyes.

It is appropriate that we should have before our eyes the sole
glory of God, and it must be the constant object of our prayers.[24]

The importance of the glory of God leads directly to the basic need for
man to worship God, a worship that expresses itself in service and
praise.[25]

When true worship is seen as man's most fundamental need, false worship, the transference of God's glory and praise to some other object,
becomes the worst possible sin. This transference is essentially superstition and idolatry. It is directly opposed to the service of the
glory of God.[26] For the glory of God cannot ever be transferred to the
sacraments or any visible reality; and any movement in this direction is
idolatry.[27] Evident here is Calvin's radical opposition to the Mass and
to the adoration of the blessed sacrament, practices which he considered
superstitious and idolatrous.[28]

Superstition and idolatry are obviated by a true concept of worship
and adoration which respects the glory of God. Such worship must be
spiritual, since God is spirit. "Adoremus Deum qui spiritus est, in
spiritu et veritate."[29] We adore God who is spirit, in spirit and in
truth.

*Pietas* is the comprehensive term which for Calvin designates the

right attitude of man towards God, an attitude which implies true knowledge and true worship.  This word, as mentioned above, Calvin used in
the very first lines of his letter to the king.[30]  It was also the very
last word of the *Institutes* of 1536.[31]  God the Father was the object of
this *pietas*,[32] and Christ was our unique model and exemplar in its practice.[33]

    *Pietas* is not given to man ready-made.  It is only acquired with
great effort on the part of man, and must be pursued with zeal (the *pietatis studium*).[34]  Christian life is a continual exercise in *pietas*.
"Because they have been called to holiness, the entire life of all Christians must be an exercise in piety."[35]  The importance of *pietas* for
Calvin is further underlined by the importance he gives to its opposite,
*impietas*.  *Impietas* is profoundly sacrilegious.  "Impiety profanes and
pollutes the very name of God."[36]

    Calvin's reply to Sadoleto's letter to the Genevans was to some ex-
tent a personal defense and expressed and underlined the major themes of
the *Institutes* of 1536.  Here again Calvin reaffirmed the predominance
of the Word and obedience to the Word.

> ...ours is the obedience which, while it disposes us to listen to
> our elders and superiors, tests all obedience by the word of God;
> in fine, ours be the church whose supreme care it is humbly and re-
> ligiously to venerate the word of God and submit to its authority.[37]

There is no other source of light or truth than the Word.[38]  The Word
became the criterion and norm for all doctrines.

> The Spirit goes before the church, to enlighten her in understand-
> ing the Word, while the Word itself is like the Lydian stone by
> which you test all doctrines...[39]

What the Word teaches is respect for the glory of God.

> Whatever I felt assured that I had learned from thy mouth, I de-
> sired to dispense faithfully to the church.  Assuredly the thing at
> which I chiefly aimed and for which I most religiously labored was
> that the glory of your goodness and justice, after dispersing the
> mists by which it was formerly obscured, might shine forth conspicu-
> ous, that the virtue and blessings of your Christ, all glosses
> being wiped away, might be fully displayed.[40]

The theme of the glory of God predominates in Calvin's reply to Sadoleto.  Here he describes Christian life in terms of "illustrating the
glory of God."

The prime motive of his existence is zeal to illustrate the glory
of God. For we are born first of all for God, and not for ourselves.[41]

Commitment to the glory of God expresses itself in the life of the
believer in true worship. True worship is central to the Christian life.

I have also no difficulty in conceding to you that there is nothing
more perilous to our salvation than a preposterous and perverse
worship of God. The primary rudiments by which we are wont to
train to piety those whom we wish to gain as disciples to Christ
are these: not to frame any new worship of God for themselves at
random, and after their own pleasure, but to know that the only
legitimate worship is that which he himself approved from the beginning. For we maintain what the sacred oracle declared that obedience is more excellent than any sacrifice. In short we train them
by every means to be contented with the one rule of worship which
they have received from his mouth and bid adieu to all fictitious
worship.[42]

Fictitious worship is characterized by externalism and leads to the complete deterioration of true piety.

In the sacraments, all we have attempted is to restore the native
purity from which they had degenerated, and so enable them to re-
sume their dignity. Ceremonies we have in a great measure abolished, but we were compelled to do so; partly because by their
multitude they are degenerated into a kind of Judaism, partly because they had filled the minds of the people with superstition,
and could not possibly remain without doing the greatest injury to
the piety which it was their office to promote. Still we have retained those which seemed sufficient for the circumstances of the
times.[43]

In the preceding text we have the motivation behind Calvin's radical
opposition to many of the sacraments and in a special fashion to the
mass, described by Calvin as "missae abominationem." Over-insistence
on the carnal and on the external led to the great peril of "trans-
ferring to others the glory which you claim for your own majesty."[44]

Here again in the *Reply to Sadoleto* as in the *Institutes* of 1536,
Calvin's spirituality was expressed in terms of *pietas*. The intention
was to avoid what for Calvin was a very serious danger, the superstition
and idolatry endemic to any outward emotionalism.[45]

The 1539 edition of the *Institutes* was a new Latin edition considerably enlarged, containing seventeen chapters. The last chapter, which
underwent no modification in the course of later editions, was in effect
a theological study of the Christian life. In this small treatise
Calvin stated his purpose in the following fashion:

For me it will be sufficient to point out the method by which a
pious man *(vir pius)* may be taught how to frame his life aright,
and briefly lay down some universal rules by which he may not im-
properly regulate his conduct.[46]

Calvin began by viewing the life of the Christian in terms of God's

call to holiness.

But what better foundation can it begin than by reminding us that
we must be holy, because God is holy.[47]

This holiness demands of us that we have no fellowship with wickedness

and impiety. In our pilgrimage toward holiness Christ is our vivifying

model.

Christ, through whom we have returned to favor with God, is set before us as a model, the image of which our selves should express.[48]

Engrafted into the body of Christ, we must exclude any defilement or

impiety "in order to show forth the glory of God."[49]

We cannot appropriate Christ as our model nor hope to be engrafted

into him without a true knowledge of him. This knowledge is not purely

conceptual, but is a doctrine of life *(doctrina vitae)*, a doctrine at

the source of our salvation.

None have intercourse with Christ but those who have acquired a
true knowledge of him from the Gospel....Doctrine is not an affair
of the tongue but of the life; it is not apprehended by the intellect and the memory merely, like other branches of learning; but is
received only when it possesses the whole soul, and finds its seeds
and avocation in the inmost recesses of the heart....To doctrine in
which our religion is contained we have given the first place,
since by it our salvation commences; but it must be transfused into
the breast, and passed into the conduct and so transform us into
itself, as not to prove unfruitful....The gospel ought to penetrate
the inmost affections of the heart, fix its seat in the soul, and
pervade the whole man a hundred times more than the frigid discourses of philosophers.[50]

This true and lived doctrine leads to an integral worship *(integrita-*

*tem cultus)*. Integrity is not immediately given, but must be gradually

acquired, for the Christian life is one of progress, a process of spir-

itual growth toward a full fellowship with God.

No one will travel so badly as not daily to make some degree of
progress. This, therefore, let us never cease to do, that we may
daily advance in the way of the Lord; and let us not despair because of the slender measure of success. How little soever the
success may correspond with our wish, our labor is not lost when
today is better than yesterday, provided with true singleness of

> mind, we keep our aim, and aspire to the goal, not speaking flatter-
> ing things to ourselves, nor indulging our vices, but making it our
> constant endeavor to become better, until we attain to goodness
> itself. If during the whole course of our lives we seek and follow,
> we shall attain it, when relieved from the infirmity of flesh we
> are admitted to full fellowship with God.[51]

The long road toward full fellowship with God is characterized according to Calvin by self-denial, which he expresses as bearing a cross
after the pattern of our Lord. Self-denial is demanded of us if we are
to serve the glory of God.

> The great point, then, is that we are consecrated and dedicated to
> God (Nos esse Deo consecratos ac dedicatos) and therefore should
> not henceforth think, speak, design or act without a view to his
> glory.[52]

Calvin insisted that we have been made sacred, that we are not ours, but
the Lord's. "Nostri non sumus, sed Domini."[53] Not being our own then,
we must devote "the whole energy of our minds to the service of God."[54]
This service is by no means limited to external formalism but demands a
complete submission to the Holy Spirit. Calvin understood this relationship of man to God in terms of Christian philosophy (Christiana philosophia).

> But Christian philosophy bids her (reason) give place and yield
> complete submission to the Holy Spirit, so that man himself no
> longer lives, but Christ lives and rules in him.[55]

Self-denial and mortification are accomplished in charity towards the
other. "We shall succeed in mortifying ourselves if we fulfill all the
duties of charity."[56] While Calvin seems at times to speak in terms of
the medieval contemptus mundi, he had a positive view of the present
life which in many ways can be enjoyed even in the process of self-
denial.

> Still the contempt which believers should train themselves to feel
> for the present life must not be a kind to beget hatred of it or
> ingratitude to God. This life, though abounding in all kinds of
> wretchedness, is justly classed among divine blessings which are
> not to be despised.[57]

This earth is a gift of God and demands on our part an attitude of
thanksgiving. Nevertheless, compared to eternal life, this worldly life
must be in some way disdained and condemned.

If heaven is our country, what can the earth be but a place of exile?

> If departure from the world is entrance into life, what is the
> world but a sepulchre, and what is residence in it but immersion in
> death?  If to be free from the body is to gain full possession of
> freedom, what is the body but a prison?[58]

Life on earth is a pilgrimage, a journey which demands the proper integration of the use of earthly pleasures and the service of God.

> This the Lord prescribes by his word, when he tells us that to his
> people the present life is a kind of pilgrimage by which they
> hasten to the heavenly kingdom.  If we are only to pass through the
> earth, there can be no doubt that we are to use its blessings only
> insofar as they assist our progress, rather than retard it.[59]

True piety demands the ability to be able to cope with privation and
abundance.

> Let it be the aim of all who have any unfeigned desire for piety to
> learn after the example of the Apostle both to be full and to be
> hungry,  both to abound and to suffer need.[60]

So there is tension between the two lives.

This brief survey of the early works of Calvin indicates the existence of a coherent spirituality expressed in terms of *pietatis studium*
or *philosophia Christiana*.  This spirituality contains a method and some
general rules regulating the conduct of all Christians desirous of
attaining holiness.[61]

Spirituality is usually understood as the process of sanctification
in the concrete life of a believer.  This concept presupposes certain
theological a prioris, such as the distinction between justification and
sanctification, the possibility of progress in sanctification, the concept of a gradual perfection to be attained and the acceptance of the
existence of ways and means of attaining such a perfection.  These theological a prioris are present in the early thought of John Calvin.

*B.  Justification and Sanctification:  The Theological A Prioris of John
    Calvin's Spirituality*

It was Luther's doctrine of the justification of the sinner that had
previously led to a denial of any spirituality in the doctrine of the
Reformation.  Luther had spoken of our salvation as being grounded in
the alien righteousness of God which signifies the merits of Jesus
Christ and not our own worthiness.  But in the different existing currents of spirituality, mystical and otherwise, of that period

justification was understood not as a forensic imputation of righteousness but as an inner transformation.  Justice or holiness in the sense of
an objective and ontological making holy brought about by God was understood as the foundation for the subjective and progressive sanctification of man.

Of central importance in this whole question of the presence or ab-
sence of a sprituality among the Reformers is the distinction introduced
by Calvin between justification and sanctification.  While acknowledging
the logical priority of justification Calvin underlined its inseparable
connection with sanctification: if justification is genuine, it is pro-
longed into a sanctification which is effective externally.

> How is it we are justified by faith?  Because by faith we take hold
> of the justice of Christ, which alone reconciles us to God.  But we
> cannot take hold of this without taking hold, at the same time, of
> sanctification.  For he is given to us as our justice, wisdom,
> sanctification, redemption (1 Cor. I, 30),  Therefore, Christ jus-
> tifies no one without also sanctifying him.  For these benefits are
> joined by an eternal bond, so that whom he enlightens by his wisdom
> he redeems, whom he redeems he justifies, whom he justifies he
> sanctifies.  But, since the whole question only touches justice and
> sanctification, we will confine ourselves to them.  Though we may
> distinguish one from the other, Christ contains them both without
> division.  Do you, then, desire to obtain justice in Christ?  You
> must first possess Christ.  But you cannot possess him without par-
> ticipating in his sanctification, for he cannot be torn apart.
> Since, therefore, the Lord never gives us the enjoyment of these
> benefits without giving us himself, he gives us both at the same
> time; never one without the other.  Thus we see how true it is that
> we are not justified without works, but yet not by works, since our
> participation in Christ by which we are justified includes sancti-
> fication as well as justice.[62]

Justification is an external change in relation; it is a juridical act
concerning the state of man before God.  Sanctification effects a change
within the person; it takes place within the interior of man for an
inner renewal.  Justification is based on what Christ has done for us;
sanctification is based on what he does within us.

Justification and sanctification are the twofold fruits of faith.

> Christ lives in us in two ways.  The one life consists in governing
> us by his Spirit and directing all our actions, the other in making
> us partakers of his righteousness, so that while we can do nothing
> of ourselves, we are accepted in the sight of God.[63]

Justification for Calvin was

> the acceptance with which God receives us into his favor as right-
> eous men and...consists in the remission of sins and the imputation
> of Christ's righteousness.[64]

This righteousness is obtained by imputation, for we are justified

> not because faith infuses into us a habit or quality, but because
> we are accepted by God. Strictly speaking then, our righteousness
> is nothing other than God's pre-acceptance of us.[65]

Sanctification, on the other hand, is the continuing regenerative work of the Holy Spirit in us. Sanctification is a continual re-making of man by the Holy Spirit, a work which implies a gradual process lead-ing to the ultimate end, holiness. Sanctification is only begun here on earth, while justification is perfect from the very first moment of its reception. It is as perfect as the righteousness of Christ.[66]

Although differentiated, for Calvin, justification and sanctification were inseparably joined together. While justification is really the imputation of righteousness, sanctification is the process of continual struggle on the part of man with the assistance of the Holy Spirit toward the restoration of the image of God.[67] According to Calvin, jus-tification is not only the initial moment of the process toward the restoration of the image of God, but it accompanies the process.

> The gratuitous pardon of sins is given to us not only once, but is
> a benefit perpetually residing in the church, that it may be daily
> offered to the faithful...thus it is, that all the saints have need
> of the daily forgiveness of sins, for this alone keeps us in the
> family of God.[68]

> Therefore it is necessary for us to ask for this blessing not just
> once, but to hold to it throughout life...the faithful, then, have
> no other righteousness, even to the end of life, than that which is
> here described.[69]

Therefore the restoration of the image of God involves two mutually re-lated dimensions.

> Our salvation consists of these two parts, that God rules us by his
> Spirit and reforms us to his image through the whole course of life,
> and also that he buries all sins.[70]

For Calvin justification and sanctification are effected continually in the Christian; they co-exist in dialectical tension.

The dialectical tension of justification and sanctification implies ongoing process and progress.

This restoration is not accomplished either in a minute of this time
nor in a day, nor in a year, but God abolishes the corruption of
the flesh in his elect in a continuous succession of time and indeed little by little; he does not cease to cleanse them of their
filth, to dedicate them to himself as temples, to reform their
senses of true piety, so that they exercise themselves all their
lives in penitence, and know that this would never come to an end
until death.[71]

Calvin's understanding of the relationship between sanctification and
justification implied an idea of growth which become predominant in his
concept of the spiritual life.[72]  Progress toward perfection should be
the constant aim of a Christian.[73]  In fact, according to Calvin, "the
highest perfection of the godly in this life is an earnest desire to
make progress."[74]  For sanctification is a process which is accomplished
through the course of an entire life, perfected only in death.[75]  In
fact,

our life is a road on which we must continue to march until we come
to our Lord Jesus Christ.  Thus the kingdom of God must increase in
us more and more.[76]

The increase of the Kingdom of God within the justified man and his
daily progress toward perfection are made possible through genuine subjective possession of Christ.  Only through union with Christ do we par-
take of the blessing of Christ:  this is the *insitio in Christum* where
justification and sanctification are intimately linked.

Communion with Christ, the *insitio in Christum*, is an indispensable
condition for receiving the grace that God gives to man.  There is no
possible union with God without being grafted into Christ.  Now, the
purpose of sanctification is ultimately a perfect union with God.

The chief good of man is nothing else but union with God; this is
attained when we are formed according to him as our exemplar.[77]

But this end is not attained unless man is united to Christ.  In fact,
the whole process of sanctification is not possible without a prior
union with Christ.

...It is also said that we are grafted into him, and that we are
clothed with him, because nothing that he possesses belongs to us...
until we have been made one with him.[78]

This incipient union with Christ is the necessary condition for the
spiritual life and Calvin described it forcibly.  He preferred to

describe the intensity of this union by his use of the word *grafted* (in French, *enter*).[79] In his commentary on Romans, he defined this word *enter* as expressing not only conformity of example, but a real union through which man passes from his nature to Christ's.[80] Through this grafting on Christ man is made one substance with him.

> We expect salvation from him, not because he stands aloof from us, but because in grafting us onto his body he not only makes us partakers of all his benefits, but also we become one substance with him.[81]

Calvin wrote of this as a mystical union.

> Therefore, to that union of the head and members, the residence of Christ in our hearts, in fine a mystical union (in Latin, *mystica*; in French, *union sacrée*) we assign the highest rank.[82]

This mystical union was described in terms of a marriage between man and Christ.

> To this union alone it is owing that, in regard to us, the gracious has not come in vain. To this is to be referred that sacred marriage, by which we become bone of his bone, and flesh of his flesh.[83]

Calvin used the marriage analogy more than once to describe the union which exists between the Christian and Christ. "Under the figure and similitude of marriage, the sacred union which makes us one with Christ."[84] The nature of this union described under the analogy of the mystical marriage is somewhat difficult to understand. It is quite evident that Calvin was not speaking here of absorption into Christ or of total identification with Christ. This union must allow the integral subsistence of the properties of man and of Christ, although we are united to Christ "more closely than our limbs with the body."[85] "Even as he is one with regard to the Father, we become one in regard to him."[86] While Calvin employed powerful physical imagery, it is clear that he was not speaking of an essential unity of Christ with his believers. Rather he was describing a mystical union, by which he meant an intimate and personal union with Christ, a union realized without confusion of persons, but which transforms us into an ever more perfect image of God.[87]

While we should not interpret this in pantheistic terms as implying a mixing of divinity and humanity, nor in terms of a substantial union, we should consider this union a communion at the deepest level and not

simply a harmony of wills.  Having based his concept of justification
and sanctification on the doctrine of union and incorporation in Christ,
Calvin preserved in his spirituality a genuine mystical element.[88]  In
so doing he treated the subjective experience of God as a real foundation for doctrine.

Calvin's doctrine of justification and sanctification stressed anew
the dynamic operation of the Holy Spirit in the spiritual life.  The
Spirit is the living bond between the Heavenly Christ and all who are
united with Him.  In the mystery of the Ascension, Christ took his human
nature beyond this earth.  The Holy Spirit became the living bond between Christ and man.  He brought down to us what Christ is and became a
Christ for us.  He has engrafted us into the living Christ.

> To this is to be referred that sacred marriage, by which we become
> bone of his bone, and flesh of his flesh, and so one with him, for
> it is by the Spirit alone that he unites himself to us.  By the
> same grace and energy of the Spirit we become his members, so that
> he keeps us under him, and we in our turn possess him.[89]

> The Lord by  his Spirit bestows upon us the blessings of being one
> with him in soul and body, and spirit.  The bond of that connection
> therefore is the spirit of Christ who unites us to him, and is a
> kind of channel by which everything that Christ has and is is given
> to us.[90]

Calvin never tired of repeating that the Holy Spirit is the bond of our
union with Christ.[91]

Proceeding from the Father and the Son, the Holy Spirit preserves
what has been constituted, sustains and animates what has been given.

> The Holy Spirit sustains, quickens and vivifies all things in
> heaven and on earth...in all things transfusing his vigor and in-
> spiring them with being, life and motion.[92]

The Spirit has not merely a sustaining influence but he is himself the
source of those gifts necessary for a full, sanctified life.

> Paul plainly testifies that judgment and knowledge and gentleness
> and all other gifts proceed from one source.  For it is the office
> of the Spirit to put forth and exercise the power of God by con-
> ferring new gifts upon man, and distributing them among them.[93]

It is the work of the Holy Spirit that consecrates us to Christ.
"For while by nature we are unholy, the Spirit consecrates us to God."[94]
It is the Spirit who forms and readies us to yield ourselves to God.

> No one is fit to offer sacrifices or any other service *(cultum)* to God but he who has been molded *(formatus)* by the hidden operation of the Spirit. Willingly indeed we offer ourselves in our all to God, and build his temples: but whence does voluntary action come except that the Lord subdues us and thus renders us teachable and obedient.[95]

The Holy Spirit also has an ecclesial function.

> All the elect are so united in Christ that as they are dependent on one head, they also grow together into one body, being joined in this together as are the limbs of the body. They are made truly one since they live together in one faith, hope and love, and in the same Spirit of God.[96]

The Holy Spirit distributes the gifts of the head to the members.[97]

Through his activity the Spirit makes the Church the *locus* of sanctification.

> The word church is used in the sacred scriptures in two senses. Sometimes when they mention a church, they understand that which is really such in the sight of God *(coram Deo)* into which none are received but those who are children of God by the grace of adoption, and by sanctification of the Spirit are the true members of Christ. And then it comprehends not only the saints who dwell on earth, but all who are elect from the beginning of the world.[98]

The Church as locus of sanctification and the work of the Spirit is essentially an inward and interior reality. The kingdom of Christ which for Calvin was the Church[99] is spiritual and not external.

> He means  that they are greatly mistaken who seek with the eyes of the flesh the kingdom of God, which is in no respect carnal or earthly, for it is nothing else than the inward and spiritual renewal of the soul. From the nature of the kingdom itself he shows that they are altogether wrong who look around here or there in order to observe visible marks. That restoration of the church he tells us which God has promised must be looked for within, for by quickening his elect into the heavenly newness of life, he establishes his kingdom within them.[100]

C. *Sanctification as the Restoration of God's Image in Man and his World. The Concept of Order and the Spiritual Life*

Calvin considered the process of sanctification with its explicit christological and pneumatological emphases, as the restoration of the image of God and the original order.

> Already in the beginning Adam was created in the image of God, in order that he might present the righteousness of God as in a mirror, but because that image has been effaced by sin, it must now be

restored in Christ.  However in truth the regeneration of the
faithful is no other thing than the restoration of the image of God
in them.[101]

God the Father, who as he has reconciled us to himself in his
anointed, has impressed his image upon us, to which he would have
us to be conformed.[102]

According to Calvin, "in the beginning," the image of God was manifested
"by light of intellect, rectitude of heart and the soundness of every
part."[103]  Reflecting the divine righteousness as a mirror ("Adam was at
first created after the image of God, and reflected as in a mirror the
divine righteousness"),[104] man lived in ordered relation to his fellow
creatures and his environment.[105]

   The image of God in man expresses itself through order.  It is not
something static impressed on man, but is expressed dynamically by man
living in response to God's grace.  Calvin's concepts of the image of
God and of order were interchangeable.  The concept of order was a fundamental category in Calvin's theology.  It served as a vehicle for
much of his thought; and viewed from the standpoint of this central
idea, a great deal of his spirituality can best be understood.[106]  Calvin held that all things are ordered according to the movement of God's
grace in creation and redemption.  The order of creation gives to every
creature, and to man particularly, his destiny and reason for existence.
In this order man lives in rectitude and integrity.  Here men are called
to follow the "law of their creation and live in the genuine order."[107]
Genuine order, whether in the cosmos or in man, or in government (or
politics) is a reflection of God's glory.

   There is presented to us in the whole order of nature the most
   abundant matter for showing forth the glory of God...But David here
   with great propriety commends the special grace toward the human
   race; for this, of all the subjects which come under our contemplation, is the brightest mirror in which we may perceive his glory.[108]

Through the Fall the original order of creation was disrupted and the
image of God disfigured.

   Although we grant that the image of God was not overly effaced and
   destroyed in him, it was, however, so corrupted that anything which
   remains is fearfully deformed.[109]

That man does not seek God's glory in his own action is the clearest
proof of this disorder.[110]  Calvin explained that in the defection of

the first man "a whole order of creation was inverted."[111] From then on
he lives in an inverted order of creation. Evil arises as man inverts
and abandons the God-given order by turning from dependence on God to
dependence on himself. He takes the rectitude with which he was blessed
and ascribes it to himself, making it a curse. The root of defection is
infidelity or faithlessness. "Infidelity was the root of all defection,
just as faith alone unites us to God."[112] According to Calvin, were we
but rightly composed in obedience to God all the elements of creation
would sing to us and we should hear in the world the angelic melody.[113]
Unbelief on the part of man, ingratitude, disobedience, concupiscence,
are the very roots of man's defection.

The whole purpose of redemption, and of the process of sanctification especially, is the restoration of a lost order, of the image of God
in man. God in his changelessness has not abandoned his desire and will
for order in the world.

> It is the glory of our faith  that God, the creator of the world,
> in no way disregards the order which he himself at first estab-
> lished.[114]

The work of Christ is precisely to restore man to order by renewing in
him the image of God.

> Christ is the most perfect image of God into which we are so re-
> newed as to bear the image of God in knowledge, purity, righteous-
> ness and true holiness.[115]

> Adam was first created after the image of God, and reflected as in
> a mirror the divine righteousness; and that image having been de-
> faced by sin must now be restored in Christ. The regeneration of
> the godly is indeed...nothing else than the formation anew of the
> image of God in them...[116]

How central these categories of order and image of God are becomes
apparent when we see how they govern Calvin's description of the Christian life as a life of obedience. At the same time, they clearly under-
line the predominant role of the Father in the process of sanctification
and lead us at the same time to a better understanding of the nature of
the imitation of Christ.

A Christian is elected to order and fulfills his purpose as he takes
his place in the harmonious structure of God's order. The whole chapter
on Christian life in Calvin's *Institutes* is simply a description of the
true order that should govern man. The word "religion," fundamental in

the mind of Calvin, means to gather, to bind up again, and thus true religion implies an orderliness which is lacking in superstition.

> ...the name is used in opposition to *vagrant licence*--the greater
> part of mankind rashly taking up whatever first comes in their way,
> whereas piety, that it may stand with a firm step, confines itself
> within due bounds.  In the same way superstition seems to take its
> name from its not being contented with the measures which reason
> prescribes, but accumulating a superfluous mass of vanities.[117]

Piety, the predominant category of Calvin's spirituality, is the attitude of a man integrated within God's order:  a pious person is one who
has taken his place within God's order.

To take one's place within God's order means to depend on God alone
in obedience and belief in God's goodness and solicitude, in movement
away from oneself and towards God, and in gratitude.

> If we do not begin with this point, calling upon our God, it is to
> pervert all order.  So then let us learn that the principal exer-
> cise and study that the faithful ought to have in this world is to
> run to their God, and, while acknowledging that he is the fountain
> of all blessings, seek good in him.[118]

With this concept of order Calvin established the sovereignty of God
at the very center and origin of all spiritual.  God is the unique cause
of our salvation, the author of our faith, the only source of any good
we may accomplish.

> All the good qualities which believers possess are due to God.  In
> using the term 'all' he (St. Paul) certainly makes God the author
> of spiritual life from its beginning to its end.[119]

Apart from the confidence generated in the faithful by the sovereignty of God experienced in his election, another direct consequence of
this principle of God's absolute sovereignty is man's discovery that he
does not belong to himself.  God must come first, before everything,
before ourselves.  This means that the honor of God is more important
than our own individual salvation.  For Calvin the ultimate end of history was not the salvation of man, but the glory of God.  In fact, one
of Calvin's fundamental intuitions is expressed in the saying, *soli Deo
gloria*.  Nothing in creation should ever obscure this glory.  The final
cause of creation and every manifestation of the divine will is the
glorification of God.  Everything in creation, good or evil, must contribute to this glory.  Every created being must work for the glory of
God.

> The great point, that is, that we are consecrated and dedicated to
> God and therefore should hence forward not think, speak, desire or
> act without a view to his glory.[120]

Therefore, the believer is not preoccupied with the question of his
salvation, however legitimate such a concern may be.  For the man who
concentrates on his salvation makes his ultimate goal himself and thus
reduces God to the means to a personal end.  The faithful man, on the
other hand, lives for the glory of God, and because he does not give
first place to his own salvation he finds it, since salvation consists
in returning to God his rightful primacy.  In reality, it is not man who
glorifies God, but God who glorifies himself in the faithfulness of his
servants.

In so insisting on the notion of the divine order, Calvin indicates
clearly the pre-eminence the Father has in his theology.  Christ is the
pattern of order, the Holy Spirit its restorer; but it is the Father who
is the source of order.  Nothing escapes the will and purpose of God.
The final cause of all creation and of every manifestation of the divine
will is the glorification of God.

Calvin's concept of order directly influenced his understanding of
the need to imitate Christ and of the nature of this imitation.  The
creation of order and the redemption of order occur in the person of
Christ.  Because of his obedience unto death Christ's life is a pattern
of order.  Because of his death

> ...sin has been abolished, salvation has been given back to men,
> and in short the whole world has been renewed and all things re-
> stored to order.[121]

In the humanity of Christ we see, according to Calvin, a perfect
pattern of order, of true moderation and harmony.[122]  When Calvin
appealed, as he frequently did, to his congregation to live according to
the order of nature, or true humanity, or according to the rule of
moderation, he was not referring to a philosophical rule of life, but to
the very person of Christ.  When Calvin spoke of the *order of nature*,
which included in his thinking the ideas of orderliness and regularity
of events within creation, of proper interrelation among all things in
creation, and of the realization by every creature of its appropriate
purpose, he was speaking of nature as it originally was, ought to be and
really is in the humanity of Christ.  In Christ is complete unity and

harmony between the will of God and the will of man.[123]

Calvin reaffirmed this christological dimension of all order in the
following text:

> Full manhood is found in Christ; but foolish men do not in a proper
> manner seek their perfection in Christ. It ought to be held as a
> fixed principle among us that all that is out of place is hurtful
> and destructive. Whoever is a man in Christ is in every respect a
> perfect man.[124]

But to be a perfect man in Christ, to be restored to order, demands more
than a simple imitation of Christ.

The concept of incorporation dominated Calvin's thinking as sanctification and the Christian life. Incorporation is a restoration of the
original order,

> as the ruin of the human race is that it is broken and scattered,
> the restoration of it consists in its being properly united in one
> body.[125]

When Calvin spoke of conformity to the pattern of Jesus Christ, he
expressed himself through the image of the union between the head and
members of the body. It is as participators in a relationship of union
with Christ that we are exhorted to imitate him as our example.

> As he has set before us God as light for an example, he now calls
> us also to Christ that we may imitate him. Yet he does not simply
> exhort us to imitate Christ, but from the union we have with him,
> he proves that we ought to be like him. A likeness in life indeed,
> he says, will prove that we abide in Christ.[126]

Christ is not only the example of righteousness, but also the very cloth
of that same righteousness.[127] Not only must we manifest Christ's death
and resurrection, but we must in some way participate in their efficacy.[128]

Calvin understood Christ not only as an exemplar of order, but as a
Savior who saves by incorporating man into his own Body. The *imitatio
Christi* is not simply mechanical copying of Christ. By his suffering
and death Christ not only shows the way--he is the Way.

D.  *Pietas as the Essential Expression of Calvin's Spirituality*

Within the Trinitarian structure of his spirituality, Calvin assigns
the Father a predominant role. Sanctification is understood as the
restoration of order willed by God. Within this context Calvin describes

the Christian life under two headings: piety and justice--that is, love
of neighbor.

> Piety and justice express the two tables of the law; therefore of
> these two attitudes the wholeness of life is constituted.[129]

In Calvin's mind piety came first.  Although neither of the two
principal parts of our duty set forth in the Law may be neglected, God
must be our first concern.

> We must give preference to the command concerning the worship and
> the service of God; afterwards, as far as we are able, we must give
> to men what is their due.  When we have obeyed God, then it is the
> proper time to think of our parents and wife and children; as
> Christ attends to his mother, but it is after he is on the cross to
> which he has been called by his Father's decree.[130]

Thus the service of God is the foundation of man's whole life and the
inspiration of his service to his neighbor.  Man's chief end is to
glorify his Maker.

We see that conscience and faith unfeigned are placed

> at the head, in other words, true piety; from this charity is de-
> rived.[131]

The proper attitude of man is one of dependence on God, expressed in
service and worship.  When man tries to depend on himself, he destroys
the order established by God and transfers glory to himself, which is in
fact pure and simple idolatry.

> Let us recognize then that the praise is due to him that we may not
> defraud him of that which belongs to him.  For if we should live as
> perfectly as angels and yet have the foolish idea that this came
> from our own free will and of our own movement, then we would miss
> the principal thing.  To what end serve all our good works lest it
> be that God in them is glorified?  But if we think ourselves the
> author of them, we see that they are corrupted in so doing, and are
> converted into vices so that they are nothing more than ambition.[132]

Man's true attitude toward God was described throughout the opening
questions of the Geneva Catechism of 1541:

> What is the way to honor God aright?  Answer:  To honor God aright
> is to put our whole trust in him, to study to serve him in obeying
> his will, to invoke him in all our necessities, seeking our salva-
> tion in all good things at his hand, and finally to acknowledge both
> both with heart and mouth that he is the light and fountain of all
> goodness.[133]

Calvin defined holiness, the very purpose of sanctification, in the

context of man's basic attitude toward God. Holiness is concerned with
the duties of piety; it is achieved by obedience to the first table of
the law, the table of the worship of God.[134] Holiness is, "that purity
which lies in being devoted to the service of God...holiness lies in the
worship of God."[135]

This holiness demands a consecration of the whole man, body and soul.

> Hence in order that you may sanctify yourself to God aright, you
> must dedicate both body and soul entirely to him.[136]

Consecration for Calvin implies a setting aside. The Holy Spirit consecrates man to God.

> The word, sanctification, signifies choice and separation. This
> takes place in us when we are regenerated by the Spirit to newness
> of life, that we may serve God and not the world. While by nature
> we be unholy, the Spirit consecrates us to God.[137]

Consecration must be taken here in the Old Testament sense of setting
aside, of separation, setting apart from the common use for the divine
purpose. God's holiness is seen in his set-apartness over all other
things. And the holiness of Yahweh has to find reflection in the holiness of his people. "You shall be holy, for I, Yahweh, your God, am
holy." (Lev. 19:2) Israel's holiness consisted fundamentally in having
been set apart for a specific purpose, set apart for the service and
praise of God in the world, consecrated to Him.

The primary element in *pietas* is the worship of God in spirit since
God is spirit.

> The worship of God is said to consist in the spirit, because it is
> nothing else than that inward faith of the heart which produces
> prayer and next, purity of conscience and self-denial that we may
> be dedicated to obedience of God as holy sacrifices.[138]

> What it is to worship God in spirit and truth appears clearly from
> what has been already said. It is to lay aside the entanglements
> of ancient ceremonies, and to retain merely what is spiritual in
> the worship of God; for the truth of the worship of God consists in
> the spirit, and ceremonies are but a sort of appendage.[139]

The spiritual dimension of worship is expressed in obedience.

> By the word worship we must understand not only the outward cere-
> mony but also according to the figure synecdoche, a holy desire to
> yield reverence and obedience.[140]

> The main part of true and right worship is to hear God speaking and
> to regard obedience of more account than offerings and sacrifices.[141]

Constituted through spiritual worship, *pietas* is an essentially interior attitude of man, invisible in nature and immeasurable through exterior expressions.[142]

True worship in spirit can result only from a true knowledge of God.

> You worship what you know not, we worship what we know. This is a sentence worthy of being remembered, and teaches that we ought not to attempt anything in religion rashly or at random; because unless there be knowledge, it is not God that we worship but a phantom or idol.[143]

In the same text Calvin reaffirmed the necessity for true knowledge of God:

> You must know this, that God is not properly worshipped but by the certainty of faith, which cannot be produced in any other way than by the word of God. Hence it follows that all of the secular world fall into idolatry; for Christ plainly testifies that an idol, or an imagination of their own brain, is substituted for God, when men are ignorant of the true God; and he charges with ignorance all to whom God has not revealed himself, for as soon as we are deprived of the light of his word, darkness and blindness rule.[144]

The whole notion of *pietas* is dominated by the reality of the knowledge of God. *Pietas* is the fruit within man of the knowledge of God and the knowledge of self.

> I call *pietas* that love of God in awe of his presence which a knowledge of his benefits brings about.[145]

*Pietas* corresponds to both of the aspects through which God is known: God as Lord and God as Father. True piety demands worship and obedience; it also demands love.[146] *Pietas* is reverence informed by love; *pietas* is essentially filial. The type of worship and obedience which it demands must be given freely.

> For until men feel that they owe everything to God, that they are cherished by his paternal care, that He is the author to them of all good things and nothing is to be sought out of him, they will never subject themselves in willing obedience; or rather I should say, unless they establish for themselves a solid happiness in him, they will never devote themselves to him without reserve truly and heartily.[147]

> We honor such a father with piety and ardent love, in such a way to devote ourselves totally to his service.[148]

Calvin's *pietas* is radically opposed to anything which could alter man's filial relation with the Father. Therefore, it is opposed to a

spirituality based on good works. *Pietas* is not a mercenary relation of
*do ut des,*[149] nor is it a form of *werkheiligkeit.* Pietas does not in
any way consist of an accumulation of prayers and good works or satis-
factions to be offered to God in a servile spirit. It demands the disposition of a mind that is ready and willing to accomplish God's will.

While theocentric by nature, Calvin's concept of piety also implies
an outgoing movement towards others. It calls for a relationship of
love and right dealings with one's fellowmen. Piety expresses our relationship to God, in love for our fellowmen. Indeed it cannot exist
without this expression.

> Piety of God, acknowledged, ranks higher than love of his brothers;
> and therefore the observance of the first table is more valuable in
> the sight of God than the observance of the second. For as God
> himself is invisible, so piety is a thing hidden from the eyes of
> men; and, though the manifestation of it was the purpose for which
> ceremonies were appointed, they are not certain proofs of its
> existence. It frequently happens that none are more zealous and
> regular in observing ceremonies than hypocrites. God therefore
> chooses to make trial of our love for himself by that love of our
> brother, which he enjoins us to cultivate.[150]

The sign of authentic piety is not found in zeal for an external worship
expressed in ceremonies but in the real love for man. Love of neighbor
is the outward sign of our love for God. The first table of the law
demands of all men the consecration of their entire self to God. From
this consecration to God flows our dedication to our fellowmen.

> But because no man, as a matter of course, observes charity in all
> respects, unless he seriously fear God, such observance is a proof
> of piety also.[151]

It is in this context that Calvin could say that all of perfection lies
in charity. "Hence the Apostle, not without cause, makes the whole perfection of the saint to consist in charity."[152]

Calvin emerged from his own religious evolution as *miles Christianus.* Man is in a moral struggle with himself, a struggle for freedom
from earthly desires and drives. Yet at the same time, participation in
the lives of others cannot be done away with in favor of a full-time
effort to save one's own soul. What is called for is not selfish brood-
ing but discipleship: the loving acceptance of one's part in the Lord's
work.

We are called by the Lord under this condition, that everyone

should strive to lead others to the truth, to restore the wandering
to the right way, to extend a helping hand to the fallen, to win
over those that are without.[153]

A true Christian will not be content with walking by himself in the
right way but will try to draw the whole world into the same way.[154]

Although Calvin held firmly that the authentic sign of real piety and
love is not found in the external forum, he recognized that because of
our weakness outward forms have importance.[155] But one must go beyond
them.[156] In prayer both the inward and the outward dimensions of the
spiritual life are combined.

The principal exercise of the humble man who knows he has nothing
which is his is prayer.

The principal exercise which the children of God have is to pray;
for this way they give a true proof of their faith.[157]

Prayer is a valid exercise for the humble man, a cry that finds its inspiration in his human need. It is never the mere fulfillment of a
devotional exercise, for all prayer, whether it takes the form of thanksgiving, supplication, or confession, "is an effusion and manifestation
of internal feelings before him who is the searcher of the heart."[158]
All prayer, therefore, is really the expression of an inward attitude
before God which can be expressed outwardly, as in speech,[159] or in a
posture of humility.[160] At times this external exercise can help our
internal attitude. The only right way to pray is from a true sense of
gratitude to God and a feeling of love.[161]

There is need for discipline and perseverance in prayer. Very often
we have to make ourselves pray despite our feelings. It is therefore
good that we observe particular and fixed hours for our prayers.[162]

As one must frequently lay on fuel to preserve a fire, so the exercise of prayer requires the aid of such help.[163]

There is also a need for meditation to make our life of prayer more
fervent.

Meditation as well as the nature of the word of God during prayer
is by no means superfluous. Let us not decline to involve the
example of David and introduce thoughts which may reanimate our
languid lines with new vigors.[164]

And in order to pray well, to live a life of prayer, we must discipline
our faculties. This demands deliberate thinking and reflection upon God.

Meditation upon the word of God is an excellent means to achieve this discipline. Calvin suggested the passion, death and resurrection of Christ, whatever reflections make us fear God and whatever helps us appreciate his goodness, as appropriate objects of meditation. He added that this should be accompanied by daily self-examination,[165] which destroys our peaceful self-confidence and makes us aware of our imperfections.[166] Thus confronted with our sins, we would become better prepared to receive the grace of God[167] and to meet our final judgment.

E.  *The Spirituality of John Calvin and the* Devotio Moderna

In 1523 Calvin entered the College of Montaigue in Paris. Montaigue had been reformed by Standonck who had established a severe discipline there and had introduced the spirit of the *Devotio Moderna.*[168] The library founded by him was chiefly composed of the mystical treatises of Groote and his followers. How deeply Calvin was influenced by his stay in Montaigue is difficult to assess. But there is no doubt that the spirituality of John Calvin shows a marked resemblance to the vocabulary, and to a lesser extent to the ideas, of the *De Imitatione Christi* and the writings of Groote.

The *Devotio Moderna* was a reaction against the exteriority of religious practices and against superstition; it counteracted this trend by referring everything back to God as the only sovereign cause. For Groote religion was a "consecration to the service of God,"[169] and man's final end was the very glory of God.[170] According to the *De Imitatione Christi* the entire life of the devout should serve the glory of God. God is sovereign, and his sovereignty is achieved through the realization of the order *(ordo)* instituted by his sovereign will.[171]

The idea of *ordo* inspired and dominated medieval thought. From St. Augustine to St. Bernard to St. Thomas Aquinas[172] *ordo* appeared as a constant theme. Everything, including man and his spiritual life, was considered in the light of an existing order or an order to be established. Aelred of Rievaulx, a disciple of St. Bernard, formulated this universal law in the following way:

> Every creature tends to its own order, seeks its own place; outside of its order this same creature is anxious, but within its own order it finds peace.[173]

Calvin's spirituality followed the same impulse as the *Devotio*

*Moderna*:  it was characterized by the predominance of the transcendence
of God.  This is clearly indicated by his preoccupation with the concepts of election, of holiness and of the glory of God.  The idea of
order, which is established by the transcendence of God and itself
establishes a pattern in the world and its history, was essential in
Calvin's synthesis.  The absolute sovereignty of God leads man to total
self-abnegation and to complete consecration and service to the glory
of God.  This instinct for the transcendental led Calvin to a greater
appreciation of worship.

It is here that we begin to see a difference between Calvin and the
*Devotio Moderna*.  The primacy of worship so characteristic of Calvin's
spirituality was not strongly defended in the *Devotio Moderna*.  Calvin's
stance on the centrality of worship reinforced his absolute opposition
to idolatry in all of its different forms.  The uprooting of idolatry
became a real mission for him.  And in this mission he followed one
guideline:  to attribute to anything other than God what is properly
his is "to deprive God of his honor and to violate his worship."[174]

For Calvin worship was the sharpest weapon in the struggle against
superstition.  True worship in spirit cannot degenerate into purely
external devotions.  To refute any misunderstanding of Christian life,
Calvin substituted the term *pietas* for *devotio*.  *Devotio* had already
acquired the pejorative connotation of exteriority; for Calvin the word
devotion was always used in a derogative sense.[175]

> By cultivating human piety, they should train themselves in the
> worship of God lest a foolish and silly devotion should divest
> them of human feelings.[176]

The interiorization of piety Calvin considered the best remedy for
superstition.  Superstition he understood as those religious practices
which tend to hide the essential behind the accidental.[177]  Piety, however, is a submission of the will to the Father, and demands an acceptance of what is given by God in revelation.  Superstition is directly
opposed to this acceptance and to piety itself.[178]  Superstition is in
complete contradiction with the theocentric movement of *pietas*.

> The sum of the commandment, therefore, is that true piety, in other
> words the worship of the deity, is acceptable and impiety is an
> abomination to him.[179]

Superstition and impiety destroy the order of God as established and reflected in man.

Idolatry for Calvin was not only making false images of God, but also making one's own deeds into works of righteousness.[180] True worship never led the worshipper to works-righteousness, *Werkheiligkeit*. The *Devotio Moderna* suffered from a certain mercenary spirit which at times required a return for one's effort. For Calvin, the work of sanctification was completely God's.[181] It is in this light that one can understand Calvin's insistence on self-denial and mortification.

Both spiritualities were formed by the admonition of Christ, "If you want to follow me, you have to abnegate yourself."[182] For Calvin piety as the love of God and neighbor could be found only in the man who had eliminated self-love through self-denial and had opened himself to God and his fellowman.

> We shall never love our neighbors with sincerity according to our Lord's intention until we have corrected the love of ourselves.[183]

So true piety was impossible without self-denial. "Self-denial may be said to be the commencement of piety."[184] The self-denial proposed by Calvin was not simply a negative attitude but also implied a positive attitude toward God and man. The renunciation of self frees man and establishes him in the brotherly love of his neighbor, and complete submission to God. Self-denial viewed in terms of respect and service to others marks a new movement in spirituality. Meritorious self-mortification is no longer valued in itself; what matters are those actions that demonstrate love and glorify God. Indeed, actions of self-denial "ought to be pursued for the sole reason, because they are pleasing to him."[185] The purpose of self-denial for Calvin was to release one's energy for those things which are pleasing to God and not in order to win salvation but in order to display God's glory. This is a clear indication that for Calvin self-denial is principally related to God. It means full commitment to God. Self-denial cannot be practiced as a means toward self-perfection. On this point, there is no ambiguity on the part of Calvin, while such ambiguity does sometimes exist in the *Devotio Moderna*.

The primacy of inwardness and interiority is recognized in both spiritualities. In insisting upon the inwardness both of worship and piety, Calvin was setting forth an idea which permeates his entire thought: the tension between flesh and spirit.

> Here is no greater variance in the world than of the spirit and the flesh; the Law is spiritual, man is carnal...here is expressed antithesis between the flesh and the spirit.[186]

Both spiritualities make use of platonic terminology: the body is considered a prison and the earthly life a transitory stage in the journey to eternal life. In this context, both spiritualities speak of "denying the world," and of "contempt for the present life." Both speak of this life as a life of continual combat,[187] a life of pilgrimage.[188]

Calvin did not hesitate to define the true attitude of man toward the world as a *contemptus mundi*.

> Whatever be the kind of tribulation with which we are afflicted, we should always consider the end of it to be that we be trained to despise the present, and thereby stimulated to aspire to the future life.[189]

Calvin's advocacy of a *contemptus mundi* differed greatly, in its setting and import, from that of the *Devotio Moderna*. As we previously described, there seem to have been two contrary tendencies in the spirituality of the *Devotio Moderna*: on the one hand, a call to withdrawal from the world, to perfection in solitude, and on the other, a summons to involvement in the world which is in need of reform. We saw that the *De Imitatione Christi* was essentially a monastic spirituality. There was no more effective way in its thinking of preparing for the coming of the kingdom of God than through contempt for the world and renunciation of it. The monastic way of life, with its strict discipline, became, even outside the monastery, a model to be followed. The Third Orders were originally intended as a substitute for real monastic life, a second opportunity for all those who for some reason had to remain in the world. This was an attempt to pattern life in the world on life in the cloister.[190]

The spirituality of Calvin represents a complete break from the monastic type and so differs radically from the spirituality of the *Devotio Moderna*. Like Erasmus', Calvin's spirituality is essentially apostolic in nature: a spirituality of the service of God in the world. Calvin's *contemptus mundi* is based on very different reasoning from that of the *De Imitatione Christi*. For Calvin, contempt of this world was achieved through comparison with the future life. Meditation on the future life makes us understand the vanity of the present.[191] But such a contempt must not "be of a kind to beget hatred of it or ingratitude,"[192]

since everything created is the work of God.  This life is but a pilgrimage; we are to use its blessings only insofar as they assist us in
our progress.[193]  To use them without danger, one must be truly free,
indifferent.[194]  The things of this world are good in themselves, but if
our lordship of this world is to be true lordship, we must refuse to be
enslaved to anything.  Speaking of David in Psalm XXIII, Calvin wrote:

> He valued all the comforts of the flesh only in proportion as they
> served to enable him to live to God.  It is therefore certain that
> the mind of David, by the aid of the simple prosperity which he
> enjoyed, was elevated to the hope of the everlasting inheritance.[195]

In order to insure our indifference we ought to use the goods of this
world in a spirit of thanksgiving, always recognizing God's liberality
and man's dependence.[196]  The Christian must live in the world, using it
in service to his neighbor and to God.  Though there is a proper place
for fasting[197] and mortification, to do so on account of some ascetic
principle or man-made law is a sign, not of true piety, but of impiety.

> Have done then with that inhuman philosophy which, in allowing no
> use of the creatures but for necessity, not only maliciously de-
> prives us of the lawful fruit of the divine beneficence, but cannot
> be realized without depriving man of all his senses, and reducing
> him to a block.[198]

The term "inner-worldly asceticism" can be used to describe the spirituality of John Calvin.  His ideal was not withdrawal from the world,
but the conquest of the world for the glory of God.

Calvin's belief in the radical depravity of man and his platonic mis-
trust of flesh and matter did not lead to the practical renunciation of
the world; his negativism was counterbalanced by his theology of creation and of *ordo*.

Within the spirituality of the *Devotio Moderna* contempt of the world
led to a monastic-ascetic ideal of perfection:  the fullness of Christian perfection could be achieved only within the walls of a monastery.
Calvin took the humanist's position on monasticism.

The humanists of the sixteenth century, as exemplified by Erasmus,
could not accept monasticism understood as the unique way to salvation.
(Nor could Luther, who developed his doctrine of vocation in opposition
to monasticism.[199]  In fact, Luther understood the monastic vocation to
be un-Christian in itself.)[200]  Erasmus developed the idea of the "monk
in the world."  Every Christian must separate himself from the world,

but this world is inside man - it is not the outside world. Erasmus was
an advocate of what is called the asceticism within the world, *inner-
weltliche Askese*, and this separation from the world, this contempt for
the world, is not guaranteed by living in a monastery. What is important is neither the habit nor the structure but the personal choice:
*monochatus non est pietas*. Piety is not contempt for created reality
but the understanding that man's inner life is what matters, a life
which is dependent on God. Created reality has a value, but it is a
relative value; it has autonomy, but a relative autonomy.

Because of its stress on interiority and a diminished appreciation of
the mediating role of the Church and her sacraments, the *Devotio Moderna*
evolved a more individualistic and personal approach to spirituality.
Calvin's spirituality was also personalistic; his individualism was un-
compromising. In his thinking, *pietas* directly connotes a relationship
to God grounded on God's election and grace. It implies consecration
and service to the holy, which is not a place nor an object but a person.
The holy one cannot be present to man except through himself. No sacramental substance can be his medium; he alone is his presence. A pan-
sacramental view of the world is thus directly opposed to Calvin's
thought. Man stands in the presence of God in isolation and without
intermediaries. Directed by God, the individual works out the certainty
of his salvation by himself and in himself. *Pietas* is for Calvin an
intimate relationship with God *solus cum solo*, set apart from any communal religiousness.

Calvin developed a theology of the Church which at first seems opposed
to his individualism and personalism. He affirmed that the sanctification of the individual takes place within the Church. Calvin considered the Church a true mother.

> As it is now our purpose to discourse of the visible church, let us
> learn from her single title mother, how useful, nay how necessary
> the knowledge of her is, since there is no other means of entering
> into life unless you conceive us in the womb and give us birth,
> unless you nourish us at her breast, and, in short, keep us under
> her charge and government until, divested of mortal flesh, we be-
> come like angels.[201]

Our sanctification is also advanced by the mutual prayer of the members
of the body of Christ.[202] Christians "cannot but be united together in
brotherly love and mutually impart their blessings to each other."[203]

Now the greater importance which Calvin attributed to the Church in comparison to Luther may lead to the misconception that, in Calvin's thinking, the action of the Holy Spirit was manifested principally in the
Church, rather than in the faithful.  In reality, however, he considered
the action of the Holy Spirit as occurring first and principally in the
individual.  The action of the Holy Spirit is directed towards the individual independent of the community.  The *Testimonium Spiritus Sancti* is
individual, entrusting to the individual the certitude of God's promise.

To protect the inwardness and interiority of his spirituality, Calvin
rejected the authority of a visible Church on matters concerning the
spiritual life.  At the same time, he succeeded in avoiding the subjectivism of the Anabaptists.  He was able to do this through the development of an epistemology which provided an intellectual foundation both
for his individualistic spirituality and for a radical reformation of
the Church.

The incipient individualism of the *Devotio Moderna*, and the individualism of the French humanists, was the product of the "inward" piety
and devoutness.  It was a limited individualism, however.  The writers
of these movements were unwilling to subordinate to it the mediation of
the visible Church, especially in its teaching office.  All these writers desired an intensification of religious feeling, yet feared subjectivism and disregard for the hierarchical authority.  Erasmus fully
·accepted the authority of the Church.  The *docta pietas*, the *philosophia
Christi*, the spiritual experience, all were to be judged by the visible
Church and subordinated to its authority.

For Calvin there was no such subordination.  His individualism was
clearly expressed in his understanding of the nature of the reformation.
This he expressed in his commentary on the First Epistle to the Corinthians.  Speaking in the context of the dispute on the Last Supper, Calvin wrote,

> It (the Epistle to the Corinthians) is a passage that ought to be
> carefully observed as showing that there is no remedy for correcting
> and purging out abuses, short of a return to God's pure institu-
> tion...Thus the Lord himself--when he was discoursing respecting
> marriage (Mt. 19:3), and the scribes brought forward customs and
> also the permission given by Moses--simply brings forward his
> Father's institution as being an inviolable law.  When we do this
> at the present day, the Papists cry out, that we are leaving
> nothing untouched...Mark then the nature of the controversy to this

day in reference to the Lord's Supper. Return then, to the original source. Thus, bidding adieu to human laws, the authority of
Christ will be maintained in its stability.[204]

The originality of Calvin's individualism rests on its new epistemology. By means of this epistemology he bridged the gap, created by
the *Devotio Moderna*, between knowledge and spirituality. The *Devotio
Moderna*, in its rejection of scholasticism, proposed a spirituality that
was anti-intellectual. Its writers made no attempt to introduce a
*sancta eruditio*. Calvin, on the other hand, did integrate knowledge and
spirituality. Like Erasmus and the other humanists, he linked the two
in a *pia doctrina*, a *docta pietas*.

In Calvin, theology and spirituality found their unity: revelation,
faith and doctrine, obedience and piety belong together. Calvin did not
admit a mystical theology that existed independent of knowledge and doctrine.[205] Piety became the criterion for judging doctrine; doctrine
that did not have as its purpose the spiritual progress of its hearers
was neither devout nor healthy.[206] At the same time, "there is no edification except there where there is doctrine."[207]

As we have seen, Calvin's spirituality differed radically from that
of the *Devotio Moderna*. Here we shall contend that the differences can
ultimately be traced to the new religious epistemology which he constructed.

## Notes

1. For an evaluation of Calvin's *De Clementia* and his *Psychopannychia*, see A. Ganoczy, *Le Jeune Calvin*, 57-74.

2. "Johannis Calvini Opera quae supersunt omnia" in G. Baum, E. Cunitz and E. Reus (eds.), *Corpus Reformatorum* (Braunschweig and Berlin, 1863). Hereafter OC.

3. OC, I, 9.

4. Preface to *Commentary on Psalms*. OC, 31, 11-35.

5. OC, I, 27.

6. *Ibid.*

7. *Ibid.*

8. *Ibid.*

9. OC, I, 28.

10. *Ibid.*

11. *Ibid.*

12. OC, I, 31.

13. OC, I, 30.

14. "Since the Church is the kingdom of Christ he rules only by his word." P. Barth, W. Niesel, D. Scheuner (eds.), *Ioannis Calvini Opera Selecta* (München, 1926-1962). Herafter OS. For above passage, cf. OS, I, 240.

15. Cf. OS, I, 25; I, 250; I, 234.

16. OS, L, 241.

17. OC, I, 51.

18. OC, I, 99.

19. "God has never manifested Himself to men except in His son who is His unique wisdom, light and truth." OC, I, 207.

20. OS, I, 41.

21. OC, I, 111.

22. OS, I, 101; 105; 108; 121; 145.

23. OS, I, 37.

24. OS, I, 109.

25. Cf. OS, I, 37; I, 23; I, 42.

26. OS, I, 45. Cf. Ganoczy, *Le Jeune Calvin*, 215, note 431.

27. "...neque in sacramentis maerere fiducia nostra debet, nec Dei gloria in ipsa transferri." OS, I, 21.

28. OS, I, 134, 152.

29. OS, I, 43; 102; 226.

30. OS, I, 21; 37.

31. OC, I, 248.

32. "...talem patrem grata pietate ardentique amore sic colamus, ut nos totos eius obsequio devoveamus." OC, I, 76.

33. OS, I, 247.

34. *Ibid.*

35. OS, I, 224.

36. OS, I, 108.

37. J. Olin (ed.), *John Calvin and Jacopo Sadoleto, A Reformation Debate* (New York, 1966) 75.

38. *Ibid.*, 83.

39. *Ibid.*, 61.

40. *Ibid.*, 84.

41. *Ibid.*, 58.

42. *Ibid.*, 59.

43. *Ibid.*, 64.
44. *Ibid.*, 68.
45. Cf. Ganoczy, *Le Jeune Calvin*, 216-220.
46. OC, I, 1123.
47. OC, I, 1124.
48. OC, I, 1125.
49. *Ibid.*
50. OC, I, 1126.
51. OC, I, 1127.
52. *Ibid.*
53. *Ibid.*
54. OC, I, 1128.
55. *Ibid.*
56. OC, I, 1132.
57. OC, I, 1145.
58. OC, I, 1146.
59. OC, I, 1147.
60. OC, I, 1151.
61. Cf. above, note 47.
62. *Inst.*, III, 16, 1. Eng. trans. H. Beveridge (London, 1845).
63. *Comm. in Gal.*, 2:20; OC, 50, 199.
64. *Inst.*, III, 11, 3.
65. *Comm. in Gal.*, 3:6; OC, 50, 204-205.
66. *Inst.*, III, 11, 11.
67. Cf. *Inst.*, III, 11, 2; 3, 9; 3, 14.
68. *Comm. in I Jn.*, 1:7; OC, 55, 305.
69. *Inst.*, III, 14, 11.
70. *Comm. Mal.*, 3:17; OC, 44, 484.
71. *Comm. I Cor.*, 1:8; OC, 49, 312.
72. *Comm. in Col.*, 1, 22; OC, 52, 90-91.
73. *Serm. on Gal.*, 5:14-18; OC, 51, 26.
74. *Comm. on Eph.*, 3:16; OC, 51, 186.
75. *Comm. on Jn.*, 17:17; OC, 47, 385.
76. *Serm. on Acts*, 1:1-4; OC, 48, 590.
77. OC, 55, 148.
78. *Inst.*, III, 1, 1.
79. *Inst.*, III, 1, 1; cf. III, 11, 10; IV, 15, 5; III, 13, 5; II, 3,
9; III, 6, 3; II, 13, 2; III, 2, 30.
80. Enter. Ce mot est de grand poids....Il ne signifie pas seulement conformité d'exemple, mais emporte une conjunction secrète, par
laquelle nous sommes tellement unis à luy (Christ) que nous donnant
vie par son Esprit il fait passer et comme descouler sa vertu en
nous....En cest *entement* spirituel non seulement nous tirons de
Christ vigueur, et comme une moelle de vie, mais nous passons de
nostre nature en la sienne.    *Comm. Rom.*, 7.5; OC, 49, 106-107.
81. *Inst.*, III, 2, 24.
82. *Inst.*, III, 11, 10.
83. *Inst.*, III, 1, 3.
84. *Inst.*, II, 12, 7; cf. II, 8, 18; IV, 12, 24; 19, 39.
85. OC, 46, 953.
86. *Serm. on I Sam.*, 2:27-36; OC, 29, 353.
87. "There is so great a unity between Christ and his members, that
the name of Christ sometimes includes the whole body." *Comm. Col.*, 1:24;
OC, 52, 93.

"Observe that the spiritual unity which we have with Christ belongs not merely to the soul, but also to the body, so that we are flesh of his flesh, etc. Otherwise, the hope of a resurrection were weak, if our connection *(coniunctio)* were not of that nature, full and complete." *Comm. I Cor.* 6:15; OC, 49, 398.

88. Karl Reuter clearly exaggerated when he wrote: "The concept of piety developed by Calvin is foreign to all mystical tendency; it leads only to a discipline." *Das Grundverständnis der Theologie Calvins* (Neukirchen, 1963) 99.

89. *Inst.*, III, 1, 3.

90. *Inst.*, IV, 17, 12.

91. F. Wendel writes, "He insists so strongly on this action of the Holy Spirit that one may justifiably wonder whether the Holy Spirit does not in his view occupy a position, in our relations with the Christ, analogous to that of Christ himself in his relation with the Father. In a good many passages, indeed, the Holy Spirit plays the part of an obligatory mediator between Christ and man, just as the Christ is the mediator between God and man. And in the same way Jesus Christ is the necessary instrument of redemption, so is the Holy Spirit the more or less necessary instrument by means of which this redemption reaches us, and justification and regeneration." *Calvin, The Origins and Development of His Religious Thought* (New York, 1963) 239.

92. *Inst.*, I, 13, 14.

93. *Comm. I Cor.*, 12, 5, 5; OC, 49, 498.

94. *Comm. I Cor.*, 1:2; OC, 99, 308.

95. *Comm. Hag.*, 1:14; OC, 44, 97.

96. *Inst.*, IV, 1, 2.

97. *Inst.*, II, 15, 2.

98. *Inst.*, IV, 1, 7.

99. *Comm. Amos*, 9:13; OC, 43, 172.

100. *Comm. Lk.,* 17, 20; OC, 45, 424-425.

101. *Comm. in Eph.*, 4:24; OC, 51, 208.

102. *Inst.*, III, 6, 3.

103. *Inst.*, I, 15, 4.

104. *Comm. Eph.*, 4:24; OC, 51, 208-209.

105. *Comm. Jn.*, 17:11; OC, 47, 382.

106. Cf. B. Milner, *Calvin's Doctrine of the Church* (Leiden, 1970).

107. *Inst.*, I, 3, 3.

108. *Comm. in Ps.*, 8:1; OC, 31, 88.

109. *Inst.*, I, 15, 4.

110. *Comm. Rom.*, 11:36; OC, 49, 232.

111. *Serm. on Job*, 5:17-18.

112. *Inst.*, II, 1, 4.

113. *Comm. Jer.*, 5:25; OC, 37, 635.

114. *Comm. Ps.*, 11:4; OC, 31, 123.

115. *Inst.*, I, 15, 4.

116. *Comm. Eph.*, 2:24; OC, 51, 208-209.

117. *Inst.*, I, 12, 1.

118. *Serm. on Job*, 22:23-30; OC, 34, 318-319.

119. OC, 1, 73.

120. *Inst.*, III, 7, 1; cf. III, 20, 43; 24, 14; 14, 17.

121. "In the Cross of Christ, as in a most splendid theatre, the incomparable goodness of God has been displayed before the whole world. Indeed, in all creatures both high and low the glory of God shines, but nowhere has it shone more illustriously than in the Cross, in which

there has taken place a wonderful change *(conversio)* of things, the con-
demnation of all men has been made manifest, sin has been abolished,
salvation has been given back to men, and in short the whole world has
been renewed and all things restored to order." *Comm. Jn.*, 13:31; OC,
47, 317.

122. Cf. *Comm. Jn.*, 11:33; OC, 47, 265.

123. "As musical sounds, though various and differing from each
other, are so far from being discordant that they produce sweet melody
and fine harmony; so in Christ there was a remarkable example of adap-
tation between the two wills, the will of God and the will of man, so
that they differed from each other without any conflict or opposition."
*Comm. Math.*

124. *Comm. Eph.*, 4:13; OC, 51, 200.

125. *Comm. Jn.*, 17:21; OC, 47, 387.

126. *Comm. I Jn.*, 2:6; OC, 55, 312.

127. *Comm. Rom.*, 5:12; OC, 49, 95.

128. Cf. note 21.

129. *Comm. Lk.*, 2:25; OC, 45, 89.

130. *Serm. on Job*, 34:4-10; OC, 35, 135.

131. *Inst.*, II, 8, 51.

132. *Serm. on Eph.*, 1:46; OC, 51, 270-271.

133. *Le Catéchisme de L'Eglise de Genève.* OC, 518.

134. *Comm. Lk.*, 1:75; OC, 45, 50.

135. "If righteousness be taken as a general term for uprightness,
holiness will be something higher, or that purity which lies in being
devoted to the service of God. I am rather inclined to consider holiness as referring to the first table and righteousness to the second
table...Plato lays down the distinction correctly, that holiness lies in
the worship of God, and that the other part, righteousness, bears a
reference to men..." *Comm. Eph.*, 4:24; OC, 51, 208.

136. *Comm. II Cor.*, 7:1; OC, 50, 79.

137. *Comm. I Cor.*, 1:2; OC, 49, 308.

138. *Comm. Jn.*, 4:23; OC, 47, 88-89.

139. *Ibid.*

140. *Comm. Ps.*, 45:10; OC, 31, 457.

141. *Comm. Jer.*, 7:21-24; OC, 37, 693.

142. On this theme, Erasmus had a great deal to say: "Corporal
works are not condemned; but invisible works are preferred. Visible
cult is not condemned; but God is not pleased except by an invisible
piety. God is spirit and he is moved by spirit." J. LeClercq (ed.),
*Erasmi Opera Omnia* (Leiden, 1703-1706) 5, 37.

143. *Comm. Jn.*, 4:23; OC, 47, 88-89.

144. *Ibid.*

145. *Inst.*, I, 2, 1. The relationship between knowledge of God and
*pietas* will be the object of the next chapter.

146. *Inst.*, I, 2, 1.

147. *Inst.*, I, 2, 2.

148. OS, I, 76.

149. OS, I, 59.

150. *Comm. Gal.*, 5:14; OC, 50, 250-251.

151. *Inst.*, II, 8, 53.

152. *Ibid.*

153. *Comm. Heb.*, 10:24; OC, 55, 132.

154. *Serm. on Job*, 4:1-6; OC, 33, 181.

155. *Comm. Ps.*, 27:4; OC, 31, 274.

156.  "For God wishes first of all for inward worship, and afterwards for outward profession. The principal altar for the worship of God ought to be situated in our minds, for God is worshipped spiritually by faith, prayer and other acts of piety. It is also necessary to add outward profession, not only that we may exercise ourselves in God's worship, but offer ourselves wholly to him, and bend before him both bodily and mentally." *Comm. Dan.*, 3:2-7; OC, 40, 624.

157.  *Serm. I Tim.*, 2:1-2; OC, 53, 125.

158.  *Inst.*, II, 20, 29.

159.  *Comm. Ps.*, 109:30; OC, 32, 158.

160.  *Inst.*, III, 20, 33.

161.  *Inst.*, III, 20, 28.

162.  *Comm. Ps.*, 55:17-18.

163.  *Comm. Ps.*, 25:8; OC, 31, 254.

164.  *Inst.*, III, 20, 13.

165.  *Serm. Deut.*, 7:6-7; OC, 26, 657.

166.  *Serm. Lk.*, 1:5-9; OC, 46, 18.

167.  *Serm. Deut.*, 7:5-8; OC, 26, 519.

168.  M. Godet, *La congrégation de Montaigu (1490-1580)* (Paris, 1912).

169.  Cf. Chap. 2, note 15.

170.  Cf. Chap. 2, note 21.

171.  *De Imitatione Christi*, I, 15; III, 2.

172.  M. Sandaert, "Le principe de l'ordination," *Collectanea O.C.R.* 8 (1946) 178-216.

173.  *Speculum Caritatis*, P.L. 21, 542 C.

174.  *Inst.*, I, 12, 1.

175.  *Inst.*, IV, 12, 21; III, 26, 23; I, 9, 9; II, 8, 33; I, 3, 2.

176.  *Comm. I Tim.*, 5:4; OC, 52, 306.

177.  OS, 3, 105.

178.  OS, I, 256.

179.  *Inst.*, II, 8, 8.

180.  OSS, I, 226.

181.  Here Calvin's doctrine should be compared to Tauler's. Tauler is adamant that the salvation of man can only be achieved through the work of God: "Moreover, salvation, to speak briefly, does not depend on any creature or on the creature's work, but it depends only on God and on his working." *Theologia deutsch*, Chap. 9. Cf. B. Hägglund, *The Background of Luther's Doctrine of Justification in Late Medieval Theology* (Philadelphia, 1971) 9.
Preparation for salvation is itself the work of the Holy Spirit: "Therefore where the Holy Spirit is to be received, he must create that receptivity for himself." *Sermons*, II, 138; Hägglund, *Background*, 9.
The understanding that all salvation is from God leads to an attitude of humility, and the acceptance of one's own nothingness. One cannot seek God's glory and at the same time attribute any glory to oneself. "Man should be utterly free from himself and that which is his, selfhood, self, I, me, mine, etc., so that he little seeks himself and what is his, and in all things acts as if he did not exist; he should think as little of himself as if he did not exist and as if another had done all his works." *Theologia deutsch*, Chap. 13; Hägglund, *Background*, 9.

182.  Calvin's understanding of abnegation and self-denial is based on a more radical understanding of the depravity of man than that found in the *De Imitatione Christi*. Calvin's concept corresponds more to that of Tauler. Cf. texts in Hägglund, *Background*, 9.

183.  *Inst.*, II, 8, 53.

184.  *Comm. Jn.*, 3:12; OC, 47, 61.

185.  *Inst.*, III, 7, 2.

186.  *Comm. Rom.*, 7:14; OC, 49, 128-129.

187.  For Calvin, see the following:  C. Hall, *With the Spirit's Sword* (Richmond, 1968); *Comm. II Cor.*, 10:4; OC, 50, 114-115; *Inst.* IV, 15, 11; III, 2, 17; 20, 46; 3, 10; II, 8, 30; III, 9, 1.

188.  Cf. *Comm. Math.*, 24:43; OC, 45, 678.

189.  *Inst.*, III, 9, 1.

190.  Y. Congar, *Lay People in the Church* (London, 1962) 384, 392ff.

191.  *Inst.*, III, 9, 1.

192.  *Inst.*, III, 9, 3.

193.  *Inst.*, III, 19, 1.

194.  *Inst.*, III, 19, 8.

195.  *Comm. Ps.*, 23:5-6; OC, 31, 242-243.

196.  *Inst.*, III, 10, 30.

197.  *Inst.*, IV, 12, 15; cf. IV, 12, 18; III, 3, 18.

198.  *Inst.*, III, 10, 3.

199.  G. Wingren, *Luther on Vocation* (Philadelphia, 1957).

200.  Cf. K. Dunkmann, *Die Lehre vom Beruf. Eine Einfuhrung in die Geschichte und Soziologie des Berufs* (Berlin, 1922) 80ff.

201.  *Inst.*, IV, 1, 4.

202.  *Comm. Ps.*, 20:10; OC, 31, 212.

203.  *Comm. I Cor.*, 12:12; OC, 49, 501.

204.  *Comm. I Cor.*, 11:22-23; OC, 49, 483-484.

205.  "...For the Christian there is no faith where there is no knowledge." *Comm. Gal.* 1:18; OC, 50, 173. "Faith does not lie in ignorance but in knowledge." *Inst.*, III, 2, 2. "That which can educate a man's piety demands a sane doctrine." *Comm. Tit.*, 2:1; OC, 52, 418.

206.  "Therefore one must always respect utility in doctrine; for that which does not help piety does not have any reason to exist." *Comm. Tit.*, 3:9; OC 52, 434. "Doctrine means the same as that which is according to piety. Unless a doctrine instructs us in the fear or cult of God, aedifies our faith, instructs us in patience, humility and all the works of charity, then it is not in accordance with piety." *Comm. I Tim.*, 6:3; OC, 52, 934.

207.  OS, II, 13.

CHAPTER V

*THE EPISTEMOLOGICAL RELEVANCE OF THE WORD AND THE SPIRIT*

*CALVIN'S CONTRIBUTION TO A NEW SPIRITUALITY*

A.  *Introduction*

The intellectualizing theology of the 16th century was in clear need
of a spirituality vigorous enough to question its essential structure.
The unfortunate dichotomy between them had resulted in a sterile theology and an undernourished spirituality.  The study of theology in many
instances had degenerated into dry, subtle and sometimes ridiculous dis-
cussions.  This precious intellectualism dissipated itself in pure speculation and lost contact with the primary sources of faith.

E. L. Surtz specifies four charges the humanists made against scholasticism:

> Its pretensions, its adulterations of the true teaching of Christ,
> its cold, barren intellectuality, and its inability to make the
> student and the teacher better men.[1]

The Christian Humanists constantly accused the scholastics of impiety.
What they objected to was not only the excessive veneration the scholastics had for Aristotle, but the very intentional direction and form of
scholasticism itself.  They considered scholasticism impious because, in
their eyes, it manipulated the Christian message in the same manner that
the profane sciences treated its objects: because it had lost all contact with the person of Christ and substituted a system of abstract concepts for a living relation with Christ in faith; because it refused to
acknowledge the mystery in faith and endlessly accumulated bits of knowledge about it instead.  The *Devotio Moderna* reacted against scholasticism and Nominalism by advocating an anti-intellectual spirituality.  As
a renewal of spirituality it made no attempt to integrate prayer and
theology and so suffered from the same lack of balance as the scholasticism it opposed.

Theology and spirituality are the products not only of faith but of
culture as well.  Cultural changes made scholasticism and Nominalism
irrelevant and demanded a new theological method able to answer basic
questions about the nature of Christian life in the world.  For it was
an increasingly independent public that theology had to address, and one

that was no longer satisfied with the monastic, hierarchical and author-
itarian spirituality of conventional Christendom.

A renewal took place within an epistemological shift. During the
Renaissance a considerable change in the understanding of truth took
place: attention shifted from conceptual truth to truth of subject, from
concept to word, from dialectics to rhetoric. The epistemological question of the relation of subjective perception to objective truth, and
the question of the certainty of our linguistic knowledge of God were
treated in the context of the Humanists' belief in language. They considered language the individual's expression of his inwardness and his
way of reaching the inwardness of other individuals.

The scholastic *adaequatio mentis ad rem* had stressed the conceptual
dimension of truth and inevitably tended to bridge the gap between concept and object by returning to the realm of the conceptual. This led to
an abstract theology. The Humanists bridged the gap between concept and
object through the word. The rhetorical relationship was interpersonal.
The Humanists' stand on eloquence stemmed from this almost unlimited
faith in the power of the word. The sweeping claims which the ancient
rhetoricians had made for the power of oratory were reiterated by the
Humanists for both the written and spoken word.[2] To Renaissance writers
eloquence meant, above all, persuasive power. The orator sought to teach
and to entertain his hearers; but his chief concern was to move them, to
persuade them. The Renaissance writers believed in the power speech had
to move the minds and hearts of men and therefore insisted on language
that was both beautiful and pleasing.

This orientation reintroduced into theology literary forms that were
utterly foreign to scholasticism: the letter, the sermon, the dialogue,
the autobiography. A tendency to introspection and a desire to stir
emotions, to move the reader or to persuade him, led religious writers
to experiment with poetry and eloquence as forms of theological expression. The *Summa* as a literary form had been characteristic of the cultural bent of the Middle Ages. These new literary expressions were indi-
cations of a profound difference in reality and understanding.

It was the concept of the Word of God which shaped and directed the
Christian Humanists' understanding of theology. The Italian Humanists,
moved by a concern for "practical wisdom," combined the tasks of the
theoretical theologian and the practical preacher in what they called

*theologia rhetorica* or *theologia poetica*.[3] One of the first statements
about a *theologia poetica* can be found in one of Petrarch's letters to
his brother. Poetics, he says, is not at all opposed to theology: the
scriptures themselves demonstrate by the language they use that theology
is poetry about God. Somewhat later, Coluccio Salutati developed an
epistemology which affirmed the necessity for poetic expressions of theological truths. In fact, according to Salutati theological truths
could only be expressed poetically. This poetic epistemology was an
attempt to bridge the gap between concept and word in our knowledge of
God; it confronted the problem of expressing the unknowable and the in-
expressible. I quote him at length since his  position is extremely
interesting.

> In origin, indeed, all writing and speech is intellectual and con-
> ceptual before it is vocal or public; from this it happens that
> nothing can be voiced which does not first exist in the mind.
> Whence it follows as a corollary that the names which we use can
> signify nothing at all except what is tied together by our intel-
> lect, and which indeed we express through the congruity of grammar,
> we prove by the force of logic, we persuade by flourishing of rhet-
> oric. When, however, we wish to speak about God, since we do not
> know him, lacking a concept, words also are lacking by which we
> could say something in the proper way concerning his indescribable
> majesty. If even the least could be said about it, it would not be
> entirely indescribable. Mortals wishing to meet that necessity are
> driven to think up another most excellent method of speaking inso-
> far as it can be done. However, this procedure could not belong to
> grammar, the function of which is to explain simple concepts simply,
> by simple names and words. And whereas men cannot see God in front
> of them, yet they see many of his effects, they are able to recog-
> nize him only from effects, that is, from behind. And they begin
> to speak of the manifestation of divinity as though it might be
> some man, since they have nothing more sublime than man, whom they
> know, and whom they understand by means of the senses whence our
> knowledge is moved. Therefore whatever we say about God is imag-
> ined and borrowed from us and our actions. As Cicero said, 'Homer
> imagined this and transferred human qualities to the gods.' Nor do
> we do this only when we speak of God, but also as our same Cicero
> said, 'They imagine it to be done with the shades of the underworld,
> which could not be brought to exist or be conceived without bodies.
> For they were unable to comprehend self-subsisting souls and sought
> some figure or shape for them.' From this, although it is self-
> evident, it is clear that not only when we speak of God but also
> when we talk about incorporeal beings we speak of them improperly
> and according to the outer shell and what we say is false. This
> mode of speaking is poetic carrying a falsity of appearance on the
> outside, but containing within the hidden truth. From this we can
> easily see that all transfers of meaning or metaphors, figures,
> tropes, metaplasms and allegories, as well as tropology and parables

peculiarly pertain to this faculty. Poetry should therefore be defined as that mode of speaking which understands both things and
words as something other than it shows them....Necessity invents
this mode, custom receives and extends it, not only when necessity
compels but also when beauty inspires....Do you not see the divine
literature in the entire holy scriptures consists entirely of this
kind of speaking and nothing else? For when we speak of God or
incorporeal creatures nothing is true according to the letter and
there is nothing under that falsity of skin but the truth.[4]

The purpose of *theologia poetica* was not primarily illumination, but
persuasion. Man by nature is volitional. Since rhetoric is only effective when it is affective, when it carries the conviction that the
speaker's feelings are genuine, rhetorical theology demanded a certain
disposition on the part of the theologian. Together with his knowledge
of divine realities, the theologian had to possess modesty, integrity of
life and true piety. These requirements are those of a preacher.

In this epistemological framework, the Humanists preferred a more
affective type of theology, one which could double as a spirituality.
The object of their theology was a personal Being who had a name. There
existed between Him and man concrete and loving relations. The consideration of this personal God produced certain definite reactions on the
part of man: these were veneration, love, and worship.

In his *Ratio Seu Methodus* Erasmus outlined the task of theologians as
one of convincing and exhorting.[5] Theology must seek Christ uniquely.
The theologian must have the necessary qualities to accomplish this
task: piety, purity, detachment, and humility. Theology must be a
nourishment for the soul.[6]

Later writers, such as the Spaniards Juan de Valdes and Ignatius of
Loyola, wrote about the knowledge of God in terms of feeling, of a *sentire*. According to Valdes, our knowledge of God belongs to the realm of
experience.

> Those regenerated by the Holy Spirit are endowed with natural in-
> stinct, experience, and science, and in addition with divine in-
> spiration and revelation...And I understand experience not only in
> natural and human things, as is the case with other men, but like-
> wise in spiritual and divine things...All men who are without the
> Holy Spirit are without experience in spiritual and divine things.[7]

Without experience, true knowledge remains inaccessible.[8] This experience is not without intensity of feeling. The experience of God is the
"tasting and feeling of God" *(conocer, gustar y sentir a Dios).*[9]

> Finally, when you shall feel and taste so much of the sweetness and love of Christ here in this life as to be felt and tasted, taking this taste and feeling for an earnest of what you will yet have to taste and feel for in the other life to which you will expect certainly to go, to rejoice perpetually with Christ, you will not hesitate to confess the life eternal.  And now, when you have within yourself such experience, yours will be a living and true faith, because you will have the experience of it within you.[10]

For Juan de Valdes, Christianity is not a matter of science but of experience.

> I have stated this for this reason:  that having regarded the matter of Christianity not as a science, but as an experience I have endeavored to make this truth intelligible to individuals by numerous illustrations.  But they are incapable of understanding these Christian truths who are inexperienced in Christian subjects.[11]

For de Valdes, knowledge of divine things without actual experience of them is impossible; apart from experience there is no religious life of any intensity.  The purely abstract possession of a religious truth he denied.  The only real possession of a religious truth is a vital one, and its effect is felt in the soul.

In Valdes' thinking, the experience that accompanied knowledge became the absolute criterion in measuring the objective content of Revelation.  Valdes' sole authority was the Holy Spirit - through this power believers were able to grasp the concepts in the mind of the biblical writer.  There was but one rule of faith:  the experience of justification and regeneration.

This rule applied to the scriptures as well, which of themselves were not the source of knowledge of God.  The illumination of the Spirit was necessary to re-create the original experience of the biblical writer.

> In the reading of the Holy Scriptures I understand that the pious Christian should fix his attention only upon the inner knowledge and feelings (conoscimenti e li sentimenti interiori) which God, by means of his Holy Spirit, shall give to him in his soul.  He, then, through these means shall go on experiencing the things of the Holy Spirit.  So that taking up a book of the Holy Scriptures, he may attempt to understand what has taken place in it.  And thus, let him think that he does not understand what he did not experience; and thinking this, if he shall desire to understand it, he will seek to experience it, and will not curiously seek to know how, or what, others have therein understood.[12]

For de Valdes the interior word of the Spirit replaced the exterior word.

So I learn from scripture and so I inwardly feel, and that to such
a degree that I might have ventured to confess it even without the
scriptures.[13]

In this context the Tradition of the Church does not hand on a personal experience but only a secondary apprehension.  Personal experience
becomes the interpretative norm for the Tradition of the Church.  According to Nieto, "Here we are very close to the Reformation principle of the
inner witness of the Holy Spirit as the only norm for biblical interpretation."[14]

Faith is based then neither on the authority of the Church nor on
Scripture which includes contradictions and confusion but on the experience of the Spirit.

I think that I should have felt less satisfaction and that the
Evangelists would have offended me more had they harmonized in
everything without the least discrepancy, than finding them to be
what I do find them, who are apparently discordant upon some things,
as well because I rejoice that my faith does not depend upon Scriptures - nor is it based upon them, but it depends upon inspirations
and experiences, and it is based upon them; just as was the faith
of the Samaritans, who, after having seen Christ and heard him
speak, believing by inspiration and by experience, told the woman
that they no longer believed because of her report, but from the
experience they had.[15]

At the very center of de Valdes' spirituality was a theory of religious certitude which superseded the medieval notion of *auctoritas* and
proclaimed the normative value of internal experience.  The self-knowledge
advocated by both the *Devotio Moderna* and Erasmus was conceived of by
Valdes as an experiential type of knowledge.

De Valdes' spirituality lacked an ecclesial perspective; it was not
really anti-ecclesiastical or anti-hierarchical, but a-ecclesiastical.
Here was a religion of the spirit, profoundly non-sacramental, relying
on the immediacy of inspiration of the inner life.

*Sentire* is also a key word in the spirituality of Ignatius of Loyola,
a contemporary of Calvin.[16]  For Ignatius the whole of spiritual experience unfolded in three different stages.  The first stage he expressed
by the word "to feel," *sentire*.  In this stage the individual experienced within himself an interior knowledge, consolation and divine inspiration, which had its cause and origin not in him, but in the work of
the Holy Spirit.  The second stage consisted in "discernment" through
reflection, and the third stage was marked by the "confirmation," a

supreme gift from God which guaranteed the decision taken and gave the
soul certitude and the life it needed.  In all these stages Ignatius was
speaking in terms of an interior experience, of a divine action felt and
accepted.  We must "know," *sentire*, the way God acts in us so that we
may become faithful to what he wishes to make known to us.  This situation is described in one of Ignatius' letters:

> It happens sometimes that the Lord himself moves our souls and
> forces us as it were to this or that particular action by leaving
> our souls wide open.  This means that he begins to speak in the
> very depths of our being, without any clamor of words, he enrap-
> tures the soul completely into his love and bestows upon us an
> awareness of himself so that even if we wished we should be unable
> to resist.[17]

In opening himself to the influence of the Spirit, man is able to feel
the presence of God, to experience his touch and sense the immediacy of
his influence.  Such an experience can ultimately be expressed only
with the aid of images borrowed from the realm of sense perception.
This type of knowledge must be experienced; it cannot be thought out.

> We have however been speaking of things which it is impossible to
> render in words as they really are, or at least not without giving
> a very lengthy and detailed account.  And even then these would
> still remain matters which it is better to feel inwardly for one-
> self than to impart outwardly to others.[18]

"I beheld, sensed within myself and penetrated in spirit all the mysteries of the Christian faith."[19]

Ignatius was conscious that this experiential knowledge, this *sentire*,
was "from above" *(de arriba)*; in his own mind he measured the knowledge
gained in the course of laborious theological study against the simplicity and depth of his inward experience.  He realized that his God-given
experience and knowledge was personal, that his ability to "feel God"
was at the center of his personal life and was therefore not communal.
He understood that such personal experience could not be easily communicated.

With Juan de Valdes and Ignatius of Loyola, the experiential nature
of knowledge was underlined.  At the same time, the Humanists' concept
of theology and piety modified the anti-theological bias piety had
acquired from the *Devotio Moderna*.  The Humanists held that personal
appropriation  of theological knowledge is essential.  God cannot be
apprehended simply as an object.  The Humanists appealed to the words of

St. John: "If any man do the Father's will, he shall have knowledge of doctrine." (John, 7, 17) There can be no separation between thought and action. While insisting on the distinction between religious knowledge and other kinds of knowledge, the Humanists affirmed the place of reason in matters of religion. But in the limited context of their epistemology, they were unable to deal satisfactorily with two important problems: the individual and private nature of religious knowledge and its relationship to the authority of the Church and the Nominalists' denial of the possibility of intuitive knowledge of God.

The Humanists vested ultimate authority in theology and spirituality in the Church. It was in the Church that God's word was to be found. They considered the Church the meeting place of the Divine and the human. The epistemological role of the Church in the theological process the Humanists left untouched. Therefore, while the Church had lost its predominant role in spirituality and piety due to the influence of the religious movements of the 15th and 16th centuries, it retained it in the realm of doctrine. Erasmus declared himself willing to subject his views to the decision of the Church whether or not he understood her prescriptions. The uniqueness of the word of God, advocated by Lefèvre d'Etaples, was in the end only a relative uniqueness, since all words about God are mediated by the Church and in a real sense are the Church's words. The Church functioned as the mediator and custodian of divine revelation, and ultimately as the judge of every experience of God. Often this role of the Church in theology led to the canonization of a particular ecclesiastical power group's ideology. At such times, the Church was unable truly to support a personal spirituality. A Church-mediated theology tends to over-estimate the importance of conceptual and verbal expression to the detriment of the personal experience of God. The Bible, interpreted in and by the Church, must remain the criterion for evaluating the authenticity of all religious experiences.

The epistemology of the Humanists was unable to successfully counter the Nominalists' denial of the possibility of an intuitive knowledge of God.

Occam had held that there were two different types of knowledge: intuitive and abstracted. Intuitive knowledge involves direct awareness of an object either in the mind or in reality. The essence of intuitive

knowledge is that it provides a demonstration of a thing in itself; it
is the awareness of something as opposed to the understanding or judgment of it.  Abstracted knowledge is not in itself evident knowledge,
but is the mind's response to what it has experienced through the senses.
Abstracted knowledge presupposes intuitive knowledge, which is the foundation of all knowledge.[20]  Abstracted knowledge is not concerned with
demonstration but with understanding.[21]

These were the affirmations of an epistemology which refused to grant
certainty to what lay beyond experience.  Since reason cannot operate
beyond the terrain of natural experience, Occam reduced strict knowledge
to that which was individually verifiable through experience.

All this he applied to the knowledge of God.  God cannot be known by
us at all.  We must be satisfied with what faith and revelation tell us.
Concerning those things which are to be believed, *credibilia*, there is
no knowledge possible:  for the objects of belief are neither self-
evident nor derived from natural experience.  All evident, natural knowledge must meet one of these two conditions.[22]

This sharp bifurcation between intuitive and abstracted knowledge
affected the understanding of the relation between faith and reason.
Man was thrown back upon the scriptures which he received through the
tradition of the Church.  The divine authority of the Church provided
the one foundation of religious knowledge.

B.  *The Epistemology of John Major (1470-1540)*

Occam's position on the possibility and nature of our knowledge of
God was accepted by most Nominalists.  But in the early part of the 16th
century John Major, a Nominalist himself, elaborated a different theory
of the knowledge of God.[23]  Major's early works on logic, in the Occamist tradition, made him the outstanding teacher of philosophy in Paris.[24]
In theology and philosophy Major was an eclectic; in logic he sought to
reconcile nominalism and realism.[25]  Most of Major's work was concerned
with establishing the distinctions between intuitive knowledge and
abstractive knowledge, the first intention and the second intention,
significations and suppositions.  Major, more than the Occamists, tended
to relate knowledge to concrete experience; his favorite expressions are
*experientia docet, experientia teste*.[26]  Major attributed more importance in the act of perception to the objective reality than to what was

in the mind. In his view, knowledge *(notitia)* was turned toward the external authority *(ad rem ad extra)*. Both intuitive and abstractive knowledge had the same object;[27] they terminated not at the concept but the reality.[28] He did not consider images as objects terminating our perceptions but as the means through which we attain reality.[29] Ultimately, Major arrived at a position that was more realist than that of Thomas Aquinas.[30] Thought terminates, through all intermediate representations, in objective realities.

Following the tradition of Scotus and others, Major affirmed that knowledge was of the singular and not of the universal.[31] In facing the fundamental problem of the relation between language and being, between propositions and existing reality, Major affirmed a "natural" link joining language and the realities it signified.[32] Language, then, does not signify concepts but objective reality.[33]

In accordance with the position of Occam, Major defined intuitive knowledge as the direct knowledge of an actually present object, naturally caused by that object and not by another. This knowledge involved what Major called an *assensus causalis*.[34] All intuitive knowledge is dependent upon the actual presence of its object *(notitia intuitiva naturaliter esse nequit sine praesentia sui objecti)*.[35] Intuitive knowledge is a knowledge that is gained experimentally. In abstractive knowledge, on the other hand, there is no immediate experience of the known objective. For Major, all questions concerning knowledge of God hinged on the distinction between intuitive and abstractive knowledge. Is God known by man directly through immediate apprehension, or is he known indirectly through propositions? Certainly there is no naturally evident knowledge of God.[36]

Notwithstanding this affirmation, Major maintained that God could make himself known to man intuitively through his *potentia absoluta*.[37] God can will to create in us an intuitive knowledge of himself without the evident experience of the object.[38] He is known as a voluntary object, through a real activity.

God's essence is not distinguishable from his existence.[39] But God never acts toward us through necessity but freely through an act of his will.[40] God acts upon us in a personal way and thus we can know him personally *(personaliter)* through the effects of his supernatural causality.[41]

The knowledge of God is contingent upon his will. Our evidence for this knowledge is not the evidence of a natural object; it is the evidence of an absolute personal reality. The absoluteness of God is self-authenticating. At the same time, it is the ground of any genuine knowledge of him.

Thus Major concluded that even in this life intuitive knowledge of God is possible, for God speaks to us and manifests the *species audibilis*. So it may be said that our knowledge of God comes from hearing.[42] This is also true of ordinary intuitive knowledge, which relies on the experience of hearing. We receive this particular intuitive knowledge[43] of God by listening to his word.[44]  It can therefore be characterized as intuitive auditive knowledge *(intuitiva auditio)*.

The images and ideas which make up our intuitive auditive knowledge have a real relation to the divine being. Languages is not merely a means of knowledge but points to the reality known. Major expresses this in the distinctions he draws between *cognitio activa* and *cognitio factiva*. True knowledge of God is *cognitio factiva*: We do not know God through our own linguistic concepts but through his own words. The words or images God has chosen have a signitive relation to divine truth. Their function is ostensive and persuasive.

Major understood theology as a science possessing its own first principles. These were to be found in holy scripture, for Major the primary resource of theology.[45]  From scriptural affirmations Major deduced other truths through logic.[46]  In his method, the theological process begins with a systematic study of scripture, and the organization of the different scriptural affirmations into a logical whole.[47]  Theology is essentially a practical knowledge based on the scripture which leads to love *(ad caritatem)*.[48]

Major based his scriptural commentaries on Origen and St. Jerome. He avoided Nicholas of Lyre. Major found in the person of Christ the key to the understanding of scripture.[49] For Christ is the purpose *(scopus)* of all the scriptures; their harmony and coherence are from him.[50]

The incarnation of Christ serves as a model for the interpretation of scripture. Christ in his humanity and bodiliness speaks to us in bodily terms; but we must understand him spiritually. Through his humanity we must be led to his divinity.[51] The literal sense of the scriptures embodies a spiritual sense. This sense Major termed epistemological.[52]

## C. *John Calvin's Epistemology: Its Sources*

Within this context of humanism, and nominalism, as mediated by John Major, John Calvin elaborated his own epistemology. To the epistemological question of our knowledge of God he proposed a solution involving an intuitive knowledge of God in His Word and through His Spirit.[53] This knowledge of God can be described in terms of an intuitive-auditive knowledge. Calvin's formula for epistemological problems was set out in his theory of the relationship between the Word and the Spirit. The Word supplies the objective factors for the knowledge of God; the Spirit, the subjective factor. True knowledge of God is communicated through a conjoined divine action, objective and subjective. The elements of Calvin's epistemology are found in his definition of faith.

> We now see in what way faith is by hearing, and yet it derives its certainty from the zeal and earnest of the Spirit. Those who do not sufficiently know the darkness of human minds imagine faith is formed naturally by hearing and preaching alone; and there are many fanatics who disdain the outward preaching, and talk in lofty terms about secret revelations and inspirations. But we see how Christ joins these things together, and, therefore, though there is no faith until the Spirit of God seals our minds and hearts, still we must not go to seek visions or oracles in the clouds, but the word, which is near us, in our mouth and heart (Rom. 10:8), must keep all our senses bound and fixed in itself.[54]

The conjunction of the Word and Spirit result in what can be described as an auditive-intuitive knowledge, simultaneously individual and immediate.

Different factors contributed to the elaboration of Calvin's epistemology. His dissatisfaction with scholastic theology[55] and its bifurcation of the intellectual life led him to a humanistic understanding of *pietas* as *sapientia*, as *sancta eruditio*.[56] Calvin understood theological knowledge as a vital and experiential kind of knowledge firmly rooted in the Word of God. His spirituality and theology was influenced to a large extent by his understanding of the Word of God.

This primacy of the Word was also a central issue in Luther's thinking. One of the words most frequently used by Luther was "listening." He considered the Word of God as the soil and atmosphere in which life grows. Luther held that God himself speaks and hears in man.[57] Man already lives in a kingdom of hearing,[58] for the whole of deity lives in the word.[59] All of creation is divine Word. "The created world is made

through the uncreated Word; for what is all of creation but the Word of
God."[60] Nothing can stand against the divine Word; no one can control
it, or limit its channel. In his reply to Erasmus, Luther affirmed that
the divine Word cannot be bound.

> And who has given you the power or committed to you the right to
> bind Christian doctrine to places, persons, times, and causes, when
> Christ wishes it to be proclaimed and to rule most freely through-
> out the world? The word of God is not bound, says Paul, and is
> Erasmus now to bind it? Nor did God give us the word that it
> should be had with respect to places, persons or times. As Christ
> says, 'Go into all the world,' not 'Go into this place and not into
> that' as Erasmus says.[61]

This dynamic Word of God was the norm of the Reformation. The visible
Church could only be healed by faithful obedience to the authority of
the Word of God.

"The Church is born," Luther wrote in 1520, "through faith in the
Word of Promise. For the Word of God is incomparably above the Church."[62]
No expression came more readily to Calvin than *Verbum Dei, la Parole de
Dieu*. The phrase echoes through all his writings.[63]

The depth and range of Calvin's understanding of the Word of God is
revealed to us in the following passage from the *Institutes*:

> Certainly when God's Word is set before us in Scripture it would be
> the height of absurdity to imagine a merely fleeting and vanishing
> utterance, which, cast forth into the air, projects itself outside
> of God. Rather 'Word' means the everlasting wisdom, residing in
> God, from which both all oracles and all prophecies go forth. For
> as Peter testifies, the ancient prophets spoke by the Spirit of
> Christ just as much as the Apostles did, and all who thereafter
> ministered the heavenly doctrine. Indeed, because Christ had not
> yet been manifested, it is necessary to understand the Word as
> begotten of the Father before time.[64]

God by his word was the creator of the world. Every divinely uttered
revelation is rightly designated as a "Word of God"; the substantial
Word, the wellspring of all revelations, is properly given a title above
all the rest. Subject to no variety, the Word abides everlastingly one
and the same with God, and is God. The Word of God is a source of power
and authority. Calvin explains this in his *Instruction in Faith*:

> But let us remember that this power (which in the Scripture is
> attributed to pastors) is wholly contained in and limited to the
> ministry of the word. For Christ has not given this power properly
> to these men, but to his word of which he has made these men minis-
> ters. Hence, let pastors boldly dare all things by the word of God,

of which they have been constituted dispensators; let them con-
strain all the power, glory and haughtiness of the world to make
room for and to obey the majesty of that word; let them by means of
that word command all from the greatest to the smallest; let them
edify the house of Christ; let them demolish the reign of Satan...
but all through and within the word of God.  Pastors who substitute
their own fancies for the word are to be chased away as wolves.
For Christ has commanded us to listen only to those who teach us
that which they have taken from his word.[65]

For Calvin, the Word of God was an event, an intervention of God in
one's life, spoken not merely to enlighten by its teachings, but to
transform by its creative power.[66]

According to Calvin, God manifests himself only through his Word:

In this, therefore, whether God uses the agency of man or works
immediately by his own power, it is always by his word that he
manifests himself to those whom he designs to draw to himself.[67]

In his commentary on the First chapter of St. John's gospel, Calvin outlined his understanding of the nature of the Word of God.  He translated
"the Word" as "speech," because he feared that the Greek word *logos*

does not apply so well.  It means, no doubt, definition, and reasoning, and calculation; but I am unwilling to carry the abstruse-
ness of philosophy beyond the measure of my faith.[68]

The Word of God is dynamic; it cannot be considered only as "definition."
The second person of the Trinity is the Speech of God.[69]  Here God reveals himself to man and manifests his will.

He obeys God who, being instructed in his will, hastens in the direction in which God calls him.  But how are we so instructed unless by his word?  The will declared by his word is, therefore,
that which we must keep in view in acting.[70]

This Word of God has the power to effect fully what it intends.

And he is to so rule as to smite the whole earth with the mere rod
of his mouth and break them in pieces like a potter's vessel.[71]

For Calvin, the Word "is the first basis whereby faith is supported
and sustained."[72]  The word that confirms faith has an objectivity all
its own.

I only contend that so long as they insist on the word of God, they
are never so caught as to be led away to destruction, while their
conviction of the truth of the word of God is so clear and certain
that it cannot be overthrown by either man or angels.[73]

Because of the value which Calvin attributed to the Word in the

process of faith, it would be difficult to overestimate the importance
preaching had for him.  For by the preaching of the Word "God begets and
multiplies his church and this church maintains the truth and transmits
it to posterity."[74]

With his doctrine of the Word of God, Calvin put himself in the tradition of the Humanists who had advocated a *theologia rhetorica*.  This
theology could not accommodate the type of experiential and direct knowledge of God that Juan de Valdes and St. Ignatius had described in terms
of *sentire*.  The *theologia rhetorica* lacked a specific doctrine of the
Holy Spirit.  In the *Enchiridion* of Erasmus, the Spirit was conspicu-
ously absent.  The Holy Spirit was understood in its opposition to the
flesh, to the outward and external.  It had no place in the question of
the knowledge of God.

In Calvin we have a vibrant doctrine of the Holy Spirit, which he received in great part from Bucer.[75]  According to Calvin, the Holy Spirit
produces a new spiritual sense *(sensus)* within man.  This sense, which
operates through a spiritual intuition or intuitive perception, leads
the soul to a certainty surpassing all human judgment.[76]  The Holy
Spirit by its action illuminates the soul in such a way that it can perceive the truth of the word revealed in the scriptures.[77]

> For the scriptures exhibit pure evidence of its truth, as white and
> black can do of their color, and sweet and bitter things of their
> taste...[78]

All we need is a sense to discern and be convinced of its divine quality,
a sense that convinces us with the same immediacy we have from the perception of light and darkness.[79]  Calvin used the words *persuasio, notitia, sensus*, to describe the nature and the result of this perception.

> It is, therefore, such a persuasion as requires no reason; such a
> knowledge as is supported by the highest reasons and in which the
> mind rests with greater security and constancy than in any reason;
> in fine, such a sense as cannot be produced but by revelation from
> heaven.[80]

The Holy Spirit creates in man a sense of the divine that produces understanding and a conviction characterized by immediacy and finality:  in
other words, a spiritual discernment.

Calvin conceded that knowledge of this sort is beyond rational comprehension.  Believers "are rather confirmed by the persuasion of divine
truth than by rational demonstrations."[81]  With *notitia, persuasio* was a

basic element in Calvin's doctrine of the knowledge of God. This is
clearly expressed in his commentary on Ephesians:

> I answer, the effect of the spirit on faith is two-fold even as
> faith is made up of two principal parts. For he both illuminates
> the intellect *(mentes)* and confirms the mind. The beginning of
> faith is knowledge; the consummation of faith is a fixed and steady
> persuasion which admits of no opposing doubtings.[82]

In the *Geneva Catechisms* of 1542 Calvin affirmed,

> The Holy Spirit by his illumination makes us capable of understand-
> ing those things which otherwise greatly exceed our ability, in-
> forms us to a steadfast persuasion by sealing the promises of sal-
> vation in our heart.[83]

In his *Reply to Sadoleto*, Calvin maintained the difference between
knowledge received from God and knowledge received from human sources:

> So true it is that Christian faith must not be founded on human
> testimony, not propped up by doubtful opinion, not reclined on
> human authority but engraven on our hearts by the finger of the
> living God, so as not to be obliterated by any coloring of error.
> There is nothing of Christ, then, in him who does not hold the ele-
> mentary principle, that it is God alone who enlightens our minds to
> perceive his truth, who by his Spirit seals it in our hearts, and
> by his sure attestation to it confirms our conscience. This is, if
> I may so express it, that full and firm assurance commended by
> Paul, and which, as it leaves no room for doubts, so not only does
> it not hesitate and waver among human arguments as to which party it
> ought to adhere, but maintains its consistency to the whole world,
> though the whole world should oppose.[84]

The assurance we have that God is speaking to us is from the Spirit.

> Enlightened by him, we no longer believe, either on our own judgment
> or that of others, that the scriptures are from God; but in a way
> superior to human judgment, feel perfectly assured, as much so as
> if we beheld the divine image visibly impressed on it, that it came
> to us by the instrumentality of men, from the very mouth of God.[85]

The knowledge of God gained through the workings of the word and the
Holy Spirit is simultaneously characterized both by immediacy and certitude. While Calvin did speak of evidence for this knowledge, it is
clear that he was referring to self-evidence, self-authentication. This
evidence derives immediately from the impact of God's being, through the
Holy Spirit. We know the truth through the truth in accordance with
God's own witness to himself.[86]

> The true conviction which believers have of the word of God, of
> their own salvation, and of religion in general, does not spring

from the judgment of the flesh, or from human philosophical argument, but from the sealing of the Spirit; which imparts to their conscience such certainty as to remove all doubts.[87]

Calvin describes our certitude of the knowledge of God in very strong terms.

> Two different things Paul intends to teach, first that the doctrine of the gospel cannot be understood otherwise than by the testimony of the Holy Spirit; and secondly that those who have a testimony of this nature from the Holy Spirit have an assurance as firm and solid, as if they felt with their hands what they believe, for the Spirit is a faithful and indubitable witness...for nothing that is in God escapes notice of the Spirit of God.[88]

The knowledge of God possessed through the gift of the Holy Spirit is certain and complete. "The certainty which it requires must be full and decisive as is usual in matters ascertained and proved."[89]  It is a knowledge in "which the mind rests more firmly and securely than in any vision."[90]

Real certainty is possible for the believer. "We have not an uncertain God of whom we have created a confused and indistinct apprehension but one of whom we have a true and solid knowledge."[91]

The Spirit leads us to the knowledge of God more through persuasion than through cognition.

> When we call it knowledge (cognitionem) we intend not such a comprehension (comprehensionem) as men commonly have of those things which fall under the notice of their senses.  For it is so superior that the human mind must succeed and rise above itself in order to attain to it.  Nor does the mind which attains it comprehend what it perceives (sentit), but being persuaded of that which it cannot comprehend it understands more by the certainty of the persuasion than it would comprehend of any human object by the exercise of its natural capacity.[92]

Such knowledge is not the product of sense perception.  To attain to it "the mind must rise above itself."  And even then it does not comprehend but is persuaded beyond its comprehension.

> And certainly they do know (scire), but they are more confirmed by a persuasion of the divine veracity than taught by demonstration of reason.[93]

Through the testimonium internum the Holy Spirit witnesses to the knowledge of God.  This evidence lies within the realm of what may properly be called religious experience.  Calvin described this experience through his use of the word sentir, to feel.

John then takes this principle for granted, that the knowledge of God is efficacious. He then concludes that they by no means know God who keep not his precepts and commandments. Plato, though groping in darkness, yet denied that the *beautiful* which he imagined could not be known without filling man with the admiration of itself; so he says in his *Phaedrus* and in other places. How then is it possible for you to know God and to be moved by no *feeling*? Nor does it indeed proceed only from God's nature, that to know him is immediately to love him. But the Spirit also illuminates our minds, inspires our hearts with a *feeling* conformable to our knowledge. At the same time the knowledge of God leads us to fear him and to love him. For we cannot know him as Lord and Father as he shows himself without being dutiful children and obedient servants. In short, the doctrine of the gospel is a lively mirror in which we contemplate the image of God and are transformed into the same as Paul teaches us in II Corinthians 3:18. Where, therefore, there is no pure conscience, nothing can be there but an empty phantom of knowledge.[94]

Speaking of the work of the Holy Spirit in man, Calvin wrote,

In like manner, by means of him we become partakers of the divine nature, so as in a moment to feel *(sentir)* its quickening energy within us.[95]

Calvin described the same experience even more vividly:

For the pious soul has the best view of God and may almost be said to handle him, for it feels that it is quickened, enlightened, saved, justified, and sanctified by him.[96]

To "feel" *(sentir)* the presence and action of God is an expression often used by Calvin. The believer feels the majesty of God,[97] the divinity of God,[98] the action of God,[99] his fatherhood[100] and his presence.[101] The Holy Spirit has a central role in our knowledge of God through the *testimonium internum (Spiritus Sancti)* which it imparts. Calvin described the nature and mode of operation of this *testimonium* as "secret,"[102] "internal,"[103] "inward."[104] The *testimonium* is an inward teaching of the Holy Spirit which produces a certain and true knowledge of God. It is a persuasion which does not require reasons, a state of conviction not induced by argument but by direct perception. This *testimonium* is a divinely ordered insight place within the human mind. Calvin compared it to a seal.

Having denominated the gospel the word of truth, I will not prove it by the authority of men; for you have the testimony of the Spirit of God himself, who sealed the truth of it in our hearts.[105]

This *testimonium* is at the same time a witness, because it enables us to

know the truth through evidence we cannot obtain by our own investigations.

With his doctrine of the *testimonium Spiritus Sancti*, Calvin maintained that the only vitalizing knowledge of God a man can have is communicated to him through the working of the Spirit in his heart.    This
doctrine of the Spirit represented Calvin's affirmation of a real intuitive, and in some degree experiential, knowledge of God.[106]

D.  *Calvin's Epistemology:  The Correlation of the Word and the Holy*
    *Spirit*

Although Calvin stressed the importance of the Spirit (much more than
Luther did), he did not separate it from the word.  Calvin was neither
an *illuminatus* nor an "enthusiast."  He did not see the Spirit functioning as the revealer of new truths - no new revelation was to be expected.

> There are many fanatics who disdain the outward preaching and talk
> in lofty terms about secret revelations.  But we see how Christ
> joined these two things together; and therefore, though there is no
> faith until the Spirit of God seals our minds and hearts, still we
> must not go to seek visions or oracles in the clouds; but the
> word...must keep all our senses bound and fixed on itself.[107]

The work of the Spirit is not to supplement the revelation made in
scripture, nor to supersede it, but to authenticate it.

The Spirit and the Word are correlated reciprocally.  One cannot
separate the Spirit from word or word from Spirit.

> The word itself has not much certainty with us unless confirmed by
> the testimony of the Spirit.  For the Lord has joined together by a
> kind of mutual connection the certainty of his word and Spirit so
> that our minds are possessed of a genuine reverence for the word
> when the Spirit shines upon it enabling us to behold the face of
> God; and on the other hand we embrace his Spirit without fear of
> illusion when we recognize him in his image, that is in the word.[108]

The word of God has no efficacy unless the Holy Spirit is at work in man,
creating faith and opening his mind to receive the word.

> His (Christ's) preaching accomplishes nothing unless the Spirit,
> the inner teacher, open up the way to the mind.  Therefore none
> come to him but who have heard and learned from the Father.  And
> what is the nature of this hearing and learning?  It is when the
> Spirit by a wonderful special power forms the ears to hear and the
> mind to understand...we must understand therefore that no one can
> enter the kingdom of God except he whose mind has been renewed by
> the illumination of the Holy Spirit.[109]

In his commentary on Ezekiel, Calvin explained in detail the interrelationship between word and Spirit.

> The work of the Spirit, then, is joined with the word of God. But a distinction is made that we may know that the external word is of no avail by itself, unless animated by the power of the Spirit... We hold, therefore, that when God speaks he adds the efficacy of his Spirit, since his word without it would be fruitless; and yet the word is effectual because the instrument ought to be united with the author of the action.[110]

Without the Spirit of discernment the word would lead to pure positivism or legalism.

> But it may be asked, whence have we this discernment? They who answer, that the word of God is the rule by which everything that men bring forward ought to be tried, say something, but not the whole. I grant that doctrines ought to be tested by God's word; but unless the Spirit of wisdom *(Spiritus prudentiae)* is present, to have God's word in our hands will avail little or nothing, for its meaning will not appear to us...That we may be fit judges, we must necessarily be guided by the Spirit of discernment...But the Spirit will only so guide us to a right discrimination when we render all our thoughts subject to God's word.[111]

Calvin warned constantly against a tendency to deify the external word *(verbum externum)*.[112] Outward preaching is of no avail to men without the Spirit.

> You must not boast therefore of the outward preaching of the word; for it will be of no avail unless it produce its fruit by enlightening our minds.[113]

The Spirit must work within the preacher and the hearer.[114] It is through this work that the word reaches the heart of man.[115] The act of faith is grounded in the illumination of the Holy Spirit.[116] By correlating the doctrines of the Holy Spirit and the word Calvin sought to avoid both the exaggeration of the enthusiasts and the institutional claims of the Papists.

> For when they boast extravagantly of the Spirit, the tendency certainly is to sink and bury the word of God, that they may make room for their own falsehoods. And you, Sadoleto, by stumbling on the very threshold, have paid the penalty to that affront which you offered to the Holy Spirit when you separated him from the word. For, as if those who seek the word of God were standing where two ways meet destitute of any certain sign, you are forced to introduce them as hesitating whether it be more expedient to follow the authority of the church or to listen to those whom you call the inventors of new dogmas. Learn, then, by your own experience that

it is no less unreasonable to boast of the Spirit without the word
that it would be absurd to bring forward the word itself without
the Spirit.[117]

True knowledge of God is communicated through a concerted divine
action of the Word and the Spirit.  This action can thus be considered
both objective and subjective.  Calvin described two distinguishable
steps in our knowledge of God.

> God has therefore two ways of teaching; for first, he sounds in our
> ears by the mouth of men, and secondly he addresses us inwardly by
> the Spirit.[118]

The witness of the Spirit is presented by Calvin as an illumination of
the mind by which man sees that which he could not see or sees by a
means he did not know.  Through the Spirit's witness, man can "see" the
divinity already present in the word.  The efficient power of the word
does not reside in the printed words but in man's act of will and work
of the Holy Spirit.

> At the same time the prophet teaches that nothing was accomplished
> by this voice (the scripture) till the Spirit was added.  God in-
> deed worked efficiently by his own word, but we must hold that his
> efficacy is not contained in the words themselves but proceeds from
> the secret instinct of the Spirit.[119]

Both sources of man's knowledge of God demonstrate its revelatory
nature.  Dowey affirms:  "Calvin's thought has its whole existence
within the realm of God as revealer and man as knower."[120]  True and saving knowledge of God, since the Fall, can only be had through Revelation.[121]  In harmony with the Old Testament, Calvin links the revelation
of God's name with the manifestation of his power.  The knowledge of God
which we have through the revelation of his name is a knowledge given
through God's work and properties.  The name of God is

> to be understood as the knowledge of him insofar as he makes him-
> self known to us, for I do not approve of the subtle speculations
> of those who think the name of God means nothing else but God him-
> self.  It ought rather to be referred to the works and properties
> by which he is known, than to his essence.[122]

Commenting on the words, "I am Yahweh, and there is no savior besides
me," Calvin explains that the second clause is added..."that we may not
be surprised that his eternal essence only is here exhibited, but also
his power and goodness which he constantly exercises toward us and by

which he abundantly reveals himself."[123]   Calvin makes the same point in

another text:

> When the prophet speaks of the strength and power of God he does
> not mean power which is unemployed, but that which is effectual and
> actual, which is actually exerted on us and which conducts to the
> end what he has begun.[124]

The kind of knowledge of God one gains through the revelation of his

power in actions and deeds is experiential.

> We are invited to a knowledge of God, not such as, content with
> every speculation, merely flutters in the brain, but such as will
> be solid and fruitful, if rightly received and rooted in our lives.
> For the Lord is manifested by his works and properties.  When we
> feel their efficacy within us and enjoy their benefits, the knowl-
> edge must impress us more vividly than if we imagined a God from
> whom nothing penetrated to our feelings.[125]

God is a personal being who speaks to man personally in his works and

effects.  Man's listening is experiential because God's word is in no

way divorced from his deeds and actions.

> He calls God true, not only because he is ready to stand faithfully
> by his promises, but also because whatsoever he says in words he
> fulfills in deeds; for he so speaks that his command immediately
> becomes his act.[126]

God's power is contained in his word quite apart from the receptive

hearing:

> Though the word of God does not always exert its power on man, yet
> it is in a manner included in itself, as though he had said, 'If
> anyone thinks that the air is beaten by an empty sound when the
> word of God is preached he is greatly mistaken, for it is a living
> thing and full of hidden power which leaves nothing in man un-
> touched.'[127]

God is a completely voluntary object of our knowledge.  To know him is

possible only if he wills it in manifesting himself through a free in-

tervention on his part.  A double movement of will is involved in com-

municating this knowledge on God's part in his self-manifestation and on

man's part in his response.  Calvin described man's response as obedi-

ence, *aptitudo obedientiae*.  An individual has knowledge of God when he

knows facts about God and has an actual acquaintance with him.  In Cal-

vin's thought, full and certain knowledge of facts about God is arrived

at only through the personal witness of God to the individual.

> Nor does it proceed only from God's nature that to know God is
> immediately to love him.  But the Spirit who illuminates our minds
> inspires our hearts with a feeling conformable to our knowledge.
> At the same time the knowledge of God leads us to fear him and to
> love him.[128]

The Holy Spirit is God's personal presence among men; in the Spirit
we attain God in his own personal being.  The knowledge of God which
comes from the presence of the Spirit posits us as subjects vis à vis
the divine subject.  It creates a personal relationship, but one in
which God remains in control over man's judgments about him.  The *testi-*
*monium internum* of the Holy Spirit should not be understood in a subjective manner but in an objective manner:  the Holy Spirit inheres in
the objective truth of God.  Through the Spirit God's truth is personally present to man.[129]

According to Calvin, the object of the Spirit's testimony is a person.  Knowledge of God is defined as acquaintance with him.  This is why
Calvin's concept of the knowledge of God was truly personalistic:  God
speaks and man is summoned.  In Calvin's mind, the objective and subjective character of revelation coincide - the author of the word is also
the author of the receiver's faith.  We arrive not at a doctrine but at
an event.[130]

We know the truth through the truth in accordance with God's own witness to himself.  This means that we know God on the grounds that he
himself provides.  This is related to Calvin's doctrine of election.
The priority and the objectivity of God is the basis for all genuine
knowledge of him.

> Let this truth then stand sure, that no one can be called a son of
> God, who does not know himself to be such; and this is called
> knowledge by John in order to set forth its certainty.[131]

God's word in scripture shines with a majesty of its own and with unmistakable  self-authenticating power.

> The word of the Lord constrains us by its majesty, as by a violent
> impulse, to yield obedience to it.[132]

> The scripture, carrying its own evidence along with it, deigns not
> to submit to proofs and arguments, but owes the full conviction
> with which we ought to receive it to the testimony of the Spirit.[133]

Calvin understood man's knowledge of God as knowledge gained in the
immediate experience of his presence.  We know God through the direct

impact and causality of his divine being in and through his Word.  God
manifests himself and acts towards man and is present to him through his
word.  Thus knowledge of God is attained primarily by hearing rather
than by seeing.  "True knowledge of God is perceived more by the ears
than by the eyes."[134]  This hearing caused by the power of the Word of
God is experiential and the source of an intuitive knowledge.  It is
auditive since it is directly related to hearing and is caused by the
Word of God.  At the same time it is intuitive because of the quality of
relationship is establishes between God and man.

Through this notion of an intuitive-auditive knowledge of God, Calvin
was proposing a method of knowing which presumed to cut through the
shield of images and concepts separating reality from the perceiving
subject.  It depended on a personal *rapprochement* between the subject
and the object of knowledge rather than upon the ordinary subject-
object-antithesis.  In his theory of knowledge, Calvin proposed a method
of knowing in which the object takes the initiative and reveals itself
to the subject.  God presents himself to man, breaking in upon the human
consciousness from the outside.  Thus God and man are not separated by a
veil of conceptualization.  Knowledge of God does not end with a concept
of God but with God himself.

Even as Calvin elaborated his doctrine of the auditive-intuitive
knowledge of God, he was very much aware that even in revelation the
inner essence of God remains unattainable.  "God's substance is utterly
invisible and hidden from us."[135]  Revelation enables man to overcome
only part of his noetic difficulties.  Even special revelation cannot
bridge the epistemological gap that separates man from the knowledge of
God.  Calvin affirmed that God closes this gap by giving man a knowledge
that is not man's own, but God's.  The real knowledge of God does result
from an act occurring in the mind of man.  This act is effected, however,
only by the Spirit of God who, because he is God, accomplishes in man's
mind what sinful man no longer can do for himself.  The human mind can
know, it can receive the truth; but it cannot attain the full knowledge
of God, certain, permanent and productive of piety.  This is the primary
and immediate effect of regeneration:  an intuition of the authority of
scripture produced in the intellect by the witnessing of the Holy Spirit.
To know that the Bible is the word of God may not be said to be a product of human wisdom, even regenerated human wisdom.  It is not completely

separated from the intellect, since it is the mind that knows. But it
is the power of the witnessing Spirit which produces this knowledge
within the intellect. And the divine wisdom or insight is injected
directly.

Calvin held that the given knowledge of God could be described as an
immediate intuition of the mind. This intuition is not man's judgment
but God's judgment, or witness to the truth, which he simply transfers
to the mind of man. It is self-evident knowledge: God himself declares
it to be so. Through regeneration man is not given a better ability to
reason, but the gift of the witness of the Holy Spirit. By this witness, man knows the truth, but his ability to know is not due to any
improvement of the human mind but to the gift of God's judgment.

> It is foolish to attempt to convince the infidel that the scripture
> is the word of God. The evidences cannot of themselves produce a
> firm faith in scripture until our heavenly Father manifests his
> presence in it, and therefore secure implicit reverence for it.
> Then only, therefore, the scriptures suffice to give a saving
> knowledge of God when its certainty is founded on the inner per-
> suasion of the Holy Spirit.[136]

Yet this is a further obstacle to man's knowledge, which God's gift
of his personal knowledge does not wholly remove. Man's capacity to
receive truth, to know God, is still hindered by sin and by finiteness
itself. Radically speaking, man's inability to know God fully is a
necessary part of his finitude. Nevertheless, Calvin maintained that we
have a clear knowledge of God.

> For we have in the word, insofar as it is expedient for us, a naked
> and open revelation of God, and it has nothing intricate in it, to
> hold us in suspense, as wicked persons imagine; for how small a
> proportion does this bear to that vision which we have in our eyes?
> Hence it is only in a comparative sense that it is termed obscure.[137]

Yet God is so transcendent that a direct vision of him would destroy man.

> We who have not as yet reached that great height (speaking about
> angels and the vision of God) behold an image of God as it is pre-
> sented before us in the word, in the sacraments, and in fine in the
> whole of the service of the church...Our faith therefore at present
> is to behold God as absent. How so? Because it sees not his face,
> but rests satisfied with the image in the mirror; but when we shall
> have left the world and gone to him it will behold him as near as
> before his eyes...As we must understand it in this manner that the
> knowledge of God which we now have from his word is indeed certain
> and true, and has nothing in it that is confused, perplexed or
> dark, but is spoken of as comparatively obscure because it comes

far short of that clear manifestation to which we look forward; for
then we shall see face to face.[138]

Eschatological knowledge of God will be the direct face-to-face vision
of the essence of God; no longer will we see only "under symbol,"
"through a veil," "through his word." From Calvin's statements, it is
apparent that he considered all of man's present knowledge of God as indirect.

Calvin asserted the possibility of attaining God through the mediation
of preaching. This brings us to the epistemological function of the
Holy Spirit in Calvin's concept of the intuitive-auditive knowledge of
God. All language is related to God's being through the living action
of the Holy Spirit. It is the Holy Spirit that provides transparence in
our knowledge and language of God. Apart from its action, God as eternal truth does not reach us either through our language or that of the
scriptures. But by the Spirit we are made capable of distinguishing the
reality of God from the products of our own minds. That is why for Calvin man's speech could really become God's word.

> The word goes out of the mouth of God in such a manner that it
> likewise goes out of the mouth of men; but God does not speak
> openly from heaven, but employs men as his instruments.[139]

Through the preached word God is attained and known.

> Among the many noble endowments with which God has adorned the human
> race, one of the most remarkable is, that he deigns to consecrate
> the mouth and tongues of men to his service, making it his own
> voice to be heard in them.[140]

Calvin referred to preaching as a token of the presence of God and a
means by which he becomes present to us.

> The Lord is said to come when he gives any token of his presence.
> He approaches by the preaching of the word and he approaches also
> by various benefits which he bestows upon us.[141]

Calvin's solution to the problem of knowing God was an indirect but
intuitive knowledge. He arrived at this by reducing the concept of an
analogical knowledge of God to a knowledge of God through his word as
spoken by men. The word itself functions as the analogy.

> For as men are made known by the countenance and speech, so God
> utters his voice to us by the voice of the prophet and, in his
> documents, takes as it were a visible form from which he may be
> known by us according to our feeble capacities.[142]

In its analogical function the human word is a pointer. "Words are
nothing else but signs."[143]   But when God gives a sign, he comes himself
to be present.  Signs form a veil behind which God conceals his presence
in human affairs.  They are at the same time focal points for the meeting between God and man.  Calvin understood a sign to point to another
reality.

> As he was not tied to any place, so he meant nothing less than to
> tie his people to the earthly symbols, but he descends to them that
> he might take them up to himself.[144]

True symbols point beyond themselves; they must be momentary and self-
negating.  A true symbol drives the mind beyond itself to what it signifies.  Speaking of miracles, Calvin wrote,

> And for this cause are they called signs, because the Lord will not
> have men's mind to stay there but to be lifted up higher; as they
> are referred to another end.[145]

In another place, he wrote, "It pleases the Lord to employ earthly elements, as vehicles for raising the minds of men on high."[146]   For Calvin, as opposed to Occam, the function of ideas and statements in the
Bible is not to transmit a corpus of creditive ideas separated from God
but to direct and point us to God.  This is true because in the knowledge of God there is no place for the fabrications of our minds.  In the
knowledge of God we are totally dependent upon his prior activity.  We
can never subordinate the *res* to the *sermo*.  This understanding on the
part of Calvin was close to John Major's concept of the knowledge of God
as active *(cognitio activa)* but not factive *(cognitio factiva)*.  God's
purpose in revealing himself to man through signs he has chosen is to
keep man from idolatry.  Through these signs, God seeks to give man
something earthly, something he can hold on to with his mind.  Calvin's
notion of symbol is linked both to his idea of God and to his opposition
to idolatry.  There is a constant temptation for man to make God a picture of himself, to grasp God according to his capacity.  The mind of
man is a factory of idols.

Calvin's understanding of word and spirit, relating respectively to
the objective and subjective factors of knowledge, ended the antithesis
between objectivism and subjectivism.  Subjective certainty and personal
conviction were no longer dangerous obstacles to the knowledge of God.
A personal knowledge of God was not detrimental to the objective knowledge

of him.  Man's relation to God was no longer fixed by his relation to
the Church, nor even by his relation to the word, if by the word was
meant only the positivistic sense, without reference to the Spirit.  The
encounter between the divine and the human could not be limited by any
preconditions.  For such conditions would amount to a refusal to live as
an elect of God.  To ascribe divine authority to anything other than him
whom one had personally experienced would be idolatry.

Calvin argued against making any external authority the ultimate criterion of truth, whether that authority was the Church, previous historical revelation, or the Bible itself when considered only as the record
of past revelation.  According to Calvin, the Holy Spirit was not bound
to the preaching of Paul[147] nor even to that of Jesus.[148]  With this in
view, the successors to Paul and to Jesus should not presume the presence of the Spirit.

> Since therefore the Lord assigns this office to the word, let us
> know that he also gives his power to it, that it may not be offered
> in vain, but may inwardly move the heart.  Not always, indeed, or
> promiscuously but when it pleases God by the secret power of the
> Spirit to work in this manner.[149]

The Spirit is never confined to any institution.  It can work apart from
the preaching of the Church.[150]  Calvin was not an enthusiast.[151]  In
fact, in establishing the epistemological correlation of word and Spirit,
he struggled against the enthusiasts as well as the Romans.  Against the
enthusiasts, Calvin affirmed the unity of word and Spirit; against the
Romans, he denied the mediation of the Church.  This denial was made
evident in the rejection of what he called implicit faith.

> Is it faith to understand nothing, and merely submit our convic-
> tions implicitly to the church?  Faith consists not in ignorance
> but in knowledge, knowledge not of God merely, but of divine will.
> We do not obtain salvation either because we are prepared to
> embrace every dictate of the church as true and leave for the
> church the province of inquiring and determining; but when we
> recognize God as propitious Father through the reconciliation made
> by Christ and Christ as given to us for righteousness, sanctifica-
> tion and life.  By this knowledge, I say, not by the submission of
> our understanding we obtain entrance to the kingdom of heaven.[152]

He considered that real authority for man's religious life must rise out
of his personal experience and find its ultimate legitimization in the
individual.  Verification and certitude are ultimately personal and, as
such, incommunicable.  This personal certitude is not subject to public

and external judgment nor does it regain the general approval of others.

> As to others we have no testimony except from the outward efficacy
> of the Spirit; that is, insofar as the grace of God shows itself in
> them, so that we come to know it. There is therefore a great dif-
> ference because the assurance of faith remains inwardly shut up and
> does not extend itself to others.[153]

Experience is incommunicable by nature. In some of its aspects, it can
be meaningful for others. Others can understand that such an experience
occurs; others can desire to have such an experience. The religious experience is the awareness of the presence of God possessed of a distinctive feeling and tone. The inner-felt aspects of the experience and the
certitude it imparts - these cannot be communicated.

## E. *Conclusion*

John Calvin has been described as a cold logician in older scholarship as well as in more recent studies.

> He has no experiential sense of what it means to discover divinity
> dwelling within - a striking example of how remote head knowledge
> can be from visionary realization.[154]

This is certainly a caricature. John Calvin affirmed many times in his
writings the intensively experiential character of the knowledge of God.
Calvin was conscious of a Presence in the depth of his soul. This Presence was more real to him than anything else he knew.

Calvin's understanding of the nature of the knowledge of God brought
to its logical conclusion the inwardness, individualism and personalism
of the *Devotio Moderna*, yet escaped the pitfalls of pure subjectivism.
In the correlation of the Word and the Spirit Calvin established an
epistemology able to support a spirituality proceeding from the I-Thou
relationship between God and man.

Calvin spoke of a Religious knowledge, for Calvin demanded a personal
acquaintance of the subject with its object. Affective elements were
considered integral to it. Knowing involves being saved, and being
saved means experiencing a new power at work within ourselves. This
interrelation Calvin stated more explicitly in his exegesis of John 17:3.

> Now he describes the manner of bestowing life, namely, when he en-
> lightens the elect in the true knowledge of God...Where he has
> shown, we possess him by faith, and therefore we also enter into
> the possession of life; and this is the reason why the knowledge of

him is truly and justly called saving, or bringing salvation. Almost every one of the words has its weight; for it is not every
kind of knowledge which forms us anew into the image of God from
faith to faith, or rather is the same with faith, by which having been
engrafted to the body of Christ we are made partakers of the divine
adoption and heirs of heaven.[155]

Calvin was speaking here of the kind of knowledge which two people come
to have of one another through intimate conversation when the bond of
friendship has been established. Man knows God as a benevolent person
who is keenly interested in his welfare.

God is known in an existential attitude. Man and God were envisioned
by Calvin not as abstractions but in a concrete encounter. Ultimately,
the knowledge of God is a knowledge that determines the existence of the
knower.

For how can the thought of God enter your mind without immediately
giving rise to the thought that since you are his workmanship, you
are bound by the very  law of creation to be subject to his authority.[156]

This knowledge is given as man is caught by him, as he becomes aware
that in his own adulation and lowliness he is never alone and isolated
but that in himself, in his very depths, there is a life greater and
richer than his which supports and creates him. To know God is to experience that one is known by him. To know him is to be known by him
and to hope in him.[157]

This knowledge is supra-rational. It cannot be adequately formulated
in concepts, although concepts are required to communicate and share it.
Yet this knowledge is not subjective. For it is not created by man but
given as an undeserved grace. Knowing God cannot be compared to knowing
any other things. He is not an external object we discover by touching.
He is not an object of science, that can be apprehended, analyzed, or
manipulated. Knowing God does not mean that the mind has grasped another object. It is based in the experience of a subject. Calvin's
understanding of theology must be viewed within this context. Theology
cannot claim to be a *summa*, a complex of truths ordering all revealed
data by the aid of reason. Theology can only be an institution, an instruction, a kind of catechism. The title of the original edition of
Calvin's *Institutes* clearly indicated his reason for writing:

Basic instruction in the Christian religion, containing verbally

the whole sum of godliness *(pietatis)* and all that needs to be
known in the doctrine of salvation:  a work very well worth reading
for all Christians with a zeal for godliness.[158]

To remain faithful to its object, theological reflection must function at the very center of the Word of God.  It seeks to conform itself
to the Word not in order to penetrate the mystery of God but in order to
understand it in its work of summoning man.  Man is not primarily an
intellect, capable of receiving truth; he is primarily a person, open to
the Lord.

God cannot be known outside faith and obedience.  This knowledge does
not teach us propositions about him, but rather how man may unite himself with God's purposes.  We are to know not what God is in himself,
but what he is *erga nos*.[159]  We look not for scientific knowledge but
for saving knowledge.  Calvin recognized the validity of objective
knowledge.  But this is not the kind of knowledge that theology is made
of.  Theological knowledge is faith-knowledge.

Theology is not the satisfaction of the intellect.  It is a doing.
Calvin did not ask questions about God; he let himself be questioned by
God's Word.  The theologian is a man in continual dialectical relationship between the Word and the Spirit; he is sent from the Word to the
Spirit and the Spirit to the Word.  For it is not man who, under the
influence of faith, seeks to understand God's mysteries; it is God himself who reveals and unveils himself in order to save man.  There is no
autonomous role in theology for reason.  Calvin knew of no *ratio theologica* specific in itself and capable through faith of penetrating the
mysteries.[160]  For Calvin there was no such thing as scientific theology
but only wisdom *(sapientia)* which is *pietas*.

*Notes*

1.  E. L. Surtz, "Oxford Reformers and Scholasticism," *Studies in Philosophy* XLVII 4 (1950) 547-556.

2.  Cf. R. McKeon, "Renaissance and Method in Philosophy," *Studies in the History of Ideas* III (Columbia University Department of Philosophy 1935) 37-114; *idem.*, "Rhetoric in the Middle Ages," *Speculum* XVII (1942) 1-32; D. Cantimori, "Rhetoric and Politics in Italian Humanism," *Journal of the Warburg Institute* I (1937-1938) 83-102; A. Galletti, *L'Eloquenza* (Milan, 1938); E. Garin, "Note su alcuni aspetti delle Retoriche rinascimentali e sulla 'Retorica' de Patrizi," in Garin, Rossi and Vasoli (eds.) *Testi Umanistici su la Retorica* (Rome and Milan, 1953) 7-36; R. Sabbadini, *II Metodo degli Umanisti* (Florence, 1920); *idem.*, *Storia de Ciceronianismo* (Turin, 1885); C. Trabalza, *La Critica letteraria* II (Milan, 1915); G. Vallese, "Retorica medievale e retorica umanistica," *Delta* N.S. No. 2 (1952) 39-57; K. Vossler, *Poetische Theorien in der italienischen Frührenaissance* (Berlin, 1900).

3.  P. O. Kristeller wrote: "This combination of rhetoric and theology has often been taken to be peculiar to French or northern humanism but it was by no means absent from Italian humanism as the example of Petrarch or even Valla shows."
    Cf. "An Unknown Humanist Sermon on St. Stephen by Guillaume Fichet," *Mélanges Eugene Tisserant* vol. VI (Biblioteca Vaticana Studi e Testi No. 236) 487.
    We find the term *theologia sermocinalis* in the second book of the Cardinal of Cusa's *Idiota de Sapientia*. He speaks of the power of the word and the theological function of this word, the "sermonicinalis theologia."
    Nicolaus von Cues, *Texte seiner philosophischen*, ed. Dr. Alfred Petzelt, vol. I (Stuttgart, 1949) 314-315.

4.  *Novati* IV, 176-178; quoted in C. Trinkaus, *Our Image and Likeness* vol. I (London, 1970) 348.

5.  *Ratio Seu Methode...Opera Omnia* T. 5 (Leiden) col. 84.

6.  *Ibid.*, col. 77.

7.  Juan de Valdes, *Le cento e dieci considerazioni*, ed. E. Cione (Milan, 1944) Consideration 87 (trans. J. Nieto, *Juan de Valdes and the Origins of the Spanish and Italian Reformation* [Geneva, 1970] 259).

8.  Cf. Nieto, *Valdes* 259ff.

9.  Juan de Valdes, *Dialogo de doctrina cristiana*, ed. Stockwell, 114.

10. Juan de Valdes, *Alfabeto*, ed. Stockwell, 115 (trans. Nieto, *Valdes*, 272).

11. *Ibid.*, 317.

12. Juan de Valdes, *Le cento e dieci considerazioni*, ed. Cione, Consideration 55 (trans. Nieto, *Valdes*, 246).

13. Juan de Valdes, *La epistola de San Pablo a los Romanos i la I a los Corintios* (Rom. 5, 14) in *Reformistas antiguos espanoles* T. X-XI (Madrid, 1856).

14. J. Nieto, *Valdes*, 246. Cf. *ibid.*, note 170, p. 247.

15. Juan de Valdes, *Com. Mat. "proemio" in XVII Opuscules: Juan de Valdes' Minor Works*, ed. J. Betts (London, 1882) 49.

16. Pinard de la Boullaye, "Sentir, sentimiento, sentido dans le style de S. Ignace," *Archivum Historicum* S.I. 25 (1956) 416-430.

17.  *Monumenta* I, 1, 105.

18.  *Ibid.*, 106.

19.  *Fontes* II, 123, "Vidi, sensi et intellexi omnia fidei Christianae mysteria."

20.  We witness in Occam two tendencies: 1) to base knowledge on the safe ground of reality in intuitive knowledge, and 2) to eliminate any element, for instance a species, that could becloud the immediate vision of reality and prevent the mind from an immediate contact with things, thus leading it to skepticism. For if reality is not grasped immediately, how can we ever ascertain that we grasp reality at all? Cf. E. Hochstetter, *Studien zur Metaphysik und Erkenntnislehere Wilhelms von Ockham* (Berlin, 1927); E. Gilson, *The Unity of Philosophical Experience* (New York, 1937).

21.  Occam, *In Sent.* I, Pro. (Opera Plurima III; London, 1962).

22.  *Ibid.*, q. 7.

23.  During Calvin's stay at the College of Montaigu, the most important philosopher and theologian there was John Major.

24.  Magistri Anthonii Coronel, *In Posteriora Aristotelis...commentaria* (Paris, 1510) last page. For the details concerning Major's life, A. E. G. Mackay, *Memoir of John Major of Haddington* (Edinburg, 1892).

25.  J. Durkan, "John Major: After 400 Years" and "The School of John Major: Bibliography," *The Innes Review* Vol. I, 2 (1950) 131ff., 140ff.

26.  H. Elie, *Le traité "de l'Infini" de Jean Mair* (Paris, 1938); idem., *Le Complexe Significabile* (Paris, 1937). Major describes his own position in *In Sent.* IV, prol., ed. 1519. A significant fact is that his his own disciples could evolve in totally different directions. Peter Crockaert became a radical realist while Anthonio Coronel developed Major's terministic logic to exaggerated conclusions.

27.  Cf. *In Sent.* I, prol. q. 1, fol. I.4. Major very often affirms that our experience of the mirror teaches us the relationship that exists between the image and reality. Cf. *In Sent.* I, d.3, q.3, fol. XXV, 3.

28.  *In Sent.* I, d.3, q.2, fol. XXXIII, 2 and ff.

29.  *In Sent.* I, d.3, q.2, fol. XXXIV, 1.

30.  *In Sent.* II, d.3, q.3, fol. XXXVIII, 1,2; d.13, q.2, fol. LXVIII, 3; d.13, q.3, fol. LXIX, 1,3.

31.  *In Sent.* I, d.3, q.1, fol. XXXII, 2; II, d.3, q.3, fol. XXXVIII, 1, 2.

32.  *In I Sent* prol. q.4, fol. XXVI.

33.  *Lib. terminorum, Inclit*, art. lib. I, fol. VI, 3,4.

34.  *Ibid.*

35.  *In Sent.* I, prol. q.4, fol. X, 4.

36.  *In Sent.* I, prol. q.4, fol. X, 3.

37.  *In Sent.* I, prol. q.2, fol. VI, 2.

38.  *In Sent.* I, prol. q.3, fol. IX, 2.

39.  *In Sent.* I, d.3, q.1, fol. XXXI, 1.

40.  *In Sent.* I, d.9, q.1, fol. XLIV, 3.

41.  *In Sent.* I, d.6, q.1, fol. XLI, 1.

42.  *In Sent.* I, d.4, q.1, fol. XXXIX, 3.

43.  *In Sent.* I, prol. q.1, fol. I, 4.

44.  *In Sent.* I, prol. q.., fol. IX, 2.

45.  *In Sent.* I, prol. q.5, fol. XI, 3.

46.  *In Sent.* I, prol. q.4, fol. X, 5.

47.  *In Sent.* I, prol. q.4, fol. X, 3, 4.

48.  *In Sent.* I, prol. q.4, fol. X, 4.

49. *Comm. Lk.*, 2:52, fol. CCIX, 85.

50. *In Sent.* I, prol. q.6, fol. XIV, 4.

51. *Comm. Jn.*, 6:36, fol. CCLXIX, 1:20, 31, fol. CCCXL, 69; 15, 16, fol. CCCXIX, 44.

52. *In Sent.* III, d.40, q.4, fol. CLXIV, 3. Major also has an interesting doctrine on predestination. He teaches a double predestination: an eternal predestination and an eternal reprobation. Cf. *In Sent.* I, d.40, q.1 and 2, fol. XCVI, 1.

53. This epistemology may not have been his first concern; it may have evolved in part as a response to the problem of the dependence of scripture on the authority of the Church. But as a system it has its own logic and stands independently.

54. *Comm. Jn.*, 15:27; OC, 47, 354-355.

55. In the preface of the *Institutes*, Calvin accuses the scholastics of having buried the truth of Christ. "...the truth of Christ, if not properly destroyed and dispersed, lurks as if it were ignobly buried." The truth is buried under a mass of complicated and subtle arguments and theses that, according to Calvin, have no foundation in scripture, arguments that have no effective value in the work of salvation. In his vituperation it is the scholastic method of formal logic and syllogism that Calvin opposes. Cf. Erasmus,*Opera*, 4, 406 C; 461 C. Cf. also B. A. Gerrish, *Grace and Reason* (Oxford, 1962) 32-42.

The representatives of this method are called by Calvin *sophistae, scholastici sophistae, ratiocinationum architecti*. Through their syllogisms and logic, they seek to explain the incomprehensible mystery of Christ. They add to the simplicity of the scriptures through their curiosity, and in doing so, turn themselves away from the Scriptures. "All the Fathers with one heart execrated and with one mouth protested against contaminating the word of God with the subtleties of sophists, and involving it in the brawls of dialecticians. Do they keep within these limits when the sole occupation of their lives is to entwine and entangle the simplicity of scripture with endless disputes, and worse still, with that sophistical jargon? So much so that were the Fathers to rise from their graves and listen to the brawling art which bears the name of speculative theology, they would recognize it as anything but a discussion of a religious nature." (OS, I, 29) To these theologians true knowledge of God remains inaccessible. OS, 1, 96; compare Erasmus: "Hoc Philosophiae genus in affectibus situm verius, quam in syllogismis, vita est magis quam disputatio, afflatus potius quam eruditio, transformatio magis quam ratio." (*Opera*, 5, 141,E)

56. Cf. Josef Bohatec, *Budé und Calvin. Studien zur Gedankenwelt des französishen Frühumanismus* (Graz, 1950); Jean Boisset, *Sagesse et Sainteté dans la Pensée de Jean Calvin* (Paris, 1959); Victor Lawrence Nuovo, "Calvin's Theology. A Study of its Sources in Classical Antiquity" (unpublished Ph.D. thesis, Columbia University, 1964); Quirinus Breen, *John Calvin. A Study in French Humanism* 2nd ed. (1968); *idem.*, "John Calvin and the Rhetorical Tradition" in *Christianity and Humanism* (Grand Rapids Mich., 1968) 107-129; *idem.*, "Humanism and the Reformation" in Jerald C. Brauer (ed.), *The Impact of the Church Upon Its Culture* (Essays in Divinity Vol. II; Chicago, 1968) 145-171; Charles Trinkaus, "Renaissance Problems in Calvin's Theology" in William Peery (ed.), *Studies in the Renaissance* Vol. I (Austin, Texas, 1954) 59-80.

There are in the *Institutes* many clear echoes of Clavin's early concentration upon classical antiquity. His great dependence on Cicero's philosophical treatises is well known. There were at least twenty

different works of Cicero present in the library of the Academy in
Geneva. It would seem that Calvin possessed a remarkable knowledge of
Cicero the *homo religiosus* as well as Cicero the orator. In defining
the concept of religion, it is not Augustine that he has recourse to but
Cicero (*Inst.* I, 12, 1). He is also influenced by Cicero in defining
such terms as *pietas, cultus,* and *cognitio Dei*: "...ut intelligant lec-
tores, quid vere sit pietas, subiicimus verba Ciceronis ex Topicis."
(OC, 5, 102)

    Cf. also Bohatec, *Budé and Calvin*, 245ff.

    This dependence on classical authors and contemporary humanism is
seen in the very form of the *Institutes*. Its logic is that of rhetoric,
not that of syllogism. In the *Institutes* Calvin's purpose is to teach.
He aims at moving people and changing their ways. He has a love for
metaphor, personification, resounding words and phrases, alliteration.
Cf. *Inst.*, I, 5, 11; I, 5, 12; I, 5, 14.

    57. *WA*, 18, 602, 30.

    58. *WA*, 40, 401, 2.

    59. *WA*, 10, 188, 6-8.

    60. *WA*, 42, 17, 29.

    61. *WA*, 18, 626, 35; *WA*, 18, 629, 38.

    62. *WA*, 6, 560.

    63. J. Calvin, *Institution de la Religion Chrestienne*, ed. J. D.
Benoit (Paris, 1957) Vol. V, 300-303. On the influence of Luther on
John Calvin: A. Ganoczy, *Le Jeune Calvin*, 139-150.

    64. *Inst.*, 1.13, 7.

    65. OS, I, 414.

    66. R. S. Wallace, *Calvin's Doctrine of Word and Sacrament* (London,
1953) 82.

    67. *Inst.*, III, 2, 6.

    68. *Comm. Jn.*, 1:1; OC, 1, 12.

    69. "As to the Evangelist calling the Son of God the Speech, the
simple reason appears to me to be first, because he is the eternal Wisdom and Will of God and, secondly, because he is the lively image of his
purpose; for as Speech is said to be among men the image of the mind, so
it is not inappropriate to apply this to God, and to say that He reveals
himself to us by His Speech." (*Ibid.*)

    70. *Inst.*, I, 17, 5.

    71. *Letter to King Francis I*, OC, 1, 12.

    72. *Inst.*, III, 2, 6.

    73. *Reply to Sadoleto*, p. 79.

    74. *Comm. Ps.*, 22, 30; OC, 31, 236; *Comm. I Tim.*, 3:13; OC, 52, 288-
289.

    75. Bucer played an important role in the development of Calvin's
theology. As early as the *Institutes* of 1536, there is evidence that
Calvin carefully read Bucer's Commentaries. In his chapter on prayer,
Calvin reproduces the whole sequence of ideas expressed by Bucer in his
commentary on the Gospel of St. Matthew. But it was most clearly in his
Doctrine of the Holy Spirit that Bucer influenced Calvin. Cf. W. P.
Stephens, *The Holy Spirit in the Theology of Martin Bucer* (Cambridge,
1970) 196-208.

    76. The sensus-divinitatis, given by the Spirit, replaces the in-
stinctual awareness of God: "There is within the human mind, and indeed
by natural instinct, an awareness of divinity. This we take to be beyond controversy. To prevent anyone from taking refuge in the pretense
of ignorance, God himself has implanted in all men a certain understanding

of his divine majesty." (*Inst.*, I, 3, 1)  "...this conviction, namely, that there is some God, is naturally inborn in all, and is fixed deep within, as it were in the very marrow." (*Inst.*, I, 3, 3)

77. *Inst.*, I, 7, 5.
78. *Inst.*, I, 7, 2.
79. *Ibid*
80. *Inst.*, I, 7, 5.
81. *Inst.*, III, 11, 14.
82. *Comm. Eph.*, 1:13; OC, 51, 153.
83. OS, II, 8.
84. *Reply to Sadoleto*, p. 79.
85. *Inst.*, I, 7, 48.
86. *Ibid.*, II, 139.
87. *Comm. Gal.*, 1:13; OC, 50, 177.
88. *Comm. I Cor.*, 2:11 and 12; OC, 49, 341-342.
89. *Inst.*, II, 114-115.
90. *Inst.*, I, 7, 4.
91. *Comm. Ps.*, 4:2; OC, 31, 58-59.
92. *Inst.*, III, 3, 2, 14.
93. *Inst.*, III, 2, 14.
94. *Comm. I Jn.*, 2:3; OC, 55, 310-311.
95. *Inst.*, I, 13, 14.
96. *Inst.*, I, 13, 13.
97. *Inst.*, I, 3, 26.
98. *Inst.*, I, 3, 3.
99. *Inst.*, I, 2, 1; I, 5, 9.
100. *Inst.*, III, 14, 19; III, 2, 15.
101. *Inst.*, I, 1, 3.
102. *Inst.*, I, 7, 4.
103. *Ibid.*
104. *Inst.*, I, 7, 5.
105. *Comm. Eph.*, 1:13; OC, 51, 145-146.
106. C. Partee, "Calvin and Experience," *Scottish Journal of Theology* 26, 2 (1973) 169-181.
107. Cf. *Comm. Jn.*, 15:27; OC, 48, 354; *Comm. Lk.*, 24:45; OC, 45, 816; *Comm. Thess.*, 5:20; OC, 52, 176.
108. *Inst.*, I, 9, 6.
109. *Inst.*, I, 7, 4.
110. *Comm. Ezechiel*, II, 2; OC, 40, 61-62.
111. *Comm. I Jn.*, 4:1; OC, 55, 347-348.
112. *Comm. Jn.*, 14:26; OC, 47, 334; 15, 2; OC, 47, 354; *Comm. I Cor.*, 2:11.
113. *Comm. Is.*, 29:11; OC, 36, 492.
114. *Comm. Rom.*, 11:14; OC, 49, 219.
115. *Inst.*, I, 7, 4.
116. *Ibid.*
117. *Reply to Sadoleto*, p. 61.
118. *Comm. Jn.*, 14:26; OC, 47, 334.
119. *Comm. Ezekiel*, I, p. 108.
120. E. Dowey, *The Knowledge of God in Calvin's Theology* (New York, 1965) 3.
121. *Inst.*, I, 5, 13. Cf. also *Inst.*, I, 5, 13-14.
122. *Comm. Ps.*, 8:1; OC, 31, 88c. Cf. *Inst.*, I, 5, 9; III, 2, 31.
123. *Comm. Is.*, 43:11; OC, 37, 89d.
124. *Comm. Is.*, 26:4; OC, 36, 29a.

125.  *Inst.*, I, 5, 9.
126.  *Comm. Rom.*, 3:4; OC, 49, 48.
127.  *Comm. Heb.*, 4:12; OC, 55, 50.  This concept of the word of God is thoroughly biblical.  For the Israelite, the idea of "word" lies in the conception of the spoken word as a distinct reality charged with power.  The basic concept of the word is the word-thing.  The power of the word posits the reality which it signifies.  Strange as it seems, Israel does not make any distinction between a word and a thing (actions and facts).  "Dabar," "word," means as much a word pronounced or written as it does an event in nature or history.  "After these words," may also mean "after these events." (Gen. 22:1)  Words are not only said but done.  (Gen. 24:66)  All the content of this notion of word is applied to God when the O.T. says that "God speaks."  The Biblical "word of God" emerges from a cultural background in which "word" is understood as a dynamic entity with its own distinct reality.
      The word of God has a creative force.  In Genesis God's word is charged with the will and the power to create; not even Chaos can resist it.
      God's word directs the making of history; it determines events: "Things of the past I foretold long ago, they went forth from my mouth, I let you hear of them; then suddenly I took action and they came to be." (Is. 48:3)  The Word of God in the Old Testament is power in action, and its effect is creation history.  Salvation history with its own distinct reality comes into view.  (Ps. 147:15-18; Is. 44:26-28; Wisdom 18, 15; OS, 6:5; Jer. 5:14)
      The word is here considered as an externalization of the personality of God, an expression of his will.  It endures therefore as long as the will which it expresses.  There is no agent which can destroy it, corrupt it, or frustrate it.
128.  *Comm. I Jn.*, 2:3; OC, 55.
129.  Several theologians within the reformed tradition have recently insisted that in authentic Calvinism no true object of knowledge is presented.  E. Brunner maintains that there is no object of revelation; rather "revelation consists in the meeting of two subjects:  God himself is the revelation, being at the same time the revealer and the revealed."
130.  G. W. Locher, *Testimonium internum. Calvins Lehre vom Heiligen Geist und das hermeneutische Problem* (Theol. Studien, Heft 81; Zurich, 1964).  On page 15, Locher gives the essence of his argument:  "Das Ewige kam und kommt in unsere Zeit.  Darum liegt die Offenbarungskraft der Offenbarung nicht an einer überzeitlichen Wahrheit, sondern gerade an ihrer kontingenten Geschichtlichkeit.  Offenbarung ist keine Lehre, sondern ein Ereignis, nämlich die Erlösung; ein Ereignis, dem auch mit meinem Verstehen als Glaubenserkennen ein Ereignis entspricht.  Credo in Spiritum Sanctum."
131.  *Comm. Rom.*, 8:16; OC, 49, 150.
132.  *Comm. I Cor.*, 2:4; OC, 49, 335.
133.  *Inst.*, I, 7, 5.
134.  *Comm. Ex.*, 33:19; OC, 25, 109a; cf. *Inst.*, III, 2, 3; I, 6, 2.
135.  *Comm. Job*; OC, 33, 671.
136.  *Inst.*, I, 7, 5.
137.  *Comm. I Jn.*, 3:2; OC, 55, 330-331.
138.  *Comm. I Jn.*, 3:12; OC, 55, 338-339.
139.  *Comm. Is.*, 55:11; OC, 37, 291.
140.  *Comm. Mt.*, 13:37; OC, 45, 369.
141.  *Comm. Is.*, 50:2; OC, 37, 216-217.

142.  *Comm. Jn.*, 5:37; OC, 47, 124.

143.  *Inst.*, IV, 14, 26.

144.  *Comm. Acts*, 17:24; OC, 48, 412.

145.  *Comm. Acts*, 2:22; OC, 48, 37-38.

146.  *Comm. Gen.*, 9:13; OC, 23, 149.

147.  *Comm. II Cor.*, 3:6; OC, 50, 40.

148.  "As the Lord has formerly discharged the office of teacher,
with little or no improvement on the part of the disciples, he now begins to teach them inwardly by his Spirit; for words are idly wasted on
the air until the minds are enlightened by the gift of understanding."
*Comm. Lk.*, 24:45; OC, 45, 816.

149.  *Comm. Is.*, 35:4; OC, 36, 592.

150.  "He also convinced them without the word, for we know how
powerful are the secret instincts of the Spirit." *Comm. Mt.*, 15:23; OC,
45, 457.

151.  "What becomes of the word of the Lord, that clearest of all
marks which the Lord himself in designating the church so often commends
to us? For seeing how dangerous it would be to boast of the Spirit
without the word, he declared that the church is indeed governed by the
Holy Spirit; but in order that his government might not be vague and un-
stable, he bound it to the word." *Reply to Sadoleto*, 60-61.

152.  *Inst.*, III, 2, 2. Cf. A. Ganoczy, *Le Jeune Calvin*, 239-249.

153.  *Comm. Phil.*, 1:6; OC, 52, 9.

154.  Theodore Roszak, *Where the Wasteland Ends* (New York, 1972) 117.

155.  *Comm. Jn.*, 17:3; OC, 47, 376.

156.  *Inst.*, I, 2, 2.

157.  *Inst.*, III, 2, 16.

158.  *Preface to Institutes of 1536*; OC, I.

159.  *Inst.*, I, 2, 2.

160   *Inst.*, I, 1, 1.

CHAPTER VI

*CONCLUSION*

*Introduction*

To the question, "Did Calvin have a spirituality?" the reply must be affirmative. He had a spirituality possessing a discernible unity and distinct characteristics. It differed radically from the *Devotio Moderna* on three essential points: it was a spirituality of service within the world; it was accompanied by a new religious epistemology which made possible a reinterpretation of ecclesiological models and laid sound foundations for individualism in spirituality; and it asserted the inner unity of Christian life and theology.

While the distinctive ideas in Calvin's spirituality originated in response to the challenge of the sixteenth century, they have a new and unmistakable validity today. Modern emphases have deepened Calvin's seminal concepts, giving his vision of the Christian life a new and broader dimension. I see the relevance of Calvin's thought to three questions of contemporary spirituality: sanctification as world transformation; the role of the Church in the spiritual life; and spirituality and theological method.

*A. A Spirituality of Service Within the World*

In his doctrine of the creative work of the Holy Spirit within the individual and of the "ingrafting" of the individual into an organic relationship with Christ, Calvin proclaimed not only the possibility but the necessity of real oneness with God. This saving relationship begun by God involved a personal and deep response from man. Calvin posited not only a need for justification, but also a need for sanctification. Justification must be more than the forensic imputation of righteousness; it must enter into the human experience and effect an inner transformation. This inner transformation demanded, on the part of the individual, a striving in and through God's grace toward perfection. Although Calvin was convinced of the effect of sin and the need for repentance and, like Luther, stressed the *simul justus et peccator* (God justifies us while we are yet in our sin) he insisted on the perfectibility of man as well. The goal of this perfectibility was the restoration of the

image of God and of the original order, not only within man, but within
the world.

Calvin also understood salvation history as a restoration. Here it
is evident how he differed from Luther. The difference appears quite
sharply in their eschatologies. For Luther the new heaven and the coming of the Kingdom were to be accompanied by the total collapse and dissolution of the present world. For Calvin the fulfillment of the Kingdom included within it the renovation of the world, the restoration of
the created order. At the very core of Calvin's eschatology was the
belief that the coming of God's Kingdom transforms the created world.
This restoration had begun in the Incarnation, when "the world began to
be renewed and arose out of the darkness of death into the light of
life."[1]

The process of restoration is the central work of the Holy Spirit.

> ...we now begin to be formed anew by the Spirit after the image of
> God, in order that our entire renovation and that of the whole
> world may afterwards follow in due time.[2]

It is only in remembering the positive and optimistic expectation of
restoration that we can understand Calvin's rejection of the world *(contemptus mundi)*. The *contemptus mundi* does not lead to a withdrawal from
the world. It means freedom from dependence on the world, but not freedom from life in the world. There is an optimism and an element of hope,
absent in Luther, which permeates Calvin's spirituality. This outlook
is shown in Calvin's exegesis of Jn. 12:31, "Now is the judgment of this
world."

> The word judgment is taken as 'reformation' by some and 'condemna-
> tion' by others. I agree rather with the former who expound it
> that the world must be restored to due order *(legitimum ordinem)*.
> For the Hebrew word *mishpat* which is translated as judgment means a
> well-ordered constitution *(rectam constitutionem)*. Now we know
> that outside Christ there is nothing but confusion in the world.
> And although Christ had already begun to set up the kingdom of God,
> it was His death that was the true beginning of a properly ordered
> state *(status rite compositi)* and the complete restoration of the
> world.[3]

This position vis à vis the world is in marked contrast to the doctrine of the *De Imitatione Christi*, the full title of which is *On the
Imitation of Christ and Contempt for the World*. The notion of "world"
is central in the *Imitation*. Holiness is found only by adopting an

attitude of contempt toward it.  For the "world" is not in the process
of fulfillment - it is a finished work, to which no further truth can be
added.  The sum of finite realities that a person can choose or reject -
that is what the world really is.

> It is also laudable in a religious person seldom to go abroad, sel-
> dom to see others, and seldom to be seen by others.  Why will you
> consider what it is not lawful for you to have?  The world passes
> away with all its concupiscence and deceitful pleasures.[4]

There is no need to go out into the world.  Nothing new occurs in it.

> What may you see outside your chamber that you may not see within
> it?  Look, within your chamber you can see heaven and earth and
> all the elements of which all earthly things are made.[5]

The *Imitatione Christi* projects the image of a pilgrim who pays no
heed to the things around him that he may offer his entire attention to
the other world, which is eternal.[6]

Calvin would agree that we are pilgrims on this earth.  But our pilgrimage is not without consequence for the world.  Condemning the detachment of the Anabaptists from politics, he argues

> Yet this distinction does not lead us to consider the whole nature
> of government a thing polluted, which has nothing to do with Chris-
> tian men.  That is what, indeed, certain fanatics who delight in
> unbridled license should and boast:  after we have died through
> Christ to the elements of this world (Col. 2:20), are transported
> to God's Kingdom, and sit among heavenly beings, it is a thing un-
> worthy of us and set far beneath our excellence to be occupied
> with those vile and worldly cares which have to do with business
> foreign to a Christian man.  To what purpose, they ask, are there
> laws without trials and tribunals?  But what has a Christian man to
> do with trials themselves?  Indeed, if it is not lawful to kill,
> why do we have laws and trials?  But as we have just now pointed
> out that this kind of government is distinct from that spiritual
> and inward Kingdom of Christ, so we must know that they are not at
> variance.  For spiritual government, indeed, is already initiating
> in us upon earth certain beginnings of the Heavenly Kingdom, and
> in this mortal and fleeting life affords a certain forecast of an
> immortal and incorruptible blessedness.  Yet civil government has
> as its appointed end, so long as we live among men, to cherish and
> protect the outward worship of God, to defend  sound doctrine of
> piety and the position of the church, to adjust our life to the
> society of men, to form our social behavior to civil righteousness,
> to reconcile us with one another, and to promote general peace and
> tranquillity.  All of this I admit to be superfluous, if God's
> Kingdom, such as it is now among us, wipes out the present life.
> But if it is God's will that we go as pilgrims upon the earth while
> we aspire to the true fatherland, and if the pilgrimage requires
> such helps, those who take these from man deprive him of his very
> humanity.[7]

Calvin's belief in restoration, both of the individual and of the world, qualifies the nature of the existing tension in the Christian life.  Growth is a key concept for Calvin.  The power of the Resurrected Christ effects real sanctification whereby the sinner is led into a greater and ever increasing conformity with Christ.

> Paul wants to teach that outside Christ all things were upset, but that through Him they have been reduced to order.  And truly, outside Christ, what can we perceive in the world but mere ruins?  We are alienated from God by sin, and how can we but be wandering and shattered?  The proper state of creatures is to cleave to God. Such an anakephalaiosis as would bring us back to regular order, the apostle tells us, has been made in Christ.  Formed into one body, we are united to God, and mutually conjoined with one another. But without Christ the whole world is as it were a shapeless chaos and frightful confusion.  He alone gathers us into true unity.[8]

Luther said little about the growth of the sinner into the likeness of Christ.  Calvin, on the other hand, saw the existing tension in the spiritual life as the reestablishment of the image of God in man (Calvin's notion of *order*) conceived as present task and as final goal.  This order is to be accomplished not only within man; it must also be made visible within the Church and society.  Calvin expressed the visible dimension of this task in the following fashion:  "...to establish the heavenly reign of God upon earth."[9]

In a real sense the Christian must become an agent of the restoration of order throughout the world.  Within the spirituality of John Calvin was a demand for greater earthly activity and a thrust toward the conquest of the world for the Glory of God.  The individualistic dimension of Calvin's spirituality did not result in the relegation of faith to the private sphere.  Calvin's spirituality was a mystique of service. The apostolic life was no longer a consequence of love for God but the form of it.  In both its ascetical and mystical aspects, Christian perfection consisted not in formal prayer but in apostolic action undertaken for the glory of God.

The fruit of justification and sanctification is glorification.  What justification initiates by repentance and faith and sanctification supports by obedience in faith glorification completes by perfect love, both of God and of one's neighbors.  Justification, sanctification and glorification might be said to be Calvin's three stages of the spiritual life, somewhat like purification, illumination and union, the three stages of traditional Catholic spirituality.

## B.  Sanctification as World Transformation

Calvin's contribution to the understanding of sanctification as world-transformation has an unmistakable validity today.  Throughout the history of spirituality there has been a tendency towards passivity and withdrawal from active life in the world.

In a recent issue of *Concilium* entitled "Spirituality, Public or Private?"[10] Christian Duquoc, the editor, states the problem of contemporary spirituality as the necessity

> to learn to see a Christian life that is fully committed socially
> and politically as the very location of spirituality, while
> acknowledging the social and political implications of certain
> vital elements of spiritual thought.[11]

There can be no dualistic division between the private and public dimensions of the Christian life.  Speaking of the aim of that issue the editor continues:

> One of the aims of this number is to show that the dialectic of in-
> wardness and outwardness inherent in Christian spirituality is not
> virtually synonymous with the legalistic distinction between the
> private and public spheres characteristic of bourgeois society at
> the beginning of the industrial era.[12]

There is not one word on Calvin's doctrine in the entire issue.

The tension between the contemplative and the active or apostolic aspects of spirituality has divided theologians since the episode of Martha and Mary was recorded in the Gospels.  Efforts have been made throughout the history of the Church to justify the apostolate as a means of growth in the spiritual life.  But it seems that the monastic spirituality of contemplation and withdrawal has in many ways prevailed. Volume IX of *Concilium*[13] contains two radically different stands on this question in spirituality.  Clearly the tension endures.

For Hans Urs von Balthasar the quintessence of Christian existence consists in the basic attitude of "leaving everything" so that we may be totally submerged in radical surrender to God.

> He must leave everything without looking back, without trying to
> create a synthesis between Jesus and leaving one's home, between
> Jesus and burying one's father.[14]

No legitimate synthesis of Christ and the world, Christian existence and existence in the world, is possible.

A. M. Besnard advances a totally opposite view. According to him, any spirituality that is guided by concern for Christ's message, the Kingdom of God which is about to begin, must necessarily be world oriented. The Christian of today, according to Besnard, is more than anything else looking for a spirituality "in the world."

> In order for him to approach God and offer spiritual veneration he needs in no way first to forget his earthly existence and destiny, much less deny them: God's life itself is the substance of man's spiritual sacrifice; man's action, his love and his suffering, provide the ground for that dialogue with God, for that never-ending and dramatic encounter with God, in which man's destiny achieves its peak.[15]

Spirituality cannot develop in a separate religious presence, but must take place in the midst of the world, where the kingdom of God is becoming actual as a kingdom of rightousness and salvation. Worldly spirituality begins with the assumption that everyday life itself is "divine service" and that the "world" is the scene and site, the locus, of the encounter with God.

Yet the spirituality of the *Imitation of Christ* is still very much alive today. According to the *Imitation of Christ*, the Church should be composed of spiritual men whose essential task it is not to make the Church "the light of nations" but to devote themselves to the contemplative search for Christ alone, in flight from the world. This stress on inwardness characteristic of the *Imitation* seems to have led many to the denial of any effective relation between spirituality and life in the world. Lay holiness is conceived of and formulated as "living like a monk in the world."

The individualism of Calvin's spirituality made no concession to privacy. His spirituality laid the proper balance between private and public religion, between the transformation of the individual and of the community, between inwardness and outwardness. What Calvin said of saints, other men would later say of citizens. They championed the same sense of civic virtue, of discipline and of duty. Calvin envisioned an integration of holiness and virtue into the political order. His approach is relevant to the direction taken by the Catholic Church at the Second Vatican Council. According to Vatican II the Church functions as an anticipatory sign of the New Age as it concerns itself with the "this-worldly" aspects of human existence. The Council gave a new emphasis to the secular mission of the Church and to the positive evaluation of progress in all realms. This direction must also be followed in the realm of spirituality.

C. *Epistemology and Ecclesiology: The New Foundations for Individualism in Spirituality.*

The major question of the sources of authority within the spiritual life had not received sufficient treatment from the Christian Humanists. All of them, Erasmus included, accepted the traditional position of the mediating role of the Church in our knowledge of God and in the spiritual life.[16] For Erasmus the source of the *Philosophia Christi* was the revelation of God as found in the Gospel. But the Gospel came to us through the mediation of a Church which played an important role as an interpreter of the Scriptures. All things depended on the right interpretation of Scripture. But within whose competence was this?

To ascribe divine authority to anything other than the one whom one has personally experienced Calvin considered idolatry. He argued against making any external authority the ultimate criterion of truth. Without the indwelling Spirit, the Gospel could lead only to positivism or legalism. The Word and all words are related to God's Being through the living action of the Holy Spirit. In opening himself to the influence of the Spirit, man is able to feel the presence of God, to experience his touch and sense the immediacy of His presence. Through the action of the Spirit, the believer is made capable of distinguishing the reality of God from the products of his own mind.

With this doctrine of the Holy Spirit Calvin transformed the nature of the *philosophia Christi.*

> Christian philosophy bids her (reason) give place and yield complete submission to the Holy Spirit, so that the man himself no longer lives, but Christ lives and rules in him.[17]

In every generation the fullness of the Word of God reaches the believer not primarily through the Scriptures but through the work of the Spirit who inspired the writers of Scripture. The truth of the Scriptures is "sealed to our hearts" by the inner witness of the Holy Spirit; it is not simply commended to us by an ecclesiastical institution.[18]

The Holy Spirit creates within man a *sensus divinitatis* which becomes

the source of new understanding, spiritual discernment in the things of
God and man, and certainty.[19]  In the regenerated *sensus divinitatis* God
himself is discovered through his human image.  For Calvin self-knowledge
leads much further than the purely psychological or philosophical knowledge of self.  Man enters into the knowledge of himself to enter into
the knowledge of God.

At the same time, John Major's doctrine of intuitive-auditive knowledge helped Calvin avoid both positivism and subjectivism by keeping in
proper tension the knowledge received from the Word and the knowledge
received from the Spirit.

Calvin's epistemology demanded a reinterpretation of traditional
ecclesiological models.  In the Roman tradition, the Church recognizes
the Spirit not as an immanent possession subject to its direction but as
a transcendent reality by which it is directed.  For Calvin the action
of the Holy Spirit occurs principally in the individual and not in the
Church.  The Spirit acts towards the individual independent of the community.  The *Testimonium Spiritus Sancti* is individual.  It gives the
individual the certitude of God's promise.

While Calvin was not a covenant theologian in the technical sense
(what is most fundamental to his thought is the concept of an order
established by God's grace), he did think of the Church in covenantal
and contractual terms.

> All those who from the beginning of the world God adopted as his
> peculiar people were taken into covenant with him.  The covenant
> which God always made with his servants was this:  'I will walk
> among you and you will be my people.'  Those words comprehend life
> and salvation and the whole sum of blessedness.[20]

The Church that rises to this call to covenant and accepts it is the
product of a meeting of wills.  Contractual in nature, its primacy
belongs to the contracting parties.  The emergent society is secondary.
This contractualism remains valid, despite the fact that Calvin frequently described the Church in organic terms, as the body of Christ.
It is true that Calvin spoke of an *insitio in corpus Christi*.  But the
concept of the mystical body was for Calvin only a simile.  There is no
ontological link between the believer and the glorious Christ.  Only in
virtue of the promise is the believer joined to Christ.[21]  For the
glorious body of Christ is located in heaven, while the Church and the

believer are on earth.  The distance between the glorified Christ and
the believer can only be bridged by the Spirit.  And there is no need
for the body of Christ to be present on earth since the Lord

> by his Spirit bestows upon us the blessings of being one with him
> in soul, body and spirit.  The bond of that connection therefore is
> the spirit of Christ, which unites us to him and is a kind of
> channel by which everything that Christ has and is is directed to
> us.[22]

In Roman Catholicism, it is the pneumatic body of Christ that operates within the Church.  There is an ontological link between the
believer and Christ.  In Calvin's view, the power of the glorified
Christ, and not his pneumatic body, was present.  There could be no
question of any ontological link between the body of Christ and the
elect.  It is only in the light of this understanding of the mystical
body that we can see what Calvin meant by giving the Church the title of
mother.  Is the Church a mother in the sense that she gives us birth,
that she is ontologically before us?  In reaction against the Münster-
ites, a group of fanatics, Calvin insisted that there is no  solitary
road to God.

> Many are led either by pride, dislike, or rivalry to the conviction
> that they can profit enough from private reading and meditation:
> hence they despise public assemblies and deem preaching superflu-
> ous.  But, since they do their utmost to sever or break the sacred
> bond of unity no one escapes the just penalty of this unholy sep-
> aration without bewitching himself with pestilent errors and foul-
> est illusions.[23]

It would seem that for Calvin there could be no salvation outside the
visible Church.

> But as it is now our purpose to discourse of the visible Church,
> let us learn from her single title of Mother, how useful, how
> necessary the knowledge of her is, since there is no other means of
> entering into life unless she conceive us in the womb and give us
> birth, unless she nourish us at her breasts, and, in short, keep us
> under her charge and government, until divested of mortal flesh, we
> become like the angels...the abandonment of the Church is always
> fatal.[24]

But the Church is truly mother only in the measure that the Holy Spirit
acts in her.  In no way does the Church have causal relationship in the
regeneration of man.  There is an external link between the Church's
function and the role of the Spirit.  Calvin expressed this by speaking

of the *vocatio externa* of the Word, which is the preaching of the Church,
and the *vocatio interna* of the Spirit, which is the effect of the *testimonium internum*.

Through his doctrine of the Holy Spirit and his epistemology, Calvin
attempted to deal with one of the crucial problems in ecclesiology, a
problem medieval ecclesiology and the later Christian humanism had left
unsolved:  the role of the Church as a visible community active in the
world but not the Kingdom of God; as a community with specific and concrete forms, but forms which cannot be absolutized.

Although Calvin understands the Church as mother, he does not see
this same Church as the mediator or regulator of the individual believer's thought and life.  God alone is the source of any benefit.[25]
Through the words of the Holy Spirit, the ministry of the Church is
effective.  This Spirit is not an immanent possession subject to the
Church's direction but a transcendent reality by which it is directed.
The Spirit works on the existential and operative level - with no mention of consecration or cooperation on the part of the Church.  For the
Spirit cannot be institutionalized; it invokes the Holy Spirit but does
not confer it.

> All that the Scripture attributes of dignity or authority, either
> to the Prophets or Priests of the ancient Law or to the Apostles
> and their successors, is attributed not to their persons but to the
> ministry and office to which they are assigned, or, to speak more
> plainly, to the Word of God which they are called to administer.[26]

The Church has no right to define doctrine.

> God takes away from men the ability to forge any new article, so
> that he alone may be our master and teacher in spiritual doctrine.[27]

Apart from the Lordship of God in Christ, the Church has no existence.  The Church is nothing and has nothing; it is radically poor.
Christ's Lordship is never given to the Church.  The Church was not
established for its own sake. It must recognize itself only as a provisional arrangement of God and must proclaim its own eschatological tran-
sience.  For the Church is not the Kingdom of God but a function of the
Kingdom of God, subordinated to the Kingdom and obedient to it.

Although Calvin established a stringent Church discipline, he did not
entrust the unity of the Church to an external framework but to the
faith, hope, and charity produced by the Spirit of God.[28]  Calvin's

emphasis on the local Church and its Eucharistic life stems from this
concern for unity.  The Eucharistic community establishes a context for
the Christian life in which the unity of faith and fraternal concord may
be cultivated.[29]  The type of unity Calvin sought to support by his insistence on the frequency of the Eucharist was one which would respect
the individuality of the believer and at the same time avoid the anarchy
which results when institutional bounds are ignored.

John Calvin recognized the need for organization and structure but
also admitted the propriety of diversity and the possibility of plural-
ism.  He stated that "in every human society some kind of government is
necessary...and that the removal of laws would unnerve the Church, de-
face and dissipate it..."[30]

> In these ordinances, however, we must always attend to the excep-
> tion, that they must not be thought necessary to salvation, nor
> lay the conscience under a religious obligation.  They must not be
> compared to the worship of God nor substituted for piety.[31]

> ...because things of this value are not necessary to salvation, and
> for the edification of the Church, they should be accommodated to
> the varying circumstances of each age and nation...[32]

D.  *The Role of the Church in the Spiritual Life of the Contemporary*
    *Christian*

In attempting to incorporate Calvin's insights into the contemporary
Church, we are obviously forbidden from literally implementing them.
The questions of the individual and society, of control and freedom are
highly complex.  No facile parallels can be drawn.  Calvin's main contribution to us is in the area of theological principles and methodology.
In his theology of the Word and the Spirit, Calvin presents us with
sound hermeneutical principles for an ecclesiology in which the typi-
cally modern category of dialogue can be integrated into the theory of
the mediating function of the Church.

Guided by his epistemology, Calvin evolved a doctrine of the Church
that remains perpetually challenging to Christian spirituality and to
the Roman Catholic tradition today.

Within this tradition, there is present a tendency to de-institution-
alize spirituality, making it more deeply personal.  According to Karl
Rahner, the Church as the supporting element for piety is progressively
fading away.  The personal religious experience of the individual

becomes increasingly decisive.

While this is one current of thought, a great deal of contemporary
Roman Catholic spirituality has become predominantly Church-centered.
The confrontation between the divine and the human is conceived as taking place primarily by means of the Church's mediation.   In a recent
article in *Concilium*, F. Vandenbroucke wrote:

> Let us now consider finally the instrumental cause of every Chris-
> tian spirituality.  This cause is the Church with its hierarchy,
> sacraments and liturgy and Tradition.  This presupposes the accept-
> ance of the principle of the ecclesiastical economy, without which
> it is impossible to speak of Christian spirituality except in the
> broad sense in which it is said that every grace comes through the
> Church according to the formula *extra ecclesiam nulla salus*.[33]

We read in another author:

> Christianity represents us with an association based upon a shared
> faith, not the chance coincidence of a number of individual opin-
> ions, but a faith which is primordially corporate, essentially the
> faith of a society, in which faith the members of the society par-
> ticipate; their faith is their own, and yet it is not their own,
> because it comes to them from and remains always essentially the
> faith of the society.[34]

"The Church is not a voluntary religious association formed by the coming
together of individual believers," writes Christopher Dawson, "but a
supernatural divine organism which transmits the gifts of eternal life
to mankind."[35]

The doctrine echoed in these writers has led to an understanding of
the Church as a self-contained structure, a self-sufficient divine
entity, often experienced by the individual as something placed between
God and himself.  But the authority which serves as underpinning for
this ecclesiology is proving increasingly unworkable.  All authority
contains elements both of elicitation and of imposition.  The conditions
of the modern age have rendered the older forms of authority obsolete
within a contemporary model of the Church.  The shifting emphasis from
elicitation to imposition characteristic of the authority structure in
the past few centuries of Church history has made it largely into a
source of problems instead of solutions.  Innovation tends to be excluded and a tremendously dysfunctional rigidity of thought and practice takes hold.  The Church is identified, for all practical purposes,
with the hierarchy, since this closed group does and says all that is

really important to say and do.  Instead of acting as the mediator of an
intensely personal and dynamic faith, the Church functions as the mediator of its own ideology.

As an institution embodying in some way the grace of Christ and serv-
ing as a locus of the meeting between God and man, the Church is in bad
repute today.  It is not used by its members, or seen by those outside
it, as a vehicle for inwardness.

What is required are new Church structures able to sustain the authentic religious experience of the individual believer.  Within the previously described ecclesiological model, it is impossible to develop a
spirituality in which God's redeeming presence manifests itself primarily within the individual self.  For a spirituality mediated by the
Church and leading to corporate life in the Church to flourish, there
must emerge a greater awareness of the potential for community which
God's redeeming presence in man effects.  Corporateness is achieved not
strictly "from the top down," but by eliciting a consensus from the con-
stituency.  This understanding of corporateness can be developed only in
the light of a theology of the Word and Spirit.  Within such a theology,
the Church would be moved in terms of consensus.  This approach would
break the antithesis between objectivism and subjectivism and substitute
a flexible authority structure for the older, more rigid one.  Real freedom in the personal dimension of faith would then be possible.

The structure of the Church and her mediating role in the life of the
believer must be subordinated to the individual's relationship to God.
Final responsibility for the spiritual welfare of the Church's members
and ultimate authority here on earth do not reside in a corporate group.
For man cannot submit ultimately to an authority outside of himself.
Whatever submission he makes can never be absolute, for a man can never
transfer to anyone else the responsibility for his own religious faith.
Scripture and tradition enable man to grasp more fully his own inner ex-
perience; they are not substitutes for it.

E.  *The Unity of Theology and Spirituality*

In the history of Christianity, there has been a constant tendency to
separate theological reflection from spirituality.  This separation is
understandable.  Religious men are conscious of the Presence of God in
the depths of their souls.  But they are unable to describe this Presence

in the way that they describe other things. Attempts to deal with this
Presence have alternated between the two ways of negation and affirmation. Whatever can be affirmed about God can only be expressed in symbols or analogies. The function of dogma is to conserve the experience
of God and to explain it. But of its very nature it is inadequate; the
truth and reality which spring from the experience of God can only be
partially expressed in conceptual terms.

So theological reflection has usually been assigned the task of formu-
lating and examining dogmatic statements, while the experience of God
has been resumed for the realm of spirituality. This creates a false
dichotomy, limiting theological knowledge to a knowledge of things. When
this happens, the old complaint dating back to the age of the Greek
Fathers, is heard again:  that the dogmatic books are an obstacle to the
spiritual life of a man - they dessicate and destroy it.[36]  The same complaint was made in Calvin's time against the schoolmen.

It was Calvin's dissatisfaction with scholastic theology that led him
to accept the humanistic concept of *pietas* as *sapientia,* as *sancta eruditio.* Calvin understood theological knowledge as vital and experiential
in nature. He used the expression *philosophia Christi* from the very
beginning of his *Institutes* to express his concern for a renewal in theology. Its use also indicated Calvin's dependence on Erasmus, for whom
theology and spirituality were one. Erasmus' new method in theology was
not intended simply as an instrument for renewal of the intellectual
life, but for the renewal of the whole person. The *philosophia Christi*
must be understood as a principle of restoration of order.

> Moreover, what else is the *philosophy of Christ*, which He himself
> calls a rebirth, than the restoration of human nature originally
> well formed.[37]

Calvin affirmed the same thing when he said that he had given first
place to doctrine since it is through doctrine that salvation begins.[38]
For Calvin the greatest danger to the spiritual life was a false knowledge of God which made man's obligation of worship, and therefore his
piety, impossible.

*F. Spirituality and Theological Method*

The unity of theology and spirituality is still a goal to be attained
today. Theology, according to many, is too intellectualistic, and

spirituality is found lacking in theological substance.  This situation
is expressed by Hans Küng in the following fashion.

> Non-theologians also take issue with theologians in this dispute.
> They complain that our theological literature likewise has long
> been, and continues to be, by and large, esoteric and intellectual-
> istic, that it frequently disdains to rub shoulders with the real
> world, indeed that it rarely, if ever, displays real concern for
> the needs of people living today, that it fails to speak the lan-
> guage of our time, and that it almost never makes a clear and de-
> cisive call to the imitation of Christ.  In short, they object that
> our theological writing generally fails to 'edify' in the best and
> most important sense of the word.[39]

> The thinker and the man of piety, the dogmatist and the mystic, the
> theologian and the saint were each to go his separate way.  Yet so
> much of the upheaval witnessed in the theology, in the Church, and
> in the world of our century compels us to try to re-see and re-
> practice as one single theology the separate disciplines of scien-
> tific and devotional theology.  In the final analysis, a Christian
> cannot but consider learning and piety, study and devotion, and
> indeed theology and meditation as belonging essentially together.
> Theological research carried on without reverence and meditation
> easily degenerates into a speculating or historicizing scholasti-
> cism that lacks life.  Similarly, pious meditation engaged in with-
> out the sobering restraints of clear theological norms has a way of
> degenerating into an intellectually inbred or sentimental religios-
> ity that lacks substance.[40]

The situation of contemporary theological education as described by
Hugh Kerr is highly relevant to the question of the integration of spirituality and theology.

> What students today most want from the study of religion they
> hardly ever get.  The personal-mystical enthusiasm which many find
> meaningful comes too close to subjectivism for their teachers.
> Trained in the intellectualism of the typical graduate school, most
> teachers of religious subjects try to avoid anything as intangible
> as inner faith experience.  They want to demonstrate that religion
> can be studied as objectively as any other discipline.[41]

In theology, the most important decision to be made is about the
sources of theological reflection.  They are the formative factors that
determine the character of a given theology.  In Christian theology, the
fundamental source has always been Revelation, considered so basic that
theology and theological education are directly related and affected by
the understanding of its nature.  When the organizing principle of theology is the idea that revelation is primarily a deposit of propositional
truths given and transmitted by means of a history or of a Church, the

result is theological positivism. Divine truths that constitute man as man become available exclusively in Scripture or in a Church tradition. This exclusivism results in a disregard for the personal and direct encounter with the divine.

Theology becomes then a revelation-centered and Church-centered theology. The ordinary encounter between the divine and the human takes place by means of the history recorded in the Scriptures or by means of the Church. In this context theology is isolated from its roots in the religious experience of the believer and risks becoming a denominational ideology whereby a specific Church rationalizes its own existence. (Recall the mass of dogmatic theology which has served as expression of the theologian's intention to repeat faithfully the traditional formulations of his denomination.)

At the same time, the positivism of revelation regards a given divine truth as objective reality which defines man in accordance with what is most real. Theology in this context will strive for impersonal and objective knowledge, to the exclusion of man's subjective experience. Personal thinking is understood as subjectivistic and arbitary and as an obstacle to objectivity.

In his book *Personal Knowledge*, Michael Polanyi affirmed that the greatest threat to the progress of culture is the denial of the value of personal thinking.[42] One of the failings of our age is the refusal to grant existential credibility to the indefinable. We have made Wittgenstein's early dictum our own: "Of what cannot be said, thereof must one be silent." Polanyi has replaced this by, "Nothing that we know can be said precisely." Human action and man's contact with the ground of life depend in large measure upon inarticulate and unconceptualized knowledge. The constant interaction between the inarticulate and the articulate is of the utmost importance for human growth.

The exploratory drive within man, which is the primary source of creative thinking, is imbedded in his inarticulate thinking. But, when objective and impersonal knowledge are pursued as the highest possible goal, the exploratory drive and the spirit of inquiry are quenched. In the context of positivism, learning deteriorates into map reading. To find the way by means of a ready-made map is easier than to search without a map. But, as Aarne Siirala writes:

> To be sure, a traveler proceeding with the aid of a map is in an
> intellectually more advantageous position than an explorer of a new
> area who lacks a map. Yet the progress which the explorer makes
> with his groping is a higher human achievement than a well-planned
> tourist trip by the traveler with a map. The attainment of knowl-
> edge as exact as possible is an important human objective, but
> man's finest intellectual achievement is the creation of knowledge.
> The human mind is most sensitive as it brings uncharted areas under
> its control. It is then that man renews his articulate knowledge,
> the framework on which he depends in his search for knowledge. The
> genuinely new can be found only by means of the same inarticulable
> powers which the animals use in learning to find their way out of
> mazes.[43]

With our positivistic understanding of Revelation, we have made tour-

ists out of our theological students. They are trained to become map

readers, and in the process they lose their inner drive for discovery.

Theological education has become, for the most part, training for con-

ceptual analysis and verbal communication. Theology retains a remote

contact with the workings of personal experience and thought, and its

relationship with the more dynamic situation of field education can only

be but superficial.

What is needed is an empirical theology that can free man of a

Church-centered and Scripture-centered theology. An empirical theology

is one that is open to God's Word in all life. Such a theology presup-

poses a distinctive approach to Revelation. A distinction must be made

between unthematic and thematic revelation. Revelation is unthematic

inasmuch as it is experienced not as an object within the world, but as

the horizon within which the world is comprehended. It is also unthe-

matic because it is known implicitly and existentially by man before it

can possibly be understood explicitly and conceptually. God's Word is

addressed to man in a twofold manner, inwardly and outwardly. God con-

tinues to be present as revealer in the deep experiences of the be-

liever and the believing community. In a real sense, the categorical

revelation, the thematic revelation as found in Scripture and Tradition,

does not turn man away from himself to make him subject to something

outside of him. Historical revelation is an event within the world that

can serve to represent in an explicit way the truth of the graciousness

of that horizon that is already known implicitly to encompass the world.

Man cannot submit ultimately to an authority outside himself. Truth

cannot be attained unless a man is attuned to what goes on within.

No doubt the learning process in religion, as in other sciences, involves at least a provisional submission to authority. But the submission can never be absolute, for a man can never transfer to anyone else the responsibility for his own religious faith. Scripture and tradition enable man to grasp more fully his own inner experience; they are not substitutes for it.

There can be no dualism which separates theology from faith experience. Theology must be the process whereby that experience is reflexively understood, articulated in propositions and embodied in language. There is not thematization and experience, but a thematized experience. Theology, in the strict sense, is therefore merely a further development, an unfolding of that basic subjective reflection which already takes place in the obedient listening to the Word of God.

Personal faith invites discovery. The motivational force behind theological reflection is the need to explore the unknown. In fact, the only way out of absolutizing and positivism is in continuing open discussion inspired by the spirit of exploration. The task of the theologian is that of trying things on for size. Theology is consistently tentative and experimental. It should in no way support dependency, passivity and acquiescence. Robert Frost's remark applies to theological education as well as to other endeavors: "What a man needs is the courage to take a chance on his own discriminations." Theology arises from faith; creative theology arises from present faith, not past faith. The real theological questions are always contemporary and, moreover, they can be effectively handled only by someone who is sensitive to the present action of God.

Through his religious epistemology, Calvin called attention to the profoundly personal nature of the knowledge of God. God and man are not separated by an intervening veil of conceptualizations. Knowledge of God does not deal with a concept of God, but with God himself. God is not an object outside of us which we come to know through sense experience. He is not an object of science that can be apprehended, analyzed or manipulated. The knowledge of God is the experience of a subject. According to Calvin, our knowledge of God depends on what Polanyi terms a "personal coefficient." This knowledge is impossible apart from the personal involvement of the knower. Knowledge of God enhances the person's moral sensitivity and his own self-understanding. Through it, a

profound sense of commitment develops which penetrates every aspect of
the person's behavioral and conceptual existence.

On the other hand, to say that knowledge of God is composed of personal commitment does not mean according to Calvin that knowledge is
totally relative or subjective. With his doctrine of Word and Spirit
correlating to the objective and subjective factors of knowledge, Calvin
broke the antithesis of objectivism and subjectivism. He understood
theological knowledge as vital and experiential, never separated from
its sources - the Word and the Spirit.

The Holy Spirit is within us the source of all understanding. It is
never bound by any institution. Source of certainty and personal conviction for the knower, the Spirit becomes the internal and ultimate
source of authority. Calvin argues against making any external authority the ultimate criterion for truth. At the same time, he affirmed the
constant need for openness to the Word of God. That is why the theologian is a man in continual dialectical relationship between the Word and
the Spirit; he is sent from the Word to the Spirit and from the Spirit
to the Word. Within this dialectical movement, it is impossible to be
content with any objective knowledge of God as ultimate, or to lose
one's drive toward the ever new discovery of God.

## Notes

1. *Comm. on Jn.*, 13:31; OC, 45, 568.
2. OC, 45, 425.
3. *Comm. on Jn.*, 12:31; OC 47, 243.
4. *De Imitatione Christi*, c. I, 20.
5. *Ibid.*
6. Cf. I, 23; II, 1; III, 53.
7. *Inst.*, IV, 20, 2.
8. *Comm. on Eph.*, 1:8; OC, 51, 151.
9. Letter to Nicholas Radziwill, *Letter* III, 133; OC, 15, 429.
10. *Concilium*, Vol. 69, No. 7 (London, 1971).
11. *Ibid.*, p. 7.
12. *Ibid.*
13. *Concilium*, Vol. 9 (New York, 1965).
14. Hans Urs von Balthasar, "The Gospel as Norm and Test of all Spirituality in the Church," *Concilium* 9, 17-18.
15. A. M. Besnard, "Tendencies of Contemporary Spirituality," *Concilium* 9, 30-31.
16. For Juan de Valdes the Word of God meant primarily inward revelation. There is in de Valdes a strong emphasis on a religion of firsthand delivery, a religion that should be inwardly experienced and verified through an internal authority.
17. OC I, 1132.
18. "For if the Christian Church was founded at first on the writings of the prophets, and the preaching of the apostles, that doctrine, wheresoever it may be found, was certainly ascertained and sanctioned antecedently to the Church, since, but for this, the Church herself never could have existed. Nothing, therefore, can be more absurd than the fiction that the power of judging Scripture is in the Church and that on her nod its certainty depends. When the Church receives it and gives it the stamp of her authority, she does not make that authentic which was otherwise doubtful or controverted, but, acknowledging it as the truth of God, she, as in duty bound, shows her reverence by an unhesitating assent. As to the question, How shall we be persuaded that it came from God without recurring to a decree of the Church? it is just the same as if it were asked, How shall we learn to distinguish light from darkness, white from black, sweet from bitter? Scripture bears upon the face of it as clear evidence of its truth, as white and black do of their colour, sweet and bither of their taste." *Inst.*, I, 7, 2. This could be compared to Ignatius of Loyola's Doctrine on the Church as contained in the *Exercises*.
19. When Calvin was considering the problem of predestination, he declared to the Council of Geneva: "So far as I am concerned, my masters, I am quite certain in my conscience that that which I have taught and written did not arise out of my own head, but that I have received it from God, and I must stand firmly by it, if I am not to be a traitor to the truth." OC, 14, 382.
20. *Inst.*, II, 10, 1; II, 10, 8.
21. OC, 55, 71-72.
22. *Inst.*, IV, 17, 12.
23. *Inst.*, IV, 1, 5.
24. *Inst.*, IV, 1, 4.

25. *Inst.*, IV, 1, 5.

26. *Inst.*, IV, 8, 2.

27. *Inst.*, IV, 8, 9.

28. *Inst.*, IV, 1, 5.

29. *Inst.*, IV, 17, 38.

30. *Inst.*, IV, 10, 27.

31. *Ibid.*

32. *Inst.*, IV, 10, 30.

33. F. Vandenbroucke, "Spirituality and Spiritualities," *Concilium* 9 p. 55.

34. P. C. Butler, *The Church and Infallibility* (New York, 1954) 122.

35. C. Dawson, *The Formation of Christendom* (New York, 1967) 287.

36. Cf. Irenée Hausherr, *Penthos: La doctrine de la componction dans l'Orient chrétien* (Rome, 1944) 123-132.

37. *Paraclesis*, Holborn, 145:4ff. Trans. Olin, 100.

38. OC I, 1127.

39. Hans Küng, *Freedom Today* (New York, 1965) VII.

40. *Ibid.*, IX.

41. Hugh Kerr, "Education in General and Theological Education," *Theology Today* XXVII, 4 (1971) 443.

42. Michael Polanyi, *Personal Knowledge* (Chicago, 1958).

43. Aarne Siirala, *Divine Humanness* (Philadelphia, 1970) 134.

BIBLIOGRAPHY

*Sources*

Bucer, Martin. *Traité de l'Amour du Prochain.* Paris, 1949.

_____. *Martini Buceri Opera Latina* 15. Ed. Fr. Wendel. Paris-Gütersloh, 1955.

Calvin, John. *Institution de la Religion Chrestienne.* Ed. J. D. Benoit. Paris, 1957.

_____. *Ioannis Calvini Opera quae supersunt omnia.* Eds. G. Baum, E. Cunitz, E. Reuss, *et al.* 59 vols., "Corpus Reformatorum." Brunswig, 1863-1900.

_____. *Johannis Calvini Opera Selecta.* Eds. P. Barth and W. Niesel. 5 vols., Monachii in Aedibus. Chr. Kaiser, 1926-1936.

Colet, J. *Enarratio in I<sup>am</sup> Epistolam ad Corinthios.* Ed. J. H. Lupton. London, 1874.

d'Etaples, J. Lefèvre. *Commentarii initiatorii in quattuor Evangelia.* Meaux, 1522.

_____. *Epistolae divi Pauli apostoli, ex vulgata editione adiecta intelligentia ex graeco, cum commentariis.* Paris, 1512.

Dier, R. De Muiden. *Scriptum de magistro Gerardo, domino Florencio et multis aliis devotis fratribus.* Ed. G. Dumbar. Analecta I, pp. 1-113. Deventer, 1719.

Erasmus, Desiderius. *Enchiridion, Paraclesis, Methodus, Apologia.* Ed. Hajo Holborn. Munich, 1933.

_____. *Erasmi Opera Omnia.* Ed. Jean LeClerc. Leiden, 1703-1706.

_____. *Erasmi opuscula.* Ed. W. K. Ferguson. The Hague, 1933.

_____. *Opus Epistolarum Des. Erasmi Roterodami.* Eds. P. S. Allen and H. M. Allen. Oxford, 1906-1941.

Gerson, Jean le Charlier de. *De Mystica Theologia.* Ed. André Combes. Lucani, 1958.

_____. *Initiation à la vie mystique.* Ed. with preface by Pierre Pascal. Paris, 1943.

Groote, Gerard. *Consuetudines fratrum vitae communis.* Ed. Alberts W. Jappe. Fontes minores medii aevi VIII. Groningue, 1959.

_____. *Gerardi Magni Epistolae.* Ed. W. Mulder. Ons Geestelijke Erf. Antwerp, 1933.

Ignatius of Loyola. *Exercitia spiritualia sancti Ignatii de Loyola et eorum Directoria.* Ed. A. Codina. Monumenta Ignatiana, series secunda. Madrid, 1919.

_____. *Sancti Ignatii de Loyola Constitutiones Societatis Iesus.* Ed. A. Codina. Monumenta Ignatiana, series tertia. Rome, 1934-1938.

_____. *The Spiritual Exercises.* Trans. L. Puhl. Westminster, 1951.

Kempis, Thomas à. *Thomae Hemerken a Kempis opera omnia.* Ed. M. I. Pohl. 7 vols. Fribourg/BR, 1902-1922.

Major, Johannes. *In primum sententiarum; In secundum sententiarum; Super tertium sententiarum; Quartus sententiarum.* Paris, 1509, 1510, 1517, 1519.

_____. *In quatuor Evangelia expositiones luculente: et disputationes contra hereticos plurime.* Paris, 1529.

Petrarca, Francesco. *De otio religioso.* Ed. Giuseppe Rotondi (completed posthumously by Guido Matellotti). Città del Vaticano, 1958.

_____. *De sui ipsius et multorum ignorantia*. Ed. L. M. Capelli, *Le traité De sui ipsius et multorum ignorantia*. Paris, 1906.

_____. *De vita solitaria libri*. Eng. trans. with intro. by Jacob Zeitlin, *The Life of Solitude*. Urbana, 1924.

Salutati, Coluccio. *De seculo et religione*. Ed. B. L. Ullman. Florence, 1957.

*Theologia Germanica*. Intro. and Notes by J. Bernhart. New York, 1949.

Valdes, Juan de. *Alfabeto cristiano*. Ed. with commentary and notes by B. Croce. Bari, 1938.

_____. *Diálogo de Doctrina Christiana nueuamente compuesto por un Religioso*. Alcalá, 1529.

Valla, Lorenzo. *Scritti filosofici e religiosi*. Italian trans. with intro. and notes by Giorgio Radetti. Florence, 1953.

## Translations

Calvin, John

*Calvin's Reply to Sadoleto in a Reformation Debate*. Ed. J. C. Olin. New York, 1966.

*Calvin's Tracts and Treatises*. Trans. Henry Beveridge. 3 vols. Grand Rapids, 1958.

*Commentaries on the Gospels and Epistles of Saint Paul*. Trans. W. Pringle. Grand Rapids, 1948-1949.

*Commentaries*. Trans. and ed. Joseph Haroutunian and Louise P. Smith. Library of Christian Classics Vol. XXIII. Philadelphia, 1958.

*Concerning the Eternal Predestination of God*. Trans. J. K. S. Reid. London, 1961.

*Institutes of the Christian Religion*. Trans. John Allen. 2 vols., 8th rev. ed. Grand Rapids, 1949.

*Institutes of the Christian Religion*. Trans. Ford Lewis Battles. 2 vols. Library of Christian Classics Vols. XX-XXI. Philadelphia, 1960.

*Instruction in Faith*. Trans. Paul Fuhrmann. Philadelphia, 1949.

*Theological Treatises*. Trans. J. K. S. Reid. Library of Christian Classics Vol. XXII. Philadelphia, 1954.


Erasmus, Desiderius

*Desiderius Erasmus concerning the Aim and Method of Education*. Trans. W. H. Woodward. Cambridge, Mass., 1904.

*Discourse on Free Will*. Trans. E. F. Winter. New York, 1961.

*The Enchiridion*. Trans. F. L. Battles. Abridged version in W. Spinka (ed.), *Advocates of Christian Reform*. London, 1953.

*The Enchiridion of Erasmus*. Trans. Raymond Himelick. Bloomington, 1963.

*Handbook of the Militant Christian*. Trans. J. P. Dolan. Notre Dame, 1962.

*Christian Humanism and the Reformation*. Ed. and trans. J. Olin. New York, 1965. *Letter to Martin Dorp* May 1515, 55-92; *Letter to Paul Vloz* August 14, 1518, 107-134; *The Paraclesis*, 92-107.

## Secondary Literature

Adams, Marilyn M. "Intuitive Cognition, Certainty, and Skepticism in William Ockham," *Traditio* 26 (1970) 389-398.

Aldridge, J. W. *The Hermeneutic of Erasmus.* Zurich, 1966.

Asheim, I. (ed.). *The Church, Mysticism, Sanctification and the Natural in Luther's Thought.* Philadelphia, 1967.

Auer, A. *Die vollkommene Frömmigkeit des Christen nach dem "Enchiridion militis christiani" des Erasmus von Rotterdam.* Dusseldorf, 1954.

Axters, S. *La Spiritualité des Pays-Bas, l'évolution d'une doctrine mystique, Bibliotheca Mediliniensis.* Louvain-Paris, 1948.

Barhuizen, Van den Brink. *Juan de Valdes, reformateur en Espagne et en Italie, 1529-1541.* Geneva, 1969.

Bataillon, M. *Erasme et l'Espagne. Recherches sur l'histoire spirituelle du XVIe siècle.* Paris, 1937.

Battenhouse, R. W. "The Doctrine of Man in Calvin and in Renaissance Platonism," *JHI* 9 (1948) 447-471.

Battles, F. L. *The Piety of John Calvin. An Anthology illustrative of the Spirituality of the Reformer of Geneva.* Pittsburg, 1969.

Béne, C. *Erasme et Saint Augustin: ou influence de Saint Augustin sur l'humanisme d'Erasme.* Geneva, 1969.

Beradida, H. (ed.). *Pensée humaniste et tradition au XV et XVI siècles.* Paris, 1956.

Boehner, P. "The Notitia Intuitiva of Non-existents according to William Ockham," *Traditio* I (1943) 223-275.

_____. "The Realistic Conceptualism of William of Ockham," *Traditio* IV (1946) 307-335.

Bohatec, J. B. "Calvin et l'humanisme," *Revue Historique* 183 (1938) 207-241; 184 (1939) 71-104.

_____. *Budé und Calvin. Studien zur Gedankenwelt des franzosischen Frühhumanismus.* Graz, 1950.

_____. *Budé und Calvin. Studien zur Gedankenwelt des Frühhumanismus.* Graz, 1950.

Boisset, J. *Sagesse et Sainteté dans la pensée de Calvin. Essai sur l'humanisme du Réformateur.* Paris, 1959.

Bouyer, L. *Autour d'Erasme. Etude sur le christianisme des humanistes catholiques.* Paris, 1955.

Brampton, Charles K. "Scotus, Ockham and the Theory of Intuitive Cognition," *Antonianum* 40 (1965) 449-466.

Bravo, B. "Influjos de la *Devotio Moderna* sobre Erasmo de Rotterdam," *Manresa* 32 (1960) 99-112.

_____. "Gerardo Groote, Tomas de Kempis y Erasmo de Rotterdam," *Manresa* 32 (1960) 223-242.

Breen, Quirinus. *Christianity and Humanism: Studies in the History of Ideas.* Grand Rapids, 1968.

_____. *John Calvin: A Study in French Humanism.* Grand Rapids, 1931.

Brezzi, P. *Caratteri e protagonisti della spiritualita cattolica alla vine del Medio Evo.* Naples, 1960.

Busson, H. *Le rationalisme dans la littérature française de la Renaissance, 1533-1601.* Paris, 1957.

Carrière, V. *La Sorbonne et l'évangelisme au XVIe siècle, Aspects de l'Université de Paris.* Paris, 1949.

Cassirer, E. *Individuum und Kosmos in der Philosophie der Renaissance.* Leipzig, 1927.

Cave, T. C. *Devotional Poetry in France (1570-1613).* Cambridge, 1969.

Certeau, M. de.  *Le mépris du monde. La notion du mépris du monde dans la tradition spirituelle occidentale.*  Paris, 1965.

Chantraine, G.  "Théologie et vie spirituelle. Un aspect de la méthode théologique selon Erasme,"  *NRT* 91 (1969) 807-833.

Chenu, M. D.  "L'Humanisme et la Réforme au collège de Saint-Jacques de Paris,"  *Archives d'histoire dominicaine,*  t. I (Paris, 1946) 130-154.

Clamens, G.  *La dévotion à l'humanité de Christ dans la spiritualité du Thomas à Kempis.*  Lyon, 1931.

Cognet, L.  *De la Dévotion moderne à la spiritualité française.*  Paris, 1958.

Coppens, J.  "Les idées réformatrices d'Erasme dans les Préfaces aux Paraphrases du Nouveau Testament,"  *Mél. v. Cauwenberg* (Louvain, 1961) 344-371.

Coolidge, J. S.  *The Pauline Renaissance in England. Puritanism and the Bible.*  Oxford, 1970.

Courtenay, William J.  "Covenant and Causality in Pierre d'Ailly,"  *Speculum* 46 (1971) 94-119.

Courvoiser, J.  "Bucer et la discipline ecclésiastique. Réflexions sur les origines du piétisme et du Protestantisme,"  *Mélanges d'histoire offert à Henri Meylon* (Geneva, 1970) 21-29.

Crahay, R.  "De l'humanisme réformiste à la Réforme radicale,"  *Rev. Univ. Bruxelles* (1967) 1-31.

Dagens, J.  "Humanisme et Evangélisme chez Lefèvre d'Etaples,"  in *Courants Religieux et humanisme à la fin du XVI Siècle, Colloque de Strasbourg 1957* (Paris, 1959) 121-134.

Dannenfeldt, K. H.  *The Church of the Renaissance and Reformation.*  St. Louis, 1970.

Day, Sebastian.  *Intuitive Cognition, a Key to the Significance of the Later Scholastics.*  New York, 1947.

Debongnie, P.  "Les thèmes de l'Imitation,"  *Revue d'histoire Ecclésiastique* 36 (1940) 331ff.

Ditsche, M.  "Zur Herkunft und Begriffes Devotio Moderna,"  *Historisches Jahrbuch* LXXIX (1960) 124-145.

Dols, P. M. E.  *Bibliographie der Moderne Devotie.*  Nimegen, 1941.

Dörries, Hermann.  "Calvin und Lefèvre,"  *Zeitschrift für Kirchengeschichte* XLIV (1925) 544-581.

Douglas, R. M.  *Jacopo Sadoleto 1477-1545, Humanist and Reformer.*  London, 1959.

Doumerque, E.  *La piété réformée d'après Calvin.*  Paris, 1907.

Dowey, E. A., Jr.  *The Knowledge of God in Calvin's Theology.*  New York, 1952.

Dress, Walter.  *Die Theologie Gersons: Eine Untersuchung zur Verbindung von Nominalismus und Mystik im Spätmittelalter.*  Gütersloh, 1931.

Eells, H.  "Martin Bucer and the Conversion of John Calvin,"  *The Princeton Theological Review* 22 (1924) 402-419.

Elie, H.  *Le traité de l'infini de Jean Mair.*  Paris, 1938.

Emery, P. Y.  "Luther et la monachisme,"  *Verbum Caro,*  t. XX, no. 77 (Taizé, 1966) 82-90.

Epiney-Burgard, G.  *Gérard Grote (1340-1384) et les débuts de la Dévotion Moderne.*  Wiesbaden, 1970.

Ernst, H.  "Die Frömmigkeit des Erasmus,"  *Theologische Studien und Kritiken,*  t. 92 (1919) 64-77.

Esnault, R.-H.  *Luther et le monachisme aujourd'hui.*  Geneva, 1964.

Etienne, J.  *Spiritualisme érasmien et théologiens louvanistes. Un changement de problématiques au début du XVI$^e$ siècle.*  Paris, 1956.

_____. *Spiritualisme et théologiens louvanistes*. Louvain, 1956.

Evennett, H. P. *The Spirit of the Counter-Reformation*. Cambridge, 1968.

Favre-Dorsaz, A. *Calvin et Loyola*. Paris, 1951.

Febvre, L. *Au coeur religieux de XVIe siècle*. Paris, 1957.

Flew, R. N. *The Idea of Perfection in Christian Theology. An Historical Study of the Christian Ideal for the Present Life*. New York, 1968.

Fortsman, H. *Word and Spirit; Calvin's Doctrine of Biblical Authority*. Stanford, 1962.

Ganoczy, A. *La Bibliothèque de l'Académie de Calvin*. Geneva, 1969.

_____. *Le Jeune Calvin. Genèse et évolution de sa vocation réformatrice*. Wiesbaden, 1966.

Gelder, H. A. E. van. *The Two Reformations in the 16th Century. A Study of the Religious Aspects of Renaissance and Humanism*. The Hague, 1961.

Ghisalberti, Alessandro. "Il Dio dei filosofi secondo Guglielmo di Occam; fede e ragione," *Rivista di filosofia neo-scolastica* 62 (1970) 272-290.

Gioacchino Paparelli. *Feritas, Humanitas, Divinitas: Le componenti dell'Umanesimo*. Messina-Florence, 1960.

Glorieux, P. "Le chancelier Gerson et la réforme de l'enseignement," *Mélanges Étienne Gilson* (Paris, 1959) 285-298.

Goumaz, L. *La doctrine du salut (doctrina salutis) d'après les commentaires de Jean Calvin sur le Nouveau Testament*. Lausanne-Paris, 1917.

Graham, W. F. *The Constructive Revolutionary: Calvin and his Socio-Economic Impact*. Richmond, 1970.

Guibert, J. de. *La spiritualité de la Compagnie de Jésus. Esquisse historique*. Rome, 1953.

Halkin, L.-E. "La *devotio moderna* et les origines de la Réforme aux Pays-Bas," *Courants religieux et Humanisme à la fin du XVe siècle et au début du XVIe siècle* (Paris, 1959) 35-61.

Hall, B. *John Calvin, Humanist and Theologian*. London, 1956.

Hall, C. A. M. *The Role of Spiritual Warfare in the Theology of John Calvin*. Basel, 1956.

Hatzfeld, H. A. "Christian, Pagan and Devout Humanism in the 16th Century France," *Modern Language Quarterly* XII (1951) 337-352.

Hyma, A. *The Brethren of the Common Life*. Grand Rapids, 1950.

Iserloh, E. "Die Kirchenfrömmigkeit in der Imitatio Christi," in J. Daniélou and H. Vorgrimmler (eds.), *Sentire Ecclesiam* (Freiburg im BR., 1961) 251-267.

Jacob, E. F. "Gerard Groote and the Beginning of the New Devotion in the Low Countries," *Journal of Ecclesiastical History* 3 (1952) 40-58.

Jung, E. M. "On the Nature of Evangelism in the Sixteenth Century Italy," *Journal of the History of Ideas* XIV (1953) 511-527.

Junghans, Helmar, *Ockham im Lichte der neueren Forschung*. Arbeiten zur Geschichte und Theologie des Luthertums No. 21. Berlin, 1968.

Kekow, K. *Luther und die Devotio Moderna*. Hamburg, 1932.

Koch, Karl. *Studium Pietatis. Martin Bucer als Ethiker*. Neukirchen, 1962.

Kohls, Ernst-Wilhelm. *Die Theologie des Erasmus*. Basel, 1966.

_____. "Erasme et la Réforme," *Revue d'Histoire et de Philosophie Religieuse* 3 (1970) 245-256.

_____. *Die theologische Lebensausgabe des Erasmus und die oberrheinischen Reformatoren. Zur Durchdringung von Humanismus und Reformation*. Stuttgart, 1970.

Kolfhaus, W. *Vom christlichen Leben nach Johannes Calvin*. Neukirchen, 1949.

Kreck, Walter.  "Wort und Geist bei Calvin," *Wilhelm Schneemelcher* 20,
     Festschrift für Günter Dehn.  Neukirchen, 1957.
_____.  "Parole et Esprit," *Revue d'Histoire et de Phil. Religieuse*
     40 (1960) 215-220.
Kristeller, P. O.  *Renaissance Thought, Its Classical, Scholastic and
     Humanist Strains.*  New York, 1961.
Krodel, G.  "Erasmus-Luther: One Theology, One Method, Two Results,"
     *Concordia Theological Monthly* 41 (1970) 648-667.
Kruger, F.  *Bucer und Erasmus. Eine Untersuchung zum Einfluss des Eras-
     mus auf die Theologie Martin Bucers.*  Oln, 1970.
Krusche, Werner.  *Das Wirken des Heiligen Geistes nach Calvin.*  Berlin,
     1957.
Ladner, G. E.  "*Homo Viator:* Medieval Ideas on Alienation and Order,"
     *Speculum* XLII (1967) 233-259.
Landeen, W. M.  "Gabriel Biel and the Brethren of the Common Life in
     Germany," *Church History* 20 (1951) 23-36.
_____.  "The Beginning of the D.M. in Germany," *Research Studies of
     the College of Washington* 19 (1951) 161-202, 221-253; 21 (1953) 274-
     309; 22 (1954) 57-75; 27 (1959) 135-214; 28 (1960) 21-45.
Lang, August.  *Der Evangelienkommentar Martin Butzers und die Grundzüge
     seiner Theologie.*  Leipzig, 1900.
Leclerc, J.  *Histoire de la Renaissance au Siècle de la Réforme.*  Paris,
     1955.
Ledeur, E.  "Imitation," *Dictionnaire de Spiritualité* 7, cols. 1562-1587.
Leff, Gordon.  "Ockham, Knowledge and Its Relation to the Status of The-
     ology," *Journal of Ecclesiastical History* 20 (1969) 7-17.
Leith, J. H.  "A Study of John Calvin's Doctrine of the Christian Life"
     Ph.D. thesis, Yale University, 1949.
Levi, A.  "Humanist Reform in Sixteenth Century France," *The Heythrop
     Journal* 6 (1965) 447ff.
Little, D.  *Religion, Order and Law. Study in Pre-Revolutionary England.*
     New York, 1969.
Locher, G. W.  *Testimonium internum: Calvins Lehre vom Heiligen Geist und
     das hermeneutische Problem.*  Zurich, 1964.
Mann, Margaret.  *Erasme et les débuts de la Réforme française (1517-36).*
     Paris, 1933.
Mann Philipps, M.  "La *Philosophia Christi* reflétée dans les Adages
     d'Erasme," *Coll. de Strasbourg,* 1957.
Marcel, P.  "Les rapports entre la justification et la sanctification
     dans la pensée de Calvin," *Revue Reformée* V (1954) 7-18.
_____.  "L'humilité d'après Calvin," *Revue Reformée* XV, v.2 (1960) 1-
     38.
Marshall, I. H.  "Sanctification in the Teaching of J. Wesley and J.
     Calvin," *Evangelical Quarterly* XXXIV (1962) 75-82.
Massaut, J. P.  *Josse Clichtove, l'Humanisme et la Réforme.*  Paris, 1968.
Matteo, I.  *Saggio sulla filosofia di Coluccio Salutati.*  Padua, 1959.
Maurer, H. W.  *An Examination of the Form and Content of John Calvin's
     Prayers.*  Edinburgh, 1959.
McDonnell, K.  *John Calvin, the Church and the Eucharist.*  Princeton,
     1967.
McNeill, J. T.  "The Significance of the Word of God for Calvin," *Church
     History* 28 (1959) 131-146.
Mesnard, P.  "Bucer et la Réforme religieuse," *BSHPF* t. CII (Paris,
     1956) 121-136.
_____.  *Erasme. La Philosophie Chrétienne.*  Paris, 1970.

_____. "Humanisme et théologie dans la controverse entre Erasme et M. Dorp," *Filosofia* (1963) 885-900.

_____. "La conception de l'humilité dans l'Imitation de J.C.," *Mélanges de Lubac* (Paris, 1960) 199-222.

Mestwerdt, P. *Die Anfanges des Erasmus. Humanismus und Devotio Moderna.* Leipzig, 1917.

Meyer, C. "Christian Humanism and the Reformation: Erasmus and Melanchthon," *Concordia Theological Monthly* 41 (1970) 637-647.

Meylon, E. F. "The Stoic Doctrine of Indifferent Things and the Conception of Christian Liberty in Calvin's *Institutio Religionis Christianae*," *The Romantic Review* 28 (1937) 135-145.

Milner, B. *Calvin's Doctrine of the Church.* Leiden, 1970.

Monod, G. "La réforme catholique au XVI^e siècle," *Revue historique* CXXI (1916) 280-315.

Moore, W. G. *La Réforme allemande et la littérature française. Recherches sur la notoriété de Luther en France.* Strasbourg, 1930.

Morreale, M. "Devocion o piedad, Apunctaciones sobre el lexico de Alfonso y Juan Valdes," *Revista Portuguese de Filologia* VII(1956) 365-388.

Motiva, A. "Les Exercices et la Renaissance," *NRT* 70 (1948) 991-1008.

Mours, S. *Le protestantisme en France au XVI^e siècle.* Paris, 1959.

Nehring, A. "A Note on Functional Linguistics in the M.A.," *Traditio* 9 (1953) 433-434.

Nieto, J. C. *Juan de Valdes and the Origins of the Spanish and Italian Reformation.* Geneva, 1970.

Nixon, L. *John Calvin's Teachings on Human Reason.* New York, 1963.

Oberman, H. A. "From Occam to Luther: A Survey of Recent Historical Studies on the Religious Thought of the 14th and 15th Centuries," *Concilium 17: Historical Investigations* (New York, 1966) 126ff.

_____. "Some Notes on the Theology of Nominalism. With Attention to Its Relation to the Renaissance," *Harvard Theological Review* LIII (1960) 47-76.

_____. "Wir seine bettler. Hoc est verum: Bund und Grade in der Theologie des Mittelalters und der Reformation," *Zeitschrift für Kirchengeschichte* 78 (1967) 232-252.

Olin, J. C. *Christian Humanism and the Reformation.* New York, 1956.

Olphe-Galliard, M. "Erasme et Ignace de Loyola," *RAM* 35 (1959) 337-352.

Ozment, W. E. *"Homo Spiritualis." A Comparative Study of the Anthropology of Johannes Tauler, Jean Gerson and Martin Luther (1509-1516) in the Context of their Theological Thought.* Leiden, 1969.

Packer, J. I. "Calvin the Theologian" in G. E. Duffield (ed.), *John Calvin. A Collection of Essays* (Grand Rapids, 1966) 149-176.

Pannier, J. "De la préréforme à la Réforme: à propos des dernières publications de Lefèvre d'Etaples," *Revue d'Histoire et de Philosophie Religieuses* XV (1935) 530-547.

_____. *Le témoignage du Saint Esprit. Essai sur l'histoire du dogme dans la théologie réformée.* Paris, 1893.

Pauck, W. "Calvin and Butzer," *The Heritage of the Reformation* (Glencoe, 1961) 85-94.

Payne, J. B. *Erasmus: His Theology of the Sacraments.* Richmond, 1970.

Pellens, K. "Kirchendenken in der *Imitatio Christi*" in Th. Bolger (ed.), *Bibel, Liturgie und Spiritualität* (Maria Laach, 1962) 41-67.

Peremans, N. *Erasme et Bucer d'après leur correspondance.* Paris, 1970.

Picasso, G. "L'Imitazione di Christo nell' epoca della *Devotio Moderna* et nella spiritualita de sec. XV in Italia," *Revista di Storia e Letteratura religiosa* 4 (1968) 11-32.

Plattard, J. *Guillaume Budé (1468-1540) et les origines de l'humanisme français.* Paris, 1923.

Post, R. R. *The Modern Devotion. Confrontation with Reformation and Humanism.* Leiden, 1968.

Rahner, K. "The Ignatian Mysticism of Joy in the World," *Theological Investigations* III (1967) 277-293.

Reid, W. *The Present Significance of Calvin's View of Tradition.* Surrey, 1966.

Renaudet, A. *Préréforme et humanisme à Paris pendant les premières guerres d'Italie (1494-1517).* 2nd ed. Paris, 1953.

Reuter, Karl. *Das Grundverständnis der Theologie Calvins, Unter Einbeziehung ihrer geschichtlichen Abhängigkeiten.* Neukirchen, 1963.

Reveilland, M. "L'autorité de la Tradition chez Calvin," *Revue Réformée* IX (1958) 25-45.

Reymond, O. *Le problème de la perfection chrétienne d'après Calvin et John Wesley.* Lausanne, 1945.

Rice, Eugene. "Erasmus and the Religious Tradition," *Journal of the History of Ideas* 11 (1950) 387-411.

Richards, R. C. "Ockham and Skepticism," *New Scholasticism* 42 (1968) 345-363.

Rodriguez-Grabit, H. "Ignace de Loyola et le Collège de Montaigu. L'influence de Standonck sur Ignace," *Bibl. Hum. Ren.* (1958) 388-401.

Salley, C. L. "The Ideas of the Devotio Moderna as Reflected in the Life and the Writings of J. L. d'Etaples." Diss. Abstracts XIII (1953).

Schepers, M. B. *The Interior Testimony of the Holy Spirit. A Critique of the Calvinist Doctrine Establishing the Divine Authority of Sacred Scripture.* Washington, 1965.

Scholl, H. *Der Dienst des Gebets nach Johannes Calvin.* Zurich, 1968.

Scott, T. K. "Ockham on Evidence, Necessity, and Intuition," *Journal of the History of Philosophy* 7 (1969) 27-49.

Simone, F. *Il rinascimento Francese.* Turin, 1961.

_____. *Il pensiero francese del Rinascimento.* Milan, 1964.

Smedes, L. B. *All Things Made New. A Theology of Man's Union with Christ.* Grand Rapids, 1961.

Smith, S. D. "John Calvin and Worldly Religion," *Lexington Theological Quarterly* 3 (1968) 65-74.

Snyder, Susan. "The Left Hand of God: Despair in Medieval and Renaissance Tradition," *Studies in the Renaissance* XII (1965) 18-59.

Spitz, Lewis. *The Religious Renaissance of the German Humanists.* Cambridge, Mass., 1963.

Spoelhof, W. "Concepts of Religious Non-Conformity and Religious Toleration as Developed by the Brethren of the Common Life in the Netherlands, 1374-1489." Ph.D. thesis, University of Michigan, 1946.

Steinmetz, D. C. *Misericordia Dei. The Theology of Johannes von Staupitz in its Late Medieval Setting.* Leiden, 1968.

Stephens, W. P. *The Holy Spirit in the Theology of Martin Bucer.* Cambridge, 1970.

Stone, D. *France in the XVIth Century. A Medieval Society Transformed.* Englewood Cliffs, 1969.

Toffanin, G. "Il concetto di *Docta Pietas* negli Umanisti italiani," *Mél. Hauvette.* Paris, 1934.

_____. "L'Umanesimo e la teologia," *BHR* XI (1949) 205-214.

Tonkin, T. *The Church and the Secular Order in Reformation Thought*. New York, 1971.

Torrance, T. H. *Calvin's Doctrine of Man*. London, 1949.

_____. *Kingdom and Church*. Edinburgh, 1956.

_____. "Knowledge of God and Speech about Him According to John Calvin," *Revue d'Histoire et de Philosophie Religieuse* 44 (1964) 402-422.

Toussaert, J. *Le sentiment religieux en Flandre à la fin du moyen âge*. Paris, 1963.

Trinkaus, C. "Renaissance Problems in Calvin's Theology," *Studies in the Renaissance* I (1954) 59-80.

Tripet, A. *Pétrarque ou la connaissance de soi*. Geneva, 1967.

Ullman, B. L. *The Humanism of Coluccio Salutati*. Padua, 1963.

Vandenbroucke, F. "Le Christ dans l'Imitation de Jésus Christ," *La Vie Spirituelle* CX (1964) 276-290.

_____. "Le divorce entre théologie et mystique; ses origines," *NRT* 72 (1950) 372-389.

Villain, Maurice. "Le Message Biblique de Lefèvre d'Etaples," *Recherches de Science Religieuse* 40 (1952) 243-259.

Villoslada, G. "Rasgos caracteristicos de la *Devotio moderna*," *Manresa* 28 (1956) 315-350.

_____. *Loyola y Erasmo: dos almos, dos epocas*. Madrid, 1965.

Walker, D. P. "Origène en France," *Courants religieux et humanisme à la fin du XVe et au début du XVIe siècle. Colloque de Strasbourg 1957* (Paris, 1959) 113-119.

Wallace, R. S. *Calvin's Doctrine of the Christian Life*. Edinburgh, 1959.

Walzer, M. *The Revolution of the Saints. A Study in the Origins of Radical Politics*. New York, 1969.

Watson, P. S. "Luther and Sanctification," *Concordia* 30 (1959) 243-259.

Weiler, A. "Humanisme et scolastique. Le renouveau de la pensée chrétienne à la Renaissance," *Concilium* 7 (1965) 109-119.

Wendel, François. *Calvin: The Origins and Development of his Religious Thought*. Trans. Philip Mairet. London, 1963.

Wicks, J. "Luther on the Person Before God," *Theological Studies* 30 (1969) 289-311.

Wilkins, E. H. *Studies in the Life and Works of Petrarch*. Cambridge, 1955.

Williams, George Huntston and Mergal, Angel M. *Spiritual and Anabaptist Writers: Documents Illustrative of the Radical Reformation and Evangelical Catholicism*. Library of Christian Classics Vol. XXV. London, 1957.

_____. *The Radical Reformation*. Philadelphia, 1962.

Wolf, Erik. "Theologie und Sozialordnung bei Calvin," *Archiv für Reformationsgeschichte* XLII (1951) 11-31.

Wright, C. K. *A Study of Calvin's Doctrine of Sanctification*. Austin, 1956.

Zahrnt, H. *Dans l'attente de Dieu. L'Eglise avant la Réformation*. Paris, 1970.

Zijl, Th. van. *Gerard Groote, Ascetic and Reformer (1340-1384)*. Studies in Medieval History Vol. XVIII. Washington, D. C., 1963.

INDEX

MA